W9-DIL-259

THE CYCLES OF SOCIAL REFORM

Mental Health Policy Making in the United States, England, and Sweden

Philip K. Armour

UNIVERSITY
PRESS OF
AMERICA

Library of Congress Catalog Card Number: 80-6187

TABLE OF CONTENTS

PREFACE

The treatment of the mentally disordered has made significant advances since the Middle Ages. We no longer cast
the mentally ill and retarded upon rivers and seas, to rid
ourselves of a segment of society that offends our sensibi-
lities. Latter-day persons sailing in "ships of fools" are
mainly the victims of social, political, economic, racial,
and ethnic discrimination and oppression, though the recent
wave of "boat people" from Cuba did contain deviants, criminals, and social undesireables. Thus, the Medieval image of
a ship of fools does translate, however roughly into our own
age. As an image, a metaphor, it can illuminate our
attempts to understand how societies seek to manage a sub-
population of persons that do not seem to "fit."

This study is an evaluation of the organized, purposive
efforts of political and social leaders to manage the dependent population of persons viewed as mentally disturbed. As
such, this study in public policies for the mentally ill
draws on the huge literature on policy making, the sociology
mental health and illness, social epidemiology, social
psychiatry, modernization and nation building, and welfare
and health services. This study seeks to glean from this
diverse literature the relevant data on the role of reformers in creating mental health policies and programs. Since
an analysis of one nation's efforts in the regard is limi-
ting, I have adopted the cross-national historical approach
to the study of public policies for the insane.

A cross-national study of social policy is not the product of one researcher; such a complex examination also reflects the hard work and the contributions of many persons.
Thus, I have many people to thank at the completion of this
work. First of all I am indebted to my University of California, Berkeley doctoral dissertation committee members,
John A. Clausen, Harold L. Wilensky, and Ralph M. Kramer.
They provided me with continuing and sustaining intellectual
support throughout the production of this manuscript. They
continued to give substantive and critical comments which
helped to sharpen the focus of this analysis and convert
dissertation into a book. They continually challenged me to

produce the best possible product. I only hope that I have begun to live up to the standards that they hold for me and this work.

Besides my dissertation committee members there were many others who aided me in this scholarly enterprise. Richard M. Coughlin read the entire manuscript and made many valuable and insightful suggestions. His persistent backing helped me dispell doubts that I had about the viability of this enterprise. Arthur L. Stinchcombe sustained me with his expression of support of my approach to this analytic problem. Lawrence J. Redlinger kept up the pressure on me to complete this project while illuminating the notion of discretion. Robert R. Alford discussed with me the implications of his notion of structural interest groups. Jacob B. Michaelson has maintained with me a dialogue on the future of our age and especially on the unanticipated impact of well-intentioned public policies and programs. Kathleen Jones reviewed this whole enterprise with me, encouraging me to undertake a comparative analysis of developments that she has studied closely in one nation. Eugene Bardach extended my understanding of the concept of implementation. John Meyer, Tim McDaniel, and Carroll Seron helped sharpen the theoretical argument in this manuscript and suggested ways to make those points more clearly. John W. Sommer continually encouraged me to complete this work and provided valuable aid in obtaining publication of this policy study.

There are many other people whose support has been chiefly social and emotional, but no less important in enabling me to complete my dissertation. These people include Terrell and Judy Carver, Peter and Helen Elias, Phil Spencer, Adrian Read, Bill and Molly Read, Helen Reynolds, Hila Michaelsen, Robert Hughes, Paula England, Donn and Terry Rogosin, Don Hicks, Sandy and Charles McConnel, Eddy Herrera, Elizabeth Arguello, Jane and John Jordan, Murray Leaf, John Rees, Carolyn Galerstein, Shannon Vale, William Bridge, Craig Jett, Mike Casey, and Obie Obermark.

Of course, my parents Tom and Carolyn Armour and my parents-in-law Doris and Douglas Noble were deeply supportive of me in the sometimes difficult times that this project produced. And my siblings Rosalind, Anita, Matthew, and Elizabeth, my siblings-in-law Michael, Robin, and Steven, and my surrogate siblings, Aaron and Rachel, provided crucial emotional safety nets. Poetic and musical inspiration has been given by Jerry Garcia, Phil Lesh, Bob Weir, Mickey Hart, Billy Kreutzmann, the late Keith Godchaux, Donna Jean Godchaux, the late Ron McKernan, Brent Mydland, and Robert Hunter.

The financial and institutional support for the research work that sustains the arguments contained herein was provided in part by research assistantships provided by the Institute of Industrial Relations, University of California, Berkeley, 1971-72; 1973-77. The Chancellor's Patent Fund for Doctoral Dissertation Research, of University of California, Berkeley aided me with travel funds for my European research in 1975-76. The National Institute of Mental Health assisted me throughout my graduate student career with a Traineeship in Personality and Social Structure administered by the Department of Sociology, University of California, Berkeley, 1970-71; 1973-76. Research assistantship funds were also made possible by the National Science Foundation (Grant GS-37087X and Grant SOC 77-13265) and administered by the University of California, Berkeley's Institute of International Studies, 1976-77. Further support has been provided through regular faculty research support of the School of Social Sciences, University of Texas at Dallas. Additional research assistance support for the last two chapters of this work was made possible by a University of Texas Regents Organized Research Grant.

For research assistance I am appreciative to Rosemary Dawes.

Initial clerical support for this project was given by Vicki Hawk and Robin Eller. The typing and re-typing of the dissertation version of this manuscript was cheerfully conducted by Eileen Tollett. Annette Cockran re-typed parts of this manuscript. Darsa Armour (certainly a distant relative) composed this book using an Addressograph Multigraph Amtext 425. I deeply appreciate all of the clerical support I have received from the above tireless crew.

iii

Finally, I own my very deepest appreciation to Maureen L. Noble Armour. Her confidence transcended all other sources of support; her suggestions and insights propelled this work towards completion. In love and friendship I dedicate this work to her.

P.K.A.

Guinn House
Rusk, Texas

SHIP OF FOOLS

Went to see the captain
strangest I could find
Laid my proposition down
laid it on the line

I won't slave for beggar's pay
likewise golden jewels
But I would slave to learn the way
to sink your ship of fools

Ship of fools
on a cruel sea
Ship of fools
sail away from me

It was later than I thought
when I first believed you
Now I cannot share your laughter
ship of fools

Saw your first ship sink and drown
from rockin' up the boat
And all that could not sink or swim
was just left there to float

I won't leave you driftin' down
but whoa it makes me wild
For thirty years upon my head
to have you call me child

Ship of fools
on a cruel sea
Ship of fools
sail away from me

The bottle stand is empty
as they were filled before
Time there was, and plenty
but from that cup no more

Though I could not caution all
I still might warn a few
Don't lend your hand to raise no flag
atop no ship of fools

Ship of fools
on a cruel sea
Ship of fools
sail away from me

by Jerome Garcia and Robert Hunter
© 1974, Ice Nine Publishing Company, Inc.
Reproduced with the expressed permission
of the authors and publisher.

CHAPTER I

THE CYCLES OF MENTAL HEALTH REFORM

This study examines the role of social reformers and reform movements in the design, enactment, and implementation of mental health policy in the United States, England, and Sweden. Like all modern nation states these countries have struggled with the problem of providing services for the mentally disordered among their citizenry. Especially since the end of World War II, each of these nations has developed and instituted community-based programs to treat the mentally ill.[1] In varying degrees, these past and present-day programs have sought to incorporate the insights into psychological processes, the understandings of the causes and correlates of psychiatric impairment, the awareness of the deleterious impact on mental patients of improper confinement, and the possible benefits of new modes of care.

An understanding of the dimensions of the solutions to the public problems posed by psychiatric impairment requires an understanding of the role reformers, lobbyists, interest groups, and professional associations play in policy deliberations in the field of mental health. In fact, the arena of mental health policy making provides a strategic, observational setting for examining the relative impact of agents of social change as they seek to influence the outcome of legislative and administrative decision making. Given the competing and conflicting theories of mental disorders, and the concomitant diagnoses and treatment modalities that flow from the various psychiatric orientations, mental health policy makers find themselves surrounded by purveyors of a variety of therapeutic solutions. Thus, a policy study of the attempts to assess the mental health care problem can lead to an understanding of the form, behavior, and impact of lobbyists, associations, interest groups, and reform movements as they seek to adapt and translate one or more of these competing orientations into specific public policies and programs.

1

The Focus of this Study

The United States, Sweden, and England have varied in the timing of their adoption of national mental health policies. They also have varied in the success with which these programmatic elements of national policy have been implemented. This study will examine the degree of success in enacting and implementing policy goals of the mental health reformers in each of these nations.

The post-World War II policy developments in each nation rest on socio-historical foundations. Specifically, as political leaders have decided to intervene into the lives of the psychiatrically disturbed, such policy makers have determined how the mentally ill and defective, the alcoholic and drug dependent, the deviant and distressed ought to be managed. Such policy decisions, arrived at by different means, at different times, have yielded results that shape the context and terms of the future decisions. Yet, whatever the timing of the policy decision or the nature of that decision, mental health reformers and reform movements have played a part in these deliberations and in their outcomes.

A goal of this study is to examine the socio-historical conditions under which political elites have been convinced by reformers to depart from their usual concerns with taxing, war, trade, foreign relations, and domestic policy affecting the majority of the population, and concern themselves with the emotional and physical welfare of the mentally disordered among their citizenry. The questions addressed by this study are these:

- What are the social forces that shape this pattern of convergence and divergence among mental health policy in the three nations?
- Do differences in the organizational form, strength, and placement of reformers and reform movements account for these differences?
- What are the barriers to the adoption of new

2

policy and programs and hence to the success
of these movements?
- How do the different manifestations of the
reform movements in each of these
countries overcome these barriers?

The literature on policy adoption points to the need to
examine a number of factors in the search for answers to
these and related questions. Deutsch (1949), Rothman (1971,
1980), Jones (1972), Grob (1973), and others identify the
important role played by dedicated social reformers in
identifying the plight of the insane and in demanding that
governments provide humane treatment for the mentally
disordered. Krause (1968) and Foley (1975) locate the
importances of bureaucratically- and legislatively-based
reformers in their studies of the U.S. community mental
health center legislation strategies. Deutsch (1944c),
Titmuss (1950), and Abel-Smith (1964) point to modern warfare, particularly World War II, as a significant factor in
reviving interest in community care alternatives to hospitalization. Alford (1975) and Krause (1977) argue that the
organizational form of health care services shapes the
development and implementation of reform proposals by
creating barriers to and opportunities for social change.
Felix (1967), Mechanic (1969), and Swazey (1974) note the
developments in psychopharmacology as factors creating an
environment in which new treatment modalities and new mental
health policies and programs could be considered. Wilensky
(1975) and Marmor (1973) say that major policy reforms often
are the product of incremental growth based upon initial,
limited policy achievements. The analysis that follows will
assess the relative importance of these and other factors
for the successes or failures of mental health reformers and
movements in the United States, England, and Sweden.

An Overview of Mental Health Policy in England, the United
States and Sweden

Mental health policies and programs are one of the
structural uniformities of urban, industrial societies.
Though nations converge in their establishment of mental
health services, they vary in the types of services enacted,

3

in the timing of the adoption of reforms, and in the implementation strategies devised.

Variation in mental health policies. National programs to treat the mentally disturbed were instituted in an era when governments were seeking solutions to the problem of illiteracy, poverty, ill health, and criminality. The English Poor Laws, consolidated by Elizabeth I in 1601, were designed not only to deal with the increasing population of paupers and vagabonds (a development associated with enclosures, urbanization, and the first stages of industrialization), but also to cope with the growth in numbers of lunatics and feeble-minded persons (Rowse, 1950; Hill, 1969; Trattner, 1979). The poor relief methods of managing the mentally disordered were transplanted in the seventeenth century in North America. Particularly as the witchcraft phobia and its attendant horrors subsided, colonial governments in New England and other regions adopted measures based on those of England to handle the problem of the deserving poor and the pauper insane (Deutsch, 1949, cf. Grob, 1966, 1973). Similar Swedish Poor Laws were also enacted in the 17th century to cope with the new population of dependents, including the mentally disordered.

The development of mental health services is one specific example of the convergence of social policies and programs in modern societies. Yet, an examination of the services in the U.S., England, and Sweden reveals how these societies vary in their organized response to the policy mandate to provide care for the psychologically disturbed among their citizenry.

Consider the organization and financing of mental health services in these three rich nations. The services of the United States are a mixture of city, county, state, and federally-funded and administered mental health hospitals and clinics; private mental hospitals and psychiatric departments of private general hospitals; and, private practitioners of psychiatry, psychoanalysis, and other psychotherapies. In contrast to the U.S.'s mix of private and public services, the treatment of mental disorders in England and Sweden is almost exclusively carried out by the government. Since 1946, English mental health services have

4

been an integral branch of the National Health Services (NHS). Like most other services of the NHS, treatment for mental disorders in hospitals, psychiatric departments of general hospitals, and clinics is free at the time of admission. English mental health services are funded from the central government's general revenues and are now administered by the Department of Health and Social Security in conjunction with local and regional hospital and health authority boards. Control of Sweden's hospital-based mental health service was recently devolved to county and municipal governments, though the central government continues its overall directive functions through the National Board of Health and Welfare. Thus, mental health services have now been given a community-care focus as a result of this recent reorganization.

The U.S. health and mental health services. Decentralization and fragmentation are labels applied to U.S. mental health care services (Mechanic, 1969). These labels are derived from the variety of approaches used to organize and fund general medical care delivery systems: categorical federal grants for centers to treat disorders (e.g., cancer or drug addiction); federal funding of private hospital construction under the 1946 Hill-Burton Act; state mental hospital systems; county and municipal hospitals and clinics for the needy; the unique Veterans Administration network of hospitals for military personnel, veterans, and their dependents; the Public Health Service hospitals and related psychiatric services; treatment paid for by Medicare and Medicaid for the aged and needy; private health insurance providers; and, of course, the private practitioners paid on a fee-for-service basis (Anderson, 1972; Jonas, et al., 1977).[2]

The heterogeneity of the U.S. health care system is reflected in the variety found in U.S. psychiatric services. U.S. mental health services consist of a mixture of public and private services and facilities. Up until 1945, it was the sole responsibility of the states and localities to make provisions for the treatment of psychiatric patients, though the federal government operated three specialized facilities. The level of funding of these facilities and the quality of the care provided was quite variable. In 1945 the federal government became directly involved in mental health care with the passage of the National Mental Health Act that authorized federal funds for training, research, and aid to the states for community psychiatric services and created the National Institute for Mental Health to administer these funds. Beginning in 1963 with the passage of community mental health legislation, the federal government deepened its mental health commitment by funding treatment alternatives to the large, remote mental hospitals. The 1980 Mental Health Systems Act, if implemented, will deepen the direct involvement of the federal government in the provision of services.

Co-existing and prospering with the state and federal psychiatric services is the network of private psychiatric facilities, private psychiatrists, and psychotherapists. The medical marketplace offers consumers a wide variety of treatment modalities, many of which are increasingly covered by private health insurance policies.

The English health care context of mental illness treatment. In contrast to the U.S.'s mix of public and private services, the treatment of psychiatric patients in England is almost exclusively a central governmental responsibility. English mental health services have been a coordinated branch of the National Health Service since the NHS was established by Parliament during the watershed period of social welfare legislation under the post-World War II Labour government (Eckstein, 1958; Willcocks, 1967). Under the 1946 Act, the NHS was administered by a cabinet rank minister whose responsibility was to provide health care through three subservices: a regional hospital service for somatic care, psychiatric care and personnel training; general practitioner, dental, pharmaceutical, and ophthalmaic services; and local authority auxiliary health services and outpatient treatment facilities (Lindsey, 1962). After 1974 reorganization of the tripartite structure was abandoned; and an integrated health service consisted of regional, area, and district levels of management for all of NHS services.[3]

Under the tripartite system (1948-74), mental hospitals (originally controlled by counties and municipalities, royal special charters, or private corporations) were placed under the hospital boards. Local health authorities were mandated to provide outpatient care and other community-based services (Jones, 1972: 274-289). Following the original recommendation of the wartime Coalition Government's White Paper of 1944, health care is free at the time of access except for nominal charges for dental and ophthalmaic services (Titmuss, 1958: 138). Under the 1974 reorganization, mental hospital and outpatient services were administered by area and district health management committees. As a result, there ceased to be a separate mental health service. The organizational consequences of the reorganization are only being gradually understood and the impact on patient care has been even harder to assess (Klein, 1973: cf. Leavitt, 1976; Watkin, 1978; and Alaszewski, et al, 1981).

Swedish health and mental health services. Not surprisingly, Sweden's mental health services differ from those of the U.S. and Britain. Until 1967, the mental hospital service network was centrally administered by the National Board of Health and Welfare (Furman, 1965; cf. Vail, 1968). Since 1967 the responsibility for psychiatric treatment has been transferred to the counties and municipalities; now, both somatic and psychiatric care facilities are administered by the same local health authorities. This managerial consolidation of mental health services brought to an end the organizational and financial split between the older, physically-remote mental hospitals and the county council's newer psychiatric departments of general hospitals and outpatient clinics.

The devolution of control was designed to improve coordination between the two previously separate care delivery systems and to reduce the inequalities between the long-stay hospital and the newer psychiatric facilities. Like NHS reorganization in England, the restructuring of the Swedish health services offers a chance to psychiatric services to overcome their historical second-class status. Yet, Leche (1975) reports differences in the quality of care (as measured by the staffing ratios and the educational attainment of the staffs) persist despite integration. And, though there are now no legal distinctions between the two types of facilities, in fact, psychiatrists in psychiatric departments in general hospitals still refuse to admit the severely ill patients requiring compulsory commitment.

In sum, this brief overview of the current organizational features of these national somatic and psychiatric services reveals considerable variation in policies and programs. Further, the variations in these services of the United States, England, and Sweden are rooted in unique histories of such national policies. Such variation requires greater specification and leads me to adopt a historical, comparative approach in my effort to account for these differences between national policies and services.

The Cycles of Social Reform

Social reform, whatever its objectives, is by its very nature episodic: eras of intense collective concern, enthusiasm, and activity are followed by periods of indifference, neglect, and forgetfulness. Mental health reform is no exception to the pattern. Dain (1964), Rosen (1968), and Mora (1975) among others, reveal the recurrent character of enthusiasm for various psychiatric theories and treatment modalities; N. Lewis (1974); Caplan (1969), Martindale and Martindale (1971) note the cycles of governmental activity to reduce the suffering of the psychiatric patient. Further, the ideas of a reform era are often drawn from a previous era. For example, the modern, community-based approach to psychiatric care shares features with earlier orientations to mental disorders. The policy theory embedded in the U.S. Community Mental Health Centers Acts shares premises of the intervention theory that animated the enlightened 19th-century programs. These 19th-century reforms were in turn inspired by the late 18th-century moral treatment regimes at the York Asylum in England and at Bicêtre in France.

The mental hospital: an agent of reform, an object to be reformed. The modern mental hospital illustrates this cyclical character of reform. Often criticized for the detrimental impact they have had on resident patients, the asylum was the humane solution of the mid-19th century psychiatric reformers to social problems of the abuse and

8

maltreatment of the mentally disordered. In the United States' Dorothea Dix, following the lead of her mentor, Horace Mann, was appalled by the confinement of the mentally ill in prisons and workhouses and successfully campaigned for the establishment of state mental hospitals as alternatives to imprisonment for the insane (Deutsch, 1949: 169-171). In England and Sweden comparable humanistic reformers succeeded in convincing national governments to fund separate hospitals to care for the mentally ill. Thus, although the isolated and factory-like mental hospitals of the 19th century are now criticized and condemned, these hospitals were originally designed to provide humane treatment in a setting thought to be conducive to recovery and rehabilitation of the mentally disordered (Jones, 1972: 40-153; Retterstol, 1975: 207-221; Rothman, 1971: 109-154). The successes of these 19th century reforms were followed by a period of pessimism regarding the curability of mental disorders and criticism of the hospital-based services mode of care. Only in the late-19th and early-20th century was the optimism of an earlier reform era recaptured; renewed campaigns were launched in England, Sweden, and the United States to convince governments of the need to modify, expand, and enhance their mental health services.

An examination of the history of mental patient treatment reveals that the mentally disordered, like the poor, have been alternatively discovered, forgotten, and rediscovered. Of this rediscovery phenomenon in social policy making, Matza (1966) says:

> "The poor, it seems, are perennially hidden, and the brave explorers of each decade reiterate their previous invisibility and regularly proclaim the distinctive and special qualities of the 'new poor.'" (Matza: 289)

One could easily substitute the mentally ill in this statement. As with the poor, the "rediscovery" of the mentally disordered is often followed by policy recommendations that are translated by legislative and executive bodies into "new" programs. In this social and political process mental health reformers have played a crucial role in identifying the problem, posing policy solutions, attempting to imple-

9

ment programs to attack the problem, monitoring program operation, and suggesting further initiatives to improve services.

The Organizational Forms of Social Reform Movements

If the mental health policies adopted by national political elites have this cyclical quality, then to what can this variability in policy be attributed? In this study I am going to assess the impact reformers and their movements have had in shaping national mental health policies. That is, I intend to explore the relationship between English, Swedish, and American mental health reformers and the national policies and services adopted and implemented by political elites. The question is: What is a social reform movement? What is a social reformer?

Reform movements and the rationalization process. In this study reformers and reform movements are defined as those individuals, informal groups, and formal associations that seek to alter the normative structure of society. Smelser (1962: 270-312) states that social reformers attempt to restore, modify, protect, or create social norms directly or to convince political authorities to do so. The reformers that seek such changes often leave an agency, law, association, and the like as a product of their concerted efforts.

Further, to discover the variable impact of social reformers and movements in the policy-making process I draw upon and modify the typology of domination developed by Weber (1978: 212-301: 901-1157). Weber's conceptualization of charismatic, traditional, and rational-legal forms of domination and authority provide a model of a theoretical formulation of the types of reform movements. The forces for mental health reform have been subject to the same forces that have rationalized our social worlds. Of Weber's concept of rationalization, two noted social scientists say:

"The principle of rationalization is the most general element in Weber's philosophy of history. For the rise and fall of institu-

10

tional structures, the ups and downs of
classes, parties, and rulers implement the
general drift of secular rationalization."
(Gerth and Mills: 1946: 51)

This study of the creation and implementation of mental
health policies will show that mental health reformers and
their social movements have also undergone a rationalization
process. Specifically, I will show that 18th- and 19th-
century solo, and often charismatic, reformers gave rise to
associations and organizations dedicated to modifying the
normative structure of society. In the late-19th and 20th
centuries the further rationalization process of reform
movements meant the creation of a government bureau. This
governmental department, ministry, or agency became the
basis for further reforms activity. Thus, this transformation and rationalization of reform movement is yet another
specific illustration of a social process Weber identified.

   The theoretical implications of the rationalization of
reform movements. The theoretical consequences of this suggested neo-Weberian typology of reform movements are these:
the variation in the national cycles of mental health policy
making are partially a product of the variation in the
degree of rationalization of the national reform movements;
the more completely bureaucratically-based mental health
reformers are, the more successful they can be in realizing
their reform objectives in a political world that is dominated by rational-legal institutions and processes. That
is, given the innovativeness, adaptability, and hence sur-
vivability of bureaus (cf. Downs, 1967: 5-22; 73n; 109-110),
the reform movement that can create for itself a well-
defined and financed base for its operations within the
government will be better able to accomplish its reform
movement's objectives. In this sense, bureaucratically-
based reformers, like their other rational-legal counterparts, are capable even of revolutionary action:

   "Since bureaucracy has a 'rational character,'
   with rules, means-ends calculus, and matter-
   of-factness predominating, its rise and
   expansion has everywhere had 'revolutionary'
   results... as had the advance of rationalism

in general. The march of bureaucracy accor-
dingly destroyed structures of domination
which were not rational in this sense of the
term." (Weber, 1978: 1002-1003)

My analysis will show that the relative success in the 20th
century of U.S. mental health reformers stems from their
creation of a bureaucratic base for their activities, specifically the creation of community mental health centers.
England and Sweden have lagged behind the U.S. in creating
community care alternatives to the mental hospitals in part
because their reformers have lacked a base for developing,
lobbying for, and implementing such community care policies.

The Methods of Analysis

    I have selected the cross-national, historical-compa-
rative method for this public policy analysis. By being
able to compare and contrast national efforts to realize the
goal of community care, I am able to deepen my understanding
of the forces operative in all these countries which determine the timing, direction, and outcome of these policy
deliberations. Thus, the technique of comparing and con-
trasting developments in different policies is one that can
throw into relief the features of a particular nation state.

    Stinchcombe (1978) says, "the central operation for
building theories of history is seeking causally significant
analogies between instances" (Stinchcombe: 7). To identify
such analogous events Stinchcombe states that constructing
an historical narrative is crucial:

    "I believe the test of any theory of social change
    is its ability to analyze such narrative sequences,
    and that the poverty of the theory of social change
    is due to paying no attention to that narrative
    detail." (Stinchcombe: 13)

In the following chapters I develop and analyze a narration
of one process of social change: the policy response to the
continuing and perplexing dilemma of how to manage the
mentally disordered. Specifically, I have attempted to

12

gather and select from the wealth of historical material on mental disorders the most theoretically-relevant elements of the event sequences in England, Sweden, and the United States. My goal in narration construction is to locate the importance of mental health reform movements--whatever form they take--for the outcome of the national policy deliberations.

Identifying analogous reform movements. If the historical, narrative method of this work can be so justified, can the comparative approach also be supported? Stinchcombe says that "conceptual profundity depends on the deep building of analogies" (Stinchcombe: 21). In the course of this study I will attempt to construct the analogies between reformers and reform movements in an attempt to explain the variation in the mental health policies adopted and implemented in England, Sweden, and the United States. I feel justified and supported in this approach to the study of mental health reformers because the historical-comparative method is an established and successful approach in the social sciences (Weber, 1947; Tocqueville, 1955; Smelser, 1959; Bendix, 1963; 1964; Moore, 1967; Vallier, 1971.)[4]

Further, the cross-national historical method is also dictated by the nature of the phenomena under study: psychiatric practice is international and thus requires an international examination of trends in etiological theories and treatment modalities. For example, the rapid, dramatic diffusion from the country of origin of the new modes of psychiatric care--whether moral management, electroconvulsive therapy, or the family of derivatives of chlorpromazine --is an illustration of the international scope of the problem and the search for solutions to the problem. More importantly, mental health movements are present in most of the developed world and many of the newly emerging nations. And though there is considerable variation in the strength of the organization of these movements, in the form of their organization, and in their influence on policy making and implementation, the fact that these movements are nearly world-wide requires a cross-national perspective.

The rationale for the selection of cases under study. I have selected the United States, England, and Sweden for a comparative study of the implementation of community care for several reasons. First, these nations are all urban-industrial, liberal-democratic polities, with long histories of internal stability and traditions characterized by the tolerance of minorities and dissidents and active citizen participation in politics through voluntary organizations. These gross, national similarities enable me to examine the role of reformers and movements in formulating mental health policy within roughly comparable social and political contexts. Second, these nations have converged in the creation of health and social welfare programs, though there are considerable detailed programmatic differences. This convergence facilitates the development of reasonably comparable policy narratives as well as measures of the operation of mental health services.

The selection of these countries is strategic for another reason not yet mentioned. Many of the significant innovations in the treatment of mental disorders have taken place in these nations I have chosen for study: e.g., "open door" policies and therapeutic communities are two such pioneering treatment programs initiated in England that had worldwide impact in the treatment of the mentally ill. By focusing on innovative nations it is possible to gain greater insights into the role of psychiatric reformers and movements in adopting new national mental health policies and programs.[5]

The data. The data herein presented have been derived from a variety of sources. First, I have relied upon as many historical accounts as I could gather on the development of the health and mental health services in each of these nations. Following Glaser and Strauss (1967: 176ff) I have treated the various archival and library material as informants of the policy events in each of these nations under study.[6]

In addition to gathering archival materials I conducted interviews with many key participants in the post-World War II mental health reform process in these three nations. These interviews enabled me to evaluate the historical material I was gathering. The accounts of those events are sometimes incomplete and inaccurate. My field interviews

14

gave me a method to assess the reliability of these histories and interpretations presented in archival material. By engaging in participant observation at public meetings and hearings as well as conducting visits to mental hospitals and clinics, I further attempted to validate the written record of national mental policy making. Wilensky (1967) has suggested that multiple and even competing sources of intelligence is a strategy that enables administrators to minimize intelligence failures and increase the probability that the policy decision made will be the correct one. Thus, by means of the interviews and participant observation I attempted to also construct multiple sources of information that would increase the accuracy of generalizations made on the basis of the historical narratives.

The Scope of this Study

In the following chapters I will explicate the causal connections between mental health reform movements, and their various permutations, and the national mental health policies of England, Sweden, and the United States. Chapter Two presents the theory of social reform movements that will be tested in this analysis of mental health policy making.

This theory of reform movements can account for the range of possible types of movements that will be identified by examining both the form these mental health movements take over time as well as the variation these movements exhibit across nations. I will draw upon theories of collective behavior, organizational theory, studies of organizational intelligence, and theories of lobbies and interest groups to forge a theory of mental health reform movements. Having explicated my theory of reform movements, I will suggest what other factors, operating in each of these countries, might intervene to limit or expand the opportunities for reform. These theoretical elements will finally be forged into the explanatory model that can account for international variation in the cycles of mental health policy making.

Chapter Three presents the historical assessment of the policy-making framework in which mental health proposals have been developed and adopted. Specifically, in Chapter Three I provide the reader with a brief history of the governmental assumption of responsibility for the poor, sick, and mentally disordered. Nation-building is one of the most crucial of the rationalization processes that have altered traditional societies. As nation-states grew in physical size and expanded the scope of their operations beyond maintenance of internal order and the reduction of external threats to their territory, such nations began to turn their concerns to domestic affairs—e.g., economic and social management. As a result, their citizenry's health and welfare became a concern to nations as political leaders. This expansion of governmental operations into health and welfare services was also a result of the disestablishment of the Catholic Church and concomitant assumption by the state of responsibilities which had hitherto been the province of the Church, e.g., care of the needy, sick, insane, and feeble-minded. Such an historical account of the rationalization of political power and authority is a necessary foundation for my analysis of post-World War II mental health policy-making and an assessment of the importance of the reform movements in England, Sweden, and the United States.

Chapter Four addresses the emergence of mental health reformers and reform movements in each of these nations. Here I will employ the typology of reform movements. One of the significant events of the 19th century was the acceptance of the notion that governments not only had the capacity to alter the lives of its citizens, but also that such alterations could be beneficial. As the nation-state was empowered to rationally shape its citizenry, institutions like public schools, reformatories, workhouses, prisons, and insane asylums became the methods of transforming human behavior and the instruments of social control. Chapter Four focuses on the establishment of the mental hospital in each of these nations and on the impact reformers had in initiating this cycle of mental health policy making. In this chapter I also trace the sources of disillusionment with products of the first phase of reform activity, as the instruments of treatment themselves became part of the problem; that is, as hospitals became overcrowded and understaffed, the initially hopeful expectations were dashed; and, reformers turned to other strategies to relieve the suffering of the mentally disordered.

Chapter Five has several foci. First, I identify the late-19th and early-20th century developments in psychiatric practice that created a period of renewed optimism about the treatability of mental disorders, and, hence a new climate for mental health policy innovations. Specifically, I trace the emergence of the main 20th-century orientations to mental disorders. These advances provided reformers both within and without the psychiatric profession with a renewed sense of confidence that governmental intervention could make a difference in the lives of the disordered. Indeed, the 20th century reconstruction of the reform movements was in part assisted by members of an increasingly medically-trained psychiatric profession. In this chapter I will document this interaction and interpenetration of the psychiatric profession, mental health reform movements, and the allied social work and child guidance movements, to demonstrate how the character of psychiatric reform had been altered by the 1920's.

Chapter Six suggests how modern, total war created a new opportunity for advances by mental reformers. Ironically, warfare has involved governments in the health and welfare of their citizens. And major wars in this century have further deepened the involvement of governments in the lives of the mentally ill. For mental health reformers war provided a number of crucial experiences in the direction of national psychiatric services. I contend that such "training" assisted such reformers as they attempted to alter national mental health policies in the post-war period.

Chapter Seven presents a comparison of the post-World War II mental health policy adoption process in each nation to determine what impact organizational form of reformers has had on the creation of new national policies. The post-World War II period was a crucial policy development juncture. The issue was whether or not national mental health reformers could capitalize on the renewed optimism at this stage in the cycle of mental health reform. In the

U.S. reformers succeeded in creating a separate mental health bureau that could cooperate actively with other elements in the reform movement to further their mutual goals. In England and Sweden a separate organizational base for reform activities was not created. I will show that when mental health reformers lack a powerful bureaucratically-based ally in their reform efforts that these reform activities will be less successful than reform efforts assisted by a bureau. This chapter also examines the role of psychopharmacology in reform. Advances in psychopharmacology made new modes of outpatient, community-based care possible for a larger number of patients than had been thought possible. This factor aided reformers and helps to explain cross-national policy-making outcomes.

Chapter Eight extends the analysis of the differential impact of the mental health reform movements by tracing the policy adoption and implementation process in the 1960's and 1970's. In this chapter, I am concerned with how the different organizational form of reform movements determines how effective such movements are in their efforts to consolidate previous policy advances, restructure services, and adopt new policies. Further, Chapter Eight will document the success of the U.S. reform movement in creating a bureaucratic base and will show how this base accounts for the U.S. policy innovations that have outstripped policy developments in England and Sweden.

Chapter Nine provides an overview of the policy dilemmas facing mental health reformers in the 1980's. This decade will test the capacity of mental health reformers to maintain policy advances and will pose problems that might severely limit the scope of new policy innovation. Particularly inflation, tax-welfare backlash, and devolution of responsibility for welfare and health services to local governments pose challenges that these movements have never faced. I will suggest a strategy that might maximize chances of the mental health reformers maintaining the gains won in the previous decades.

Chapter Ten reviews the theoretical models developed and employed in this policy study. In this chapter, I will modify and extend the models and suggest how they might be utilized in future policy studies.

18

1. Mental illness is incredibly difficult to define. This difficulty stems from a lack of consensus among psychiatrists, psychologists, social psychologists, sociologists, and others as to what constitutes health and illness of the mind. Mechanic (1969) attempts to bring some coherence to this still raging definitional dispute. He says:

   "Although mental illness is identified by aberrant acts and expression, the definition extends beyond these acts to implicate the person's entire identity and personality. Thus when we define such behavior we say not only that the person is behaving in a manner discordant with his circumstances, but also that he is mentally ill or that his mind is disordered." (Mechanic, 1969: 2-3)

   Exploring this social process of identifying aberrant behavior and inferring from that behavior the mental health or illness of a person is beyond the scope of this study. Suffice it to say that mental illness is a broad category, encompassing a wide range of disorders. Thus, in this study I will speak of mental illnesses and disorders in recognition of the heterogeneous nature of these phenomena (cf. Clausen, 1956, 1966).

2. Many observers view the U.S. health care industry with alarm; it is out of control and consuming an ever increasing fraction of our gross national product (now about 9%), increasing the nation's level of health (Illich, 1976; Wildavsky, 1977; Enthoven, 1978).

   Total (public and private) U.S. health care costs as a percent of gross national product have risen from 3.6% in 1929 to 8.2% in 1975. Over the same period there was a 3201.8% increase in health-care expenditures. Since the introduction of Medicaid-Medicare, there has been a dramatic percentage change in percent of GNP devoted to health. In the period from 1950-65 these expenditures rose at an annual rate of 9%; following Medicare-Medicaid's enactment, this rate increased to an annual average of 14%, a 55.5% increase that is attributable to federalizing health insurance for the elderly and poor (Klarman, 1977: 215-134).

The estimates of real per capita spending on health care --i.e., in constant dollars--increased 79% from 1965 to 1976; doctors services increased 74%; hospital care 110%. Enthoven (1978) estimates that from fiscal 1976 to 1978 Medicare costs increased nearly 50%, from 17.8% billion to $26 billion. And that the increased property tax burden borne by states participating in the Medicaid scheme has directly contributed to the explosion in property taxes, and hence, the tax payer revolts and welfare backlash (cf. Wilensky, 1975).

Critics of U.S. health care can be found on all parts of the political ideological spectrum. There are those who favor maximizing consumer choice, increasing competition, eliminating discontinuity of health care coverage, and altering the nexus of the fee-for-service physician, private hospitals, and third party payment (Enthoven, 1978).

This free-market model based critique of health care converges with some of the criticisms of the neo-Marxists (cf. Navarro, 1977). For example, the elements of Krause's (1977) description of the U.S. system and explanation of its failures are remarkably similar to Enthoven's. Krause stresses the domination by physicians, hospitals, and private insurance firms: that all have a vested interest in maintaining the fee-for-service system. Both perspectives view Medicare and Medicaid as simply a new third-party payee that contributes to higher health care cost (cf. Wildavsky, 1977).

Further, Enthoven, Navarro, Krause, and Wildavsky agree that government regulation and health planning have not and will not prove to be effective in either containing the costs of insuring equity. Health-care reform has been on the agendas of Congress and the President since the early 1960's: President Nixon's health insurance proposal, the enactment in 1974 of the Health Planning and Resources Development Act, and President Carter's, Senator Kennedy's and others proposals for hospital cost containment and national health insurance. But the passage of legislation which will contain costs, break the power of vested interests, increase consumer choice and make maximum use of market mechanisms is still to be proposed let alone enacted.

3. From its inception, England's National Health Service's tripartite organization was criticized as a barrier to providing coordinated dual comprehensive health care; this criticism was especially valid for the mental health services within the NHS. The control of the Victorian and Edwardian era mental hospitals devolved to the NHS, and yet the local authorities charged with the after-care of discharged mental patients were not given funds nor were there any formal arrangements to foster community care as an alternative to hospitalization. While informal joint agreements were often negotiated, formal organizational barriers prevented the full realization of the stated community-care goals.

The 1970 local authority social services were reorganized based on the 1969 Seebohm Committee Report. This restructuring of social welfare services was followed by the historical reorganization of all local governments (cf. Redcliffe-Maud and Wood, 1972). These two reorganizations forced the issue of NHS reorganization: after reorganization of local government one of the NHS branches, local authority health services, now was forced to coordinate with totally restructured local government units and those units new social services departments. Logically, the local governmental and social service reorganizations necessitated NHS reform.

In 1974, the integration of the various sub-sectors of the NHS was undertaken that abolished the three separate administrative units for hospitals, general practitioners, and local authority health services. The new NHS organizational structure divided the country into regional, area, and district health authorities. Each of these authorities now has as its responsibility the coordination and provision of all health care services, facilities, and personnel. Under this integrated scheme, the difficulties with referrals, liaison, and service delivery could be reduced; also it was envisioned that the correspondence of the health area authorities with the recently reorganized local governmental units would result in the more efficient and effective delivery of services where the treatment and follow-up responsibilities of health and social services overlap (cf. Cawley and McLachlan, eds., 1973).

4. Stinchcombe (1978) goes on to note:

> "Classifying A and B together is, in a science, an empirical assertion. It says that there is a consequential analogy between A and B. Logically, any class is a statement that, for all the pairs of members of the class, and for a (large) series of general statements made about the class, element A is analogous to element B, B analogous to C, A to C, A to D, etc. That is, a class is a set of pairwise equivalence relations, among elements of the class, with respect to the predicates that apply to the class. We would, in ordinary language, say that the analogy between A and D was a 'deep' analogy, if a great many statements true of A are also true of D. A class in which the equivalences are deep analogies is an important concept. In a science, if these statements are of an important causal character, the concept is important." (Stinchcombe: 21)

Thus, the task of this study is to generate statements of a causal character by the process of identifying the manifestations between reform movements over time within one nation as well as to locate the forms which move-

ments take between nations (cf. Moore, 1967, xivff).
Having located these equivalencies I can gain confidence
in the concept of reform movements, and ultimately suggest how a theory of the formation of reform movements
might be constructed.

5. Following Taylor (1965: 25-25), when I speak of England,
   I also mean Wales, though this will offend Welsh nation-
   alists. This makes sense because of the history of the
   integration of the administration of England and Wales.
   Further, I will be excluding Scotland from my study for
   analogous historical reasons. Since the union of Scotland with England and Wales in 1707, the Scottish
   peoples have maintained, and indeed they are today
   expanding, the independence of the direct control over,
   many of their institutions--legal, educational, and
   social welfare. Thus, when legislation was enacted in
   1946 to establish a National Health Service for England
   and Wales, separate services were established for Scotland and Northern Ireland. For this reason, the health
   service data base is non-comparable for the four
   countries making up the United Kingdom.

6. Glaser and Strauss (1967), speak of the advantages of
   this approach:

> "Like interviews and field work, library
> sources can yield materials about the
> past, but with the immense advantage
> that they allow us to listen to and
> observe (if metaphorically) long-dead
> persons as if they were actually still
> alive." (Glaser and Strauss: 176)

Like actual informants, the library and other archival
data permitted me to develop a narrative and therefore
to gain access to the key participants in past mental
health reform movements in the three nations under
study. Further, many of the writers of accounts of
mental health policy making were, and some still are,
active participants in the mental health reform process:

23

Clifford Beers, Enoch Powell, Kathleen Jones, Richard Titmuss, Robert Felix, Mike Gorman to name only a few. As such, their written accounts are versions of the policy developments in their country that constitute, on the one hand, a chronological record of events and, on the other, one of many policy perspectives on a reality that require verification from other sources.

I worked in the libraries of the University of California, Berkeley; London School of Economics; Bedford College (University of London); England's York University; University of Texas at Dallas; University Health Science Center at Dallas; and Southern Methodist University. I used numerous other libraries by means of inter-library loans. Also, I employed the archives of the English National Association for Mental Health, Bedford College's Social Research Unit, the European Office of the World Health Organization in Copenhagen, and Sweden's Socialstyrelsen. I am indebted to all the helpful staffs of these facilities for assisting me in gathering the data to construct my narrative.

CHAPTER II

A THEORY OF REFORM MOVEMENTS

Students of the public policy making process have observed that a variety of organizational methods have been employed by advocates of intentional social change. Smelser (1962) has classified reform movements into value-oriented and norm-oriented reform movements depending upon the level and scope of social change attempted by such reformers. Ripley and Franklin (1980) have developed the concept of the sub-government; such sub-governments include individuals and organizations within and without bureaucracies and legislatures that seek to create and implement social policies. Alford (1975) uses the notion of structural interests to capture the phenomenon of forces that are mobilized to block social reforms. Estes (1979) speaks of networks of advocates, administrators and analysts, that are created by and help perpetuate social reforms. This analysis of mental health policy making will present a formal, theoretical statement of the process of the formation of the bases for social action of reformers and reform movements.

Conceptual Clarification of Reform Movements, Interest Groups, and Lobbyists

A variety of concepts are used to discuss the forces involved in social policy formulation and implementation. Among the most widely employed are reform movements, structural-interest groups, and lobbyists. In my view, social reform movements, structural-interests groups, and lobbyists must be analytically distinguished one from another in order to more fully develop the linkages between these concepts. Reform movements are the broadest category of these three potential, social change agents; they may range from groups committed to revitalizing fundamental social values to groups interested in readressing specific grievances (cf. Smelser, 1962). In contrast to this broad category of reform movements, the concept of structural-interest groups is narrower and may or may not generate social reform movements

(Alford, 1975). Following Dahrendorf (1959), I view such groups as growing out of the conflicts and contradictions inherent in the division of labor and structure of distribution of power and rewards.[1] Narrowly-based conflict groups may seek to defend their status, power, wealth, or class position against other groups, and thus may not generate a broad-based reform movement: e.g., the American Medical Association is such an interest group, with specific concerns which do not easily lend themselves to formation of a reform movement. Finally, unless reform movements and structural interest groups accept as ligitimate the given political-institutions and procedures they are unlikely to engage in lobbying activity designed to further those reform goals or defend or advance their structural interests. Lobbyists, then, are the most narrowly defined of these concepts: lobbyists and lobbies must at least appear to accept the normative procedures for reaching decisions and being willing to work within the given normative environment to accomplish their goals, or those of their employers.

Rationalization of authority. In my study of mental health reform in England, Sweden, and the U.S. I will note that as nation-states assumed a greater role in the provision of social-welfare services these services have increasingly come under rational-legal (i.e., bureaucratic) control. More specifically, as reform policies were instituted to insure citizens against the risks of old age, disability, unemployment and disease, these programs have increasingly come under bureaucratic control. As a result the advocates of these programs have often times themselves become bureaucratically-based tribunes for the heterogeneous population they seek to represent and serve (Armour, et al, 1978; cf. Wilensky, 1975).

In programs for the mentally disordered this same rationalization process can be observed. This concept of rationalization is employed in the same technical sense that Weber (1978) intended; that is, rationalization in the realm of power and authority applies to the social process whereby the exercise of governmental action is increasingly placed on a formal, written legal basis. This rationalization process in policy making is marked by the initiation of and expansion of services to treat or solve a set of socially-recognized ills. Specifically, in mental health policy this rationalization process began in the 19th century when concerned citizens and humanitarian social reformers succeeded in convincing governments to establish specialized facilities for the treatment of the mentally disordered. Inspired by the moral treatment regimes of asylum directors William Tuke of England and Philippe Pinel of France, mental health reformers hoped to cure the mentally ill by asylum treatment only to find that the problems of administering, staffing, and funding these facilities created a whole host of unanticipated problems, not the least of which was the deterioration of care in overcrowded hospitals. Thus, these hospitals increasingly came under bureaucratic control as governments sought to gain control over their costs and to organize the network of asylums that had been constructed in an unsystematic fashion in response to the specific demands of the mental health reformers (cf. Deutsch, 1949; Dain, 1964; Caplan, 1969; Rothman, 1971; Jones, 1972; Grob, 1973).

In the 20th century, this process of mental health reform has continued, but the increasingly rational-legal content of policy design and implementation has changed the terms in which reforms can be conceived (Clausen, 1956, 1966; Mechanic, 1969). In the United States in the post-World War II era, the advocates of mental health reform themselves helped create and administer a federal agency, the National Institute of Mental Health. The NIMH became an important force in a campaign to transform psychiatric treatment in the United States (Barton and Sanborn, 1977).

Reform movements. Smelser (1962) has categorized persons who adhere to a "norm-oriented belief" as often also envisioning:

> "...the restoration, protection, modification, or creation of social norms. More particularly, they may demand a rule, a law, a regulatory agency, designed to control the inadequate, ineffective, or irresponsible behavior of individuals." (Smelser, 1962: 109)

Such norm-oriented beliefs generate social reform movements that seek to mobilize people for action, frequently creating a norm or an organization. I will call norm-oriented movements social reform movements and will attempt to link such reform movements with the concepts of lobbyists and interest groups.

Unlike the value-oriented movements (Smelser, 1962: 313-381) that seek often times to revolutionize the overarching value structure of society, social reform movements' more specific objectives lead them to deal with existing social, political, and economic institutions in the effort to realize the reform objectives.[2]

Further, such social reform movements may or may not have their origins in the conflicts and contradictions inherent in the division of labor and the differential distribution of economic rewards, social status, and political power. I consider structural-interest groups more closely linked to the economic reward structure of society, hence I differentiate interest groups from reform movements on this criterion.

Reform movements may or may not decide to lobby political leaders to obtain movement objectives. The decision to lobby is based on the assumption that political institutions and processes are ligitimate and capable of effecting the desired social change or reform. Without this presumption of legitimacy and relevance a person who dealt intimately with legislators and administrators would find it difficult to work convincingly and effectively within the sometimes arcane and arbitrary conventions governing the decision-making process.[3]

Thus, for my purposes social reform movements are broadly-based organizations of individuals, coalescing around a key issue, or issues; and, such movements intentionally direct their activity to realize their reform goals. Further, a particular social reform movement may not always employ given political institutional means of effecting social change; often reform movements bypass the conventional political procedures; in some cases, they are committed to the reconstruction of those institutions. The The U.S. and English mental health associations that lobby national and local governments illustrate the connection between two of these concepts. The lobbies of these movements have their roots in the 19th-century social reform movements that were committed to the reconstruction of society through the establishment of asylums and other rehabilitation institutions (Rothman, 1971; Grob, 1973; cf. Jones, 1972).

Structural-interest groups. Structural-interest groups can form cohesive units and develop into formal associations for the purpose of advancing and defending those interests. These interest groups may seek to defend those interests, and, hence, engage in lobbying activities. Yet, such actions may block policy initiatives attempted by reform movements.

Alford (1975) developed the concept of structural-interest groups in order to illuminate the role of health professionals and organizations in resisting the reform of municipal health services. I believe such interest groups can not only attempt to coopt and thwart reforms; such structural interests may initiate reforms themselves by working with existing movements, or directly initiating their own lobbying campaign to influence decision makers.

Lobbyists. The literature on lobbies and lobbyists abounds with discussions of their role in the legislative and executive decision-making process (Schriftgiesser, 1951; Milbrath, 1963; Olson, 1965; McConnell, 1966). I suggest that to make theoretical sense of reform movements the connection between the reform movement objectives and their lobbying activities needs to be explicated. The concepts of the lobby and of the lobbyist are often used without much analytic precision in studies of the proceedings and outcomes of policy deliberations. Clearly the dictionary definition of a lobby and a lobbyist is not adequate for my purposes.[4]

The studies of the cycles of mental health reform reveal that lobbyists can be based in governmental bureaucracies, or represent formally organized voluntary associations, or act as agents for an ad hoc, special-purpose organization. In some cases the lobbyist is synonymous with structural-interest group. This diversity of potential lobby or lobbyist must be captured in any analytic typology of concepts which presumes to be exhaustive and useful.

Lobbyists—ranging from an individual through organized associations to departments of the government—act directly by means of informal personal contacts, written appeals, formal testimony, and the like, to alter the outcome of governmental deliberations, be they executive, legislative, or even judicial. More importantly, for my purposes, lobbyists may or may not represent structural-interest groups. Thus, I define lobbyist as one who seeks to influence the outcome of governmental deliberations—executive or legislative—by direct personal contact, e.g., testimony, personal conversations, letter writing, and the like. Such lobbyists may or may not be connected with a structural-interest group or social reform movement.

Intelligence and Reform Movements

The analytic distinctions drawn thus far can be enhanced if the forms of intelligence employed by these reformers, interest groups, and their lobbyists can be discerned. Intelligence of all kinds is crucial for the success of agents of change. A precise definition of social intelligence is required in order to link it to these various types of social change agents.

Wilensky (1972) defines intelligence broadly enough to be useful for understanding its role in the policy-making process. He says:

"Intelligence denotes the information—question, insights, hypotheses, evidence—relevant to policy. It includes both scientific knowledge and political or ideological information, scientific or not, overt or covert." (Wilensky, 1972: 2)

This definition is analytically useful because it places intelligence squarely within the process of policy making. Further, such a policy-relevant definition of organizational intelligence has important implications for a theory of reform movements. Since intelligence spans the scientific as well as the ideological, one might expect that conceptual connections could be drawn between forms of policy-relevant intelligence and forms of the agents of social change, i.e., reform movements (cf. Perrow, 1979: 190-194).

My analysis of mental health policy making will suggest that such connections between organizational form of reform movements and intelligence do exist. For example, in the 1950's and 60's United States Senator Lester Hill assumed a leadership role in the deliberations over mental health legislation; he required mental health reform relevant intelligence (i.e., information about the nature of mental diseases, estimates of their prevalence and incidence, data on the social, economic, and political costs of untreated and treated episodes) to justify enacting federal government programs to combat mental diseases. In short, Hill had a need policy intelligence; it was given to him formally and informally by elements of the mental health reform movement: mental health lobbyist Mike Gorman; NIMH administrator Dr. Robert Felix; NIMH's other professional and technical staff; medical and social scientific professional associations; and, professional psychiatric and psychological associations. Some of these elements of the reform movement that were based federal bureaucracy, with close links with state mental health officials, university-based experts, and formally organized professional associations constituted what Ripley and Franklin (1980) call a sub-government (Felix, 1967; cf., Foley, 1975; Barton and Sanborn, 1977).

The ligitimation function of organizational intelligence. Organizational intelligence is not only necessary for the policy maker to select from among a range of programmatic options, it is also an important source of the legitimacy claimed by policy advocates recommending one option over another; further, such intelligence can later serve the ends of law makers seeking to defend their decisions and to build public acceptance of options decided upon. Wilensky (1967) notes the importance of this legitimation function of intelligence:

"Even if technical intelligence never persuades
anybody (and we have seen that this assumption
is grossly exaggerated) the 'window dressing'
function goes beyond the rationalization of
policy to the creation of the verbal environment of an organization--hardly a trivial
matter." (Wilensky: 19)

An analytic typology that purports to be useful must take
into account this legitimation function of organizational
intelligence. In the public policy making process there is
often time fierce competition between proponents of various
policy options characterized by campaigns to insure that the
"right kind" of evidence dominates the policy deliberations.

For example, for the reform organizations, lobbyist
intelligence can play a crucial role in their activities. I
will demonstrate that it is not only the political clout of
a lobby which impresses a member of Parliament, Congress, or
Riksdag, but also the intellectual foundation and credibility of the arguments made. Thus, the technical and scientific bases of the evidence presented formally and informally are an important elements in the presentation of
lobbyists and, hence, ought to be part of any analytic model
that attempts to impose intellectual order on the range of
phenomena (Jewell and Patterson, 1977: 286ff).

Weberian Model of Ideal-Type Construction

Comparative studies of social systems and processes can
not help but draw on the methods of pioneering social scientist Max Weber. His encyclopedic knowledge, his conceptual
insights, his meticulous, analytic methods remain awesome
even in an age of quantitative analysis. Among Weber's
notable contributions to the lexicon social science methods
is his ideal-typical mode of analysis; among the most significant of these pure types is the typology of domination
(herrschaft) (Bendix, 1960: 285ff; Roth, 1978: xxxiii-cx).

Weber's typology proposed to render the range of modes
of domination and control move intelligible by the use of
three analytic concepts: charisma, tradition, and bureau-

cracy. Each of these represents a mode of domination which is associated with specific forms of legitimacy, i.e., the bases of compliance and acceptance of these forms of control and methods of organizing political, economic, and other forms of human action.[5]

Weber's ideal types of domination can be adapted for the goal of building a theory of reformers, reform movements, lobbyists, and structural interest groups operating in the policy arena. My examination of the history of mental health reform will demonstrate that reformers and lobbyists may or may not be linked with formal associations; these solo-charismatic reformers and lobbyists (e.g., America's 19th-century reformer, Dorothea Dix) can be quite effective and do not necessarily generate an organization for the express purposes of perpetuating their work. Also, the data will show that lobbyists may be both reform minded and members of the governmental bureaucracy (e.g., Dr. Robert Felix of the U.S. National Institute of Mental Health). A lobbyists-reformer can be linked to a number of informally organized reformers whose tenacity and strategic placement lends success to their activity (e.g., Mike Gorman of the National Committee Against Mental Illness). Further, evidence will show that members of a legislative body also can play a role as founding members of reform associations, act on behalf of the mentally ill in a legislative body, sit on an executive board to inspect the treatment of mental patients, and be recognized as the chief spokesman for mental patients (e.g., England's 19th-century champion of the poor, Lord Shaftesbury). Finally, a reformer may not be primarily concerned with altering by political means the services provided for the mentally disordered; reformers may be chiefly concerned with innovating or adapting new treatment modalities (e.g., England's psychiatric pioneer William Tuke).

Thus far several conceptual tasks have been achieved. Three basic types of mental health reformers and lobbyists have been discerned and linked to these reformers and movements; the conceptual connection between the solo reformer and the charismatic leader of Weber's typology of authority and the analogy between the bureaucratically-based, professionaly-trained reformers and the officials of Weber's type of rational-legal domination have been made.

The task now is to construct a typology of reform movement that integrates these concepts.

A Typology of Reformers and Reform Movements

From the range of data on reformers and reform movements three broad categories of phenomena can be gleaned. First, the history of social reform is replete with individuals who take upon themselves the tasks of investigating and solving a social problem. These individuals most closely approximate the charismatic leadership mode of control that Weber elaborated (Weber, 1978: 241-254). A second phenomenon that the history of social reform reveals is the rise of associations of reform-minded persons who seek to accomplish their social-change objectives by means of a formally-constituted organization. These associations are analogous to the traditional modes of authority that Weber notes are inherently more stable and predictable than the highly personalized, unique foundations of charismatic rule. Finally, the further transformations undergone by reform movements in this century have resulted in the bureaucratic placement of reformers. Such further routinization and rationalization of social reform action is obviously a specific example of the pervasive process of rationalization that has been and is revolutionizing our social worlds. Let me further specify the implications of each of these concepts of reform actors and organizations. In this specification process I also will note how forms of reform intelligence are linked to each of these types of actors—individual and collective— that seek to alter society's normative order.

The charismatic-social reformer. This notion of charismatic-social reformer most closely approximates Weber's conception of charismatic leader (cf. Eisenstadt, 1968).[6] A charismatic-social reformer is a person who by force of his personal qualities—impeccable life-style, energetic commitment, uncorruptability—is able to fully devote his whole life to the cause of gaining public approval for the reform advocates. In the pure type, the whole personality of the charismatic reformer can be fused with the movement or cause. For example, Dorothea Dix so zealously pursued the goal of establishing a network of state mental hospitals that she became tied in the public's mind with the cause of the mentally ill. Like other charismatic leaders, she had complete faith in her cause and in her powers of persuasion. And her total devotion to the cause attracted attention and convinced others of the necessity of taking her testimony on behalf of the insane seriously (Deutsch, 1949: 158-185).

Following the analogy with Weber's model of charismatic authority, I believe that the charismatic reformer's authority rests in part with the selflessness with which such an advocate pursues his cause. For example, the arguments presented by Dorothea Dix had credibility because Dix's demands for social change were perceived to be made by a person who had little if anything to gain—financial or otherwise—from her efforts on behalf of a socially worth-while cause. One might predict that when the self-interestedness of a charismatic advocate is revealed, their credibility is greatly reduced, if not destroyed. This destruction of a reformer's charisma is analogous to the legitimacy crisis posed by the corruption of charismatic, moral or spiritual leaders.

<u>Forms of intelligence and charismatic reform.</u> Like the forms of charismatic authority elaborated by Weber, the charismatic-social reformer exhibits a kind of "irrationality." That is, charisma's appeal is, by definition, based upon a unique set of qualities that attract people and grip their imaginations. In the case of 18th- and 19th-century charismatic reformers this "irrationality" is revealed by the underdevelopment of the social scientific justifications for their plans for social change.

In fact, even today, the technical, scientific, or rationally coherent evidence for the positions advocated by the charismatic reformer is less important than the belief in the sincerity and impeccability of those arguing for a reform porposal. To return to the case of Miss Dix, the low-level of development of the physical and social sciences in the 19th century obviously meant she was unable to offer evidence which we would today consider adequate support for the institutionalization policy. This lack of the rational, scientific bases of her arguments did not mean that the mid-19th century support of mental hospitals in the U.S. and England did not make use of intelligence as we have broadly

defined it.   Following Wilensky's definition of intelligence, Dix's evidence of the effectiveness of institutional
treatment can be classified as ideological information and
quasi-scientific evidence (Deutsch, 1949).

The routinization of charismatic reform.   Like Weber's
charismatic leaders, solo reformers exhibit many of the same
qualities of instability and unpredictability that other
charismatic leaders manifest.   Further, like their religious
and warrior counterparts, charismatic social reformers must
create, or have created for themselves, organizations that
can perpetuate their goals and activities.   Hence, the
emergence of reform movements, associations, unions, fellowships, and societies. Such organizations enable a charismatic reformer to both share the work of social reform and
continue this work once the charismatic leader retires or
dies.   This solution to the problem of continuing the reform
activities when the charismatic leader has left the scene
was given the label routinization by Weber.   The study of
reform movements reveals that this routinization process
always takes place in the arena of intentional social
change.   For example, Clifford Beers' profound, personal
encounter with mental disease and his experience of the
horrors of the treatments for mental illness was presented
in his autobiography.   Yet Beers' struggle against madness
and the maltreatment of the mentally ill was not a personal
one; he formed a National Committee for Mental Hygiene, the
precursor of a national organization designed to convince
state legislators and governors of the need to invest more
money to improve the quality of patient treatment.

Routinization of charismatic reformers and Weber's concept of traditionalism.   By the routinization of charismatic
-social reformers I do not mean to imply that a direct
organizational   successor   (e.g.,   National   Committee   for
Mental Hygiene) is analogous to Weber's traditional mode of
domination and social control.   By traditionalism Weber
means something very specific:

    "...the psychic attitute-set for the habitual work-
    aday and the belief in the everyday routine as an
    inviolable norm of conduct. Domination that rests
    upon this basis, that is, upon peity for what......

actually, allegedly, or presumably has always existed, will be called 'traditional authority.'" (Weber, 1946: 296)

Social movements, and their specialized lobbying components, are usually not involved in accepting "what is" as inviolable, but rather, are actively engaged in affecting changes in the social order, i.e., transforming perceptions of the status quo, pointing to its inadequacies, and suggesting specific institutional changes. Rather than accepting the extant, normative order, social reform organizations often take on the job of effecting normative changes. And in actively altering the political, social, and economic environment, they may not necessarily be seeking personal benefits, or benefits for others, but may truly be self-effacing and altruistic.

Reform organizations are able to transcend the barriers that can normally restrict a solo reformer or lobbyist. The continuity provided ensures that the issues that originally motivated the individual will survive, to be pursued by another committee generation. Thus, the thorough routinization of a social reform movement does not necessarily involve a commitment to the norm or routine, but rather entails the routinization of social change or at least a continuing commitment to it.

Finally, the creation of social reform organizations in the mental health field was a 19th-century phenomenon, analogous to the formation of voluntary associations and movements to deal with a wide range of social ills (cf. Smelser, 1962: 270-312). These organizations sometimes sought to further the understanding of mental diseases, to eliminate the popularly held "myths" of mental illnesses, and to create a much more favorable climate for the reception and adoption of their proposals for reform. In addition, some voluntary organizations became directly involved in the provision of mental health services, in an attempt to fill gaps in national services and to demonstrate the effectiveness of new treatment modalities.

Intelligence and reform associations. The formation of reform associations marks a rationalization of the organizational form of purposive agents of social change. Associated with this development is the improvement of the intelligence base for social reform that placed this work on a more stable, predictable basis. I will demonstrate that the rise of reform associations is linked to advances in the knowledge of the probable causes and correlates of mental disorders. Particularly in the 20th century, advances in psychiatric practice were often incorporated into the reform campaigns of various associations. This intelligence was employed to lend greater credibility to calls for specific reform proposals as well as to evaluate the effectiveness of the new methods of treatment.

Bureaucratically-based reform movements. For Weber the central tendency in the modernization of traditional societies was the extension into the application of the principle of rationalization (cf. Giddens, 1977:169-184).[7] In the field of authority and administration this rationalization tendency is expressed most fully in rational-legal forms of administration. In the arena of social reform this rationalization process can be seen in the emergence of governmental departments, bureaus, and agencies that embody the reform movement's objectives for social change.

The crucial analytic distinction that needs to be drawn here is this: the conception of reform as bureaucratized does not necessarily convey the sense of rigidity, impersonality, and detachment that Weber suggests inheres in the pure type of rational-legal rule. Weber's pure type of bureaucracy certainly contains that element of calcification; but, Weber's formulation also explicitly views the rationalization of authority as having a revolutionary impact on social life. This transforming potential of the government bureau has been perceived by reformers and their associations.

Scientific intelligence and bureaucratic-based reform movements. In contrast to solo reformers and voluntary organizations, the greater success of bureaucratically-based reformers lies in part in improvements in the quality of intelligence available to bureaucratic reformers. For

38

example, by virtue of being part of the national government, the reformers in the U.S. National Institute of Mental Health commissioned, possessed, and acquired the policy-relevant, organizational intelligence that was used in order to further their reform goals. By understanding the need for Congressional allies to secure ever larger budgetary appropriations, NIMH was able to develop relationships with strategically placed Members of Congress who were both favorably disposed to NIMH's goals and positioned to assist in the accomplishment of those goals (cf. Chu and Trotter, 1974).

Further, the NIMH staff, in contrast to the early social reformers and members of many of the voluntary reform organizations, were not only in possession of important organizational intelligence, but also at an advantage compared with their 19th century reform counterparts by virtue of their medical science and social scientific training and professional experience. This more scientific basis of mental health practice gave greater legitimacy to the proposals for reform that were suggested by the national experts lodged in government bureaus.

As will be shown, the policy advocate—whether the 19th century charismatic-social reformer, the staff of a reform organization, or the bureaucratically-based reform lobbyist —all require policy intelligence. What is new in the 20th century business of advising leaders is the transformation of both the nature of intelligence and the methods used to gather and analyze it. One expression of the rationalization process is best seen in the adoption of the scientific method of gathering intelligence and in the emergence of the scientific expert advisor. In mental health, the expansion of knowledge of mental disorders, both medical and social scientific assisted policy-makers in designing more successful programs to treat mental illness.

The Formal Typology of Social Reform Movements

The solo reformer and reform movements (i.e., norm-oriented movements) in a variety of forms can be logically classified according to the organizational type and the modes of intelligence employed by such reformers. Thus, Smelser's concept of norm-oriented social reform movements, a neo-Weberian typology of reform movements, and Wilensky's concept of organizational intelligence can be analytically linked. Figure 1 presents the elements of an analytic typology that will guide this study. The three main dimensions of this typology are: (1) the degree of specificity of the reformer or reform movement's objectives ranging from movements and individuals that have broad aims for their reform activities are analytically separable from those with more limited objectives (cf. Smelser, 1962: 120-129; 313ff); (2) the degree of rationalization of the organizational determines the form of the reform movement, i.e., solo-charismatic, formal associational, and bureaucratic; and, (3) the forms of intelligence employed by reformers and reform movements can be classified as political ideological, impressionistic evidence, and rational-scientific.

The specific examples of each type of reform movement in Figure 1 will be provided in the course of the analysis; a completed version of the table will be presented in Chapter Ten. At this stage in the study it is sufficient to point to the elaboration of the forms of reform movements, and the associated forms of intelligence, that will guide this study of social reform movements.

The uses of this typology. The variation in the outcomes of the mental health reform campaigns has several determinants. The typology presented in Figure 1 is designed to more exactly conceptualize the variable causal impact of national reform movements in the policy-making political process. Specifically, this typology focuses attention on the variable form of reform movements and suggests the relations between reform movements and other factors that help determine the outcomes of policy making. Obviously, reformers and reform movements, whatever their organizational form and intelligence bases, are not the sole cause of the changes in national mental health policy. The interaction between reform movements and other factors will be traced in subsequent chapters. These factors will include: (1) the differing organizational forms of national governments; (2) the form and the degree of development of national health and welfare services; (3) the stage, form of

FIGURE 1

BROAD-AIM REFORM AND SPECIFIC REFORM MOVEMENTS, ORGANIZATIONAL FORMS, AND INTELLIGENCE BASES*

FORMS OF INTELLIGENCE EMPLOYED BY REFORMERS AND REFORM MOVEMENTS				
RATIONAL-SCIENTIFIC INTELLIGENCE	IMPRESSIONISTIC EVIDENCE FORMS OF INTELLIGENCE	POLITICAL IDEOLOGICAL INTELLIGENCE		
	HORACE MANN	BENJAMIN RUSH	SOLO CHARISMATIC REFORMERS	BROAD-AIM REFORM MOVEMENTS
			FORMAL ASSOCIATION BASED REFORM ORGANIZATIONS	
UK MIN. OF HEALTH UNDER 1945-50 LABOUR GOVERNMENT	NEW YORK STATE CHARITY BOARDS OF THE 19TH CENTURY		BUREAU-CRATICALLY BASED REFORMERS	
	DOROTHEA DIX	WILLIAM TUKE OF THE YORK RETREAT	SOLO CHARISMATIC REFORMERS	SPECIFIC REFORM MOVEMENTS
	C. BEERS' NATIONAL COMMITTEE FOR MENTAL HYGIENE		FORMAL ASSOCIATION BASED REFORM ORGANIZATIONS	
U.S. NATIONAL INSTITUTE OF MENTAL HEALTH	ENGLISH METROPOLITAN LUNACY COMMISSION	PHILIPPE PINEL AS ADMINI-STRATOR OF BICETRE	BUREAU-CRATICALLY BASED REFORMERS	

* A COMPLETED VERSION OF THIS CONCEPTUAL FIGURE WILL BE PRESENTED IN CHAPTER 10

41

development, and policy relevance of mental health and allied professional associations; (4) the differential impact of national crises that may create reform opportunities; (5) the variable effect of the innovations in the methods of treating mental disorders and the etiological theories attached to these treatment modalities.

In my opinion, the revolutionizing rationalization process is the force that shapes most of these elements that are connected in a causal mental health policy-making process. The flow of such a causal process should look something like Figure 2.

Figure 2 captures the connections (and interconnections) between the forces that determine mental health policy-making processes and the policies that emerge from the legislative and administrative deliberations. First, beginning with the left side, Figure 2 suggests that changing causal (etiological) theories of mental disorders shapes (and in turn is shaped by) the organizational form of mental health reformers and reform movements (and their related intelligence bases). Second, Figure 2 notes that the "discovery" (or "rediscovery") of the mentally ill can be determined by the changing causal theories of mental illnesses. This diagram also locates national crises (e.g., mobilizing, total warfare) that may contribute to this discovery of the insane, and hence the identification of a social problem that requires a policy solution. Third, Figure 2 links the organizational forms of reform movements and their related intelligence bases, and the mental health professional associations in the creation of a mental health reform lobby. This lobby may be more or less tightly organized as it seeks to play a role in the policy-making process. Fourth, this figure also represents the variable organizational form of national governments. This is a factor that sets the terms for policy deliberations, the "rules of the policy-making and implementing game." National governmental forms are also one of the determinants of the organization of health and welfare services, and such governments must deal with, and in turn are altered by, national crises, hence, the connections shown in Figure 2. Fifth, the organizational form of national health and welfare services give rise to bureaucratic-based lobbyists and

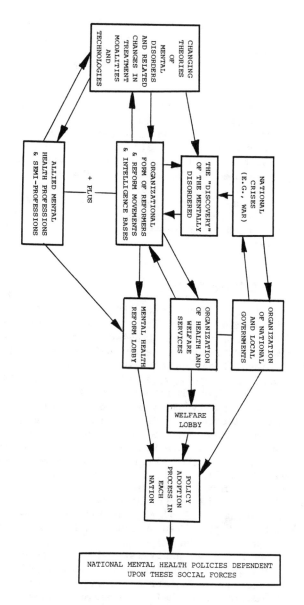

FIGURE 2

CAUSAL RELATIONSHIPS OF THE PRINCIPLE ELEMENTS IN MENTAL HEALTH POLICY ADOPTION

CHANGING THEORIES OF MENTAL DISORDERS AND RELATED CHANGES IN TREATMENT MODALITIES AND TECHNOLOGIES

ALLIED MENTAL HEALTH PROFESSIONS & SEMI-PROFESSIONS

ORGANIZATIONAL FORM OF REFORMERS & REFORM MOVEMENTS & INTELLIGENCE BASES

THE "DISCOVERY" OF THE MENTALLY DISORDERED

NATIONAL CRISES (E.G., WAR)

+ PLUS

MENTAL HEALTH REFORM LOBBY

ORGANIZATION OF HEALTH AND WELFARE SERVICES

ORGANIZATION OF NATIONAL AND LOCAL GOVERNMENTS

WELFARE LOBBY

POLICY ADOPTION PROCESS IN EACH NATION

NATIONAL MENTAL HEALTH POLICIES DEPENDENT UPON THESE SOCIAL FORCES

43

their allies that seek to influence policy deliberations. Since mental health is one topic of social welfare policy deliberations, the lobbyists concerned with the broad array of welfare state services will be involved in mental health policy making.

In sum, Figure 2 locates the mental health reformers in the policy-making process. Given that the organizational and intelligence forms of reform movements are variable, the policy-making impact of such reformers will be dependent upon the form such movements take. In this way, the typology of reform movements (Figure 1) and the mapping of the relationships of the factors determining mental health policy making (Figure 2) are linked. These specific linkages will be drawn and illustrated in subsequent chapters that trace the cycles of policy making in the United States, England, and Sweden.

Concluding Theoretical Remarks

In this chapter, I have drawn the analytic distinctions that have not been made before or not clearly drawn: specifically, the differences and linkages between reformers, reform movements, structural interest groups, and lobbyists. This analytic identification process was a prelude to constructing an analytic typology of reform movements. Second, I identified organizational intelligence as a concept that should be included in a typology of reform movements. Third, I defined and illustrated the concepts of charismatic, associational, and bureaucratic reform movements; I noted how the rationalization of the organizational form of reform movements was tied to the stages in the development of policy-relevant intelligence. This merging of the ideal-typical forms of reform movements and intelligence yielded an analytic typology that will guide my analysis of mental health policy-making in England, Sweden, and the United States. Finally, I presented a conceptual diagram of the policy-making process, the key elements of which I will focus on in the following analysis. This statement of the connections between governmental forms, health and welfare services, advances in psychiatric theory, national crises, and reform movements and their professional associational allies, suggests how these forces are connected in the social process that yields mental health policies.

Chapter Three builds on these theoretical discussions by tracing the rationalization and expansion of political authority in each of the countries under study. This analysis points to the different form the nation-state took in each country and how this transformation of political authority was coupled with the assumption by secular authorities of the responsibility for the mentally disordered among the populations of many dependent persons. I contend that to understand present-day, cross-national variations in mental health policy making one must have a clear understanding of these socio-historical foundations of governmental services for the mentally disordered.

1. The concept of conflict groups is still best illuci-
dated by Dahrendorf (1959). In his attempt to clarify
and thereby improve, the utility of Marx's concept of
class, Dahrendorf pointed to an important fact of modern
industrial life: conflict groups in society are founded
upon the contradictions in and differential distribution
of power and authority in the organization of work and
other social processes. That is, given the division of
labor, groups in work situations come into conflict
because they perceive their interests as different
(e.g., control over the pace of the assembly line,
determination of the number of persons required to
perform a task, etc.). Thus, such groups have different
interests which are at the root of their conflicts, and
such interests can be called structural when we can
identify the specific loci of these conflicts in the
social-organizational structure (cf. Giddens, 1973:
51-59; 275ff).

2. Smelser's (1962: 120-129; 313ff) analysis differen-
tiates value-oriented from norm-oriented beliefs and
movements along a number of dimensions. He says that
value-oriented movements

> "...attempt to restore, protect, modify, or
> create values in the name of a generalized
> belief. Such a belief necessarily involves
> all components of action; that is, it envi-
> sions a reconstitution of values, a redefi-
> nition of norms, a reorganization of the
> motivation of individuals, and a redefini-
> tion of situational facilities." (Smelser,
> 1962: 313)

Smelser makes other useful theoretical points. First,
his analytic distinction between general- and specific-
reform movements is useful and can be incorporated into
the schema I have developed for analyzing the relation-

ship between forms of organization and their intelligence bases. That is, general, humanitarian movements
of the late-18th and early-19th centuries "lay behind a
vast number of more specific reforms not only in the
fields of international peace, but also with regard to
the status of slaves, criminals, children, animals, and
the insane" (Smelser: 273). Obviously, this study is
focused on the specific reform movement in the struggle
for reforming treatment of the insane in the U.S.,
Sweden, and England. But a theory of reform movements
of all kinds must account for the broad-aim movements of
an associational nature, emphasizing political-ideological intelligence. A movement may pursue its goals
outside of the formal political channels of influence
and information, and may seek to represent its cause in
marches, appeals, and protests (e.g., the 1960's and
70's anti-war movements). In contrast, many specific
reform movements did use direct contacts with officials
in an effort to put an end to the fight (e.g., Viet Nam
Veterans Against the War).

The "general" and "specific" distinction requires refinement in order to locate the forces that can initiate
a movement; i.e., a charismatic reformer. Smelser
(1962) notes that many movements simply bypass the
charismatic phase and move to the associational level:

> "Many social movements in the U.S. have had
> their beginnings in hastily convened,
> unstable associations and then evolved into
> institutionalized pressure groups through
> which grievances are channeled routinely."
> (Smelser: 277)

Smelser contrasts the early Grange with the latter day,
Washington, D.C.-based farm organizations, though in
periods of acute economic distress, the institutionalized pressure groups are often bypassed by associations of militants who seek recognition of their plight
and redress for their grievances directly.

3. For example, American and European environmental-ecological movements, the societies for prevention of cruelty to animals, or the prohibitionist parties did not spring directly from class conflict as defined by Dahrendorf (1959). Other reform movements are generated in the struggle for control of the work place, or access to the ballot box, or the distribution of society's wealth, e.g., trade unions, suffrage campaigns, civil rights movements, or revolutionary parties (cf. Thompson, 1968 and Marshall, 1964).

4. Webster's Third International Dictionary defines the work lobbyist as,

> "Persons who frequent the lobbies of a legislative house to do business with the members; specifically, not members of a legislative body and not holding government office who attempt to influence legislators or other public officials through personal contact; particularly groups of such personnel representing a special interest."

In these terms a lobby and lobbyists consist of a person, group of persons, or organizations who seek to influence the outcome of a legislative process. It is clear that this dictionary definition of the lobby and the lobbyist is too limited; it does not capture the range of phenomena which can be categorized under the heading: activity designed to influence the outcome of legislative or other governmental deliberations. The case of the United States NIMH lobbying on behalf of policies it designed reveals the brittleness of this definition; the evidence of the bureaucratically-based mental health officialdom, actively seeking to shape the outcomes, legislative proceedings, and thereby insuring their ultimate control over the implementation of a resulting policy, reveals the dictionary definition's weakness to aptly describe the extent and complexity of lobbies and lobbying.

5. Merton (1967) presents a useful insight into the nature of a theory construction in the social sciences. He states that unlike the natural and physical sciences, social sciences much more dependent upon the "classics" for theory-building purposes:

> "The record shows that the physical and life sciences have generally been more successful than the social sciences in retrieving relevant cumulative knowledge from the past and incorporating it in subsequent formulations. This process of obliteration by incorporation is rare in sociology. As a result, previously unretrived information is still then to be usefully employed as new points of departure." (Merton: 35)

My effort to draw upon and integrate Weber's type of authority for the purpose of constructing a typology of reform movements is an illustration of this dependence upon classical theory; but, my work also suggests how past theoretical strategies can be adapted for present analytic objectives.

6. Weber (1946) noted that the charismatic leader's authority was unstable not only because the unique qualities which attracted and held people's attention might fail the charismatic figure, but also because the control such a leader enjoyed over people tended to vanish once this charmed leader departed. Of charismatic authority he says:

> "...the charismatic structure knows nothing of a form or of an ordered procedure of appointment or dismissal. It knows no regulated 'career,' 'advancement.' salary, or regulated and expert training of the holder of charisma or of his aids. It knows no agency of control of appeal, no local bailiwicks or exclusive functional jurisdictions; nor does it embrace permanent institutions like our bureaucratic 'departments,'

> which are independent of persons and of
> personal charisma." (Weber, 1946: 246)

Similarly, the moral crusade launched by the solo-charismatic reformer could continue only if reformers' goals and proposals were routinized in a reform organization which survived any one leader and could continue to struggle for mental patients' rights or asylum construction, or whatever the specific goals of the moment. The solution to this problem of charismatic authority's instability is to routinize the reformer's charisma.

Such routinization may take many forms. The rise of traditional modes of domination, based on kinship lineage, election, and the like, is a solution to this inherent transitory nature of charismatic rule. In the field of social movements (and a specific form of these pressure groups), the formation of societies and associations is a response to the instability of a mode of organizational action which is dependent on one individual (cf. Eisenstadt, 1968).

7. Weber noted the rationalization process in music and law, in public administration and industry, in religion and art. In the area of public authority and private economic activity, this rationalization tendency found its fullest expression in governmental or corporate bureaucracy. Thus, in Weber's characterization, bureaucracy has a number of elements—fixed office and official jurisdictional areas, structured regular activities; authority distributed in stable, predictable ways; rules governing the performance of duties; restrictions on who can hold offices; and many others (cf. Weber, 1946: 196-244).

Bendix (1960) notes that Weber's concepts of charismatic, traditional, and rational-legal forms of authority provide the basis for his analysis of social transformations:

"All three concepts provide a framework for analysis of social change; each of them allows the possibility that 'too much' arbitrariness, 'too many' demands for the proof of charisma, and 'too much' concern for justice at the expense of formal legality will alter the respective types of domination. The opposite extremes would be equally disruptive." (Bendix: 484n)

An example of modification of ideal typical case is provided by Bendix's observation that bureaucrats are legally bound to implement a lawfully promulgated policy, but may not do so because bureaucrats develop interests of their own, and "in practice they often attempt to modify the policies they are supposed to execute" (Bendix: 485). Thus, we see in Weber a conception of the variable role of bureaucrat. The rational-legal officials may not necessarily conform to the pure-type bureaucrat. For a cross-national assessment of the professional government official's discretion in implementing laws and regulations, see Chapman (1959). Chapman says:

"'Policy' is then nothing more than the political activity of civil servants." (Chapman: 275)

This conception, though based on Weber's typology, departs dramatically from it when Chapman points to the need for civil servants to violate their professional neutrality and impartiality to protest edicts that violate basic human values.

CHAPTER III

SOCIO-HISTORICAL ORIGINS OF HEALTH

AND WELFARE POLICIES

Men and women make their own public policies, but they
do not make them just as they choose; the legacy of past
public policy makers shapes the terms in which public policies of the future must be cast (cf. Marx, 1972: 437). In
England, Sweden, and the United States the formative,
nation-building years marked the time when the main characteristics of the social welfare and health care delivery
systems emerged. In this chapter I will attempt to map the
socio-historical context in which these public policy legacies are enmeshed. Present-day welfare state critics,
policy analysts, planners, and reformers often take a short-
range view of a program's origins, and as a result lose
sight of the fundamental social structural and political
roots of these programs. In my view any study of the design
of national public policies of the post-World War II period
must note the organizational legacy of social reform campaigns. The case of mental health illustrates how this
legacy is traceable to the earliest days of nation-building,
the late-Middle Ages. Governmental provision of care for
the insane, along with the deserving poor, represents the
attempt of nascent nation-states to assume responsibility
for the care and treatment of citizens vulnerable to disease
and poverty. As such, mental health policies are a specific
case of the rationalization of forms of authority.

Modernization, Industrialization, Urbanization, and Nation-Building

The central processes and developments necessitated by
modernization are: the concentration of populations in
sprawling urban areas; the employment of high energy technologies to produce and distribute goods and services; the
development of the factory system of organizing work production; the proletarianization of the peasantry; the adoption

of bureaucratic modes of management in public and private enterprises; the development of national and international money and trading markets; the invention of double entry bookkeeping. These and other developments have been transforming the world's societies into high-energy consuming, high technology producing, urban, industrial-based economies.[1]

These developments were not confined to the economic sphere alone. In the course of modernization political institutions also have been transformed. With the decline of patrimonialism, territories and their occupants are now no longer the personal domains of kings, lords, and their vassals. The rise of the modern nation state, with its rational-legal form of control, has both expanded the operations of gorvernments and increased the rights and privileges of common citizens of the nation state.[2]

In Western Europe, the rationalization of forms of authority also meant that patrimonial rulers struggled to gain control over lands, people, and prerogatives held closely by the princes of the Roman Catholic Church. Further, the Protestant Reformation in England and other European countries reflected and sprang from not only the very profound desire to "purify" a religion corrupted by its intense and intimate involvement with profane affairs, but also the need of secular rulers to expand and secure their control over their domains (cf. Walzer, 1965).

The Protestant Reformation was linked to and became an instrument of the political restructuring of medieval society in which the populace often had to choose between their allegiance to the church or their king. These choices were not usually freely made. The intense, bloody, and protracted wars which raged in Europe in the years following Luther's proclamation attest to the unwillingness of people to readily shift their allegiances, both sacred and secular. A measure of the nationalization of the sacred realm and the rationalization of authority was marked in England and Sweden by the establishment of national churches. By fusing state and church allegiances, governments hoped that the conflicting loyalties could be minimized. Also, the nationalization of the church had an economic motive; the confis-

cated and often lucrative holdings of convents, abbeys,
monastaries, and parishes were disbursed to a rising aristocratic class loyal to the monarch. But with this nationalization of the churches, rulers were now faced with the
prospect of having to assume the charitable duties previously performed by the church (Palmer, 1965).

The Welfare Policy Consequences of Ecclesiastical Nationa-
lization

From the early days of the church, the provision of care
for the insane and feeble-minded had been the sacred official's responsibility. Usually this charitable work was
conducted by the religous orders; convents and monasteries
were willing to assume responsibility for the care of the
less fortunate, including persons that would today be diagnosed mentally ill or retarded. The confiscation of church
lands and the disestablishment of the monastic communities
posed a problem for the newly assertive North European
monarchs: how would the responsibilities of these monastic
communities be discharged (cf. Rimlinger, 1971: 13-18)?

In Sweden, King Gustavus Vasa (1523-60) founded a new,
powerful ally in the nation-building process, a state church
based on an evangelical Lutheranism; he was counseled in his
campaign to forge a united, Protestant Sweden by Laurentius
Angreae, who advocated the public ownership of church property under royal management (Dickens, 1966: 87-91). Likewise, Henry VIII solidified the Tudor regime by breaking
with the Church of Rome and placing himself at the head of a
Church of England; he confiscated monastic holdings and disbursed their vast estates to court favorites. While these
expropriations created new sources of personal wealth for
persons who came into possession of lands and their incomes,
they had the unanticipated consequence of involving the
state in the humanitarian work of the church. With the income from the land went the responsibilities, and the nation
state now was increasingly asked to assume these responsibilities (cf. Bindoff, 1950).

In the New World the self-conscious efforts of the Puritans to construct New Jerusalems were to serve as the basis

for many of the secular political institutions developed later in the 18th century. In these theocratic states the elimination of the rivalry between secular and sacred institutions was attempted, and the precedent for governmental management of and intervention into the lives of deviant members of these intentional communities was created (cf. Erikson, 1966).[3]

English Nation-Building and the Poor Laws

England was the first modern nation, i.e., a nation convulsed by the interrelated processes we call industrialization, urbanization, modernization (cf. Lipset, 1963).[4] This political modernization process was begun in the Tudor period of unification. Henry VII's reign marked the end of the fratricidal feudal wars of succession and created more stable conditions for nation-building. Beginning with the consolidation of political power, the Tudors began to extend the scope of governmental operations, increasing their control over social and economic life (Huntington, 1968). Like its Swedish and continental counterparts, the Tudors began to undertake services that rulers had not provided since the Roman Empire; finance, justice, foreign affairs, internal affairs, and defense, all were now inseparable functions of the state. Chapman (1959) says:

"With its new power, the Crown assumed new responsibilities and what had been matters for local regulation became matters of Royal concern." (Chapman: 17)

Social welfare functions of nation states. An example of this assumption of new social and economic responsibilities is the promulgation of a series of Poor Laws in England, France, Sweden, and other countries experiencing this consolidation of political power by patrimonial rulers. The Poor Laws were designed to cope with the extraordinary dislocations and disruptions associated with the demographic, agricultural, and industrial transformations of medieval society. The Poor Laws were predicated on the notion that the nation state, not the Catholic Church or some other institution, ought to take responsibility for the casualties of these processes (cf. Trattner, 1979: 1-13).[5]

Assessing the effectiveness of the Poor Laws as cushions against the socio-economic and psychological shocks of the enclosures and disestablishment of monastaries is beyond the scope of this study. What is clear is that the Poor Laws, both in Sweden and England, established a pattern of governmental intervention into the lives of persons at risk. The Post-Reformation world saw the church's historic perogatives eroded and witnessed the emergence of a central government willing to assume a variety of powers and responsibilities, hitherto the province of the church. In short, disenchantment of the universe goes hand in hand with the extention and rationalization of secular authority.

Health care under English Poor Laws. The Tudor monarchy made its first governmental provisions for the care of the ill in 1547. On his deathbed, Henry VIII became the founder of London's now famous Royal Hospitals. Under this agreement the City of London came into possession of confiscated Church property, the income from which was to be used to establish hospitals for the treatment of the London populace's ills. Thus London received an endowment to operate five foundations: St. Bartholomew's for the sick, St. Thomas's for the permanently infirm, Christ's Hospital for the maintenance and education of children, Bridewell for the vagabonds and unemployed, and finally, Bethlem for the mentally disordered. Further, the City of London pledged itself to raise an annual sum equal to the endowment to meet the costs of maintaining these facilities and providing services (Rowse, 1950: 198; Cartwright, 1977: 21-39).

The endowment of London's Royal Hospitals was meager. More importantly, their creation did not result in the establishment of a nationwide network of royal hospitals and clinics. Nevertheless, a historic pattern was set: from the 16th century, England's hospital services were a product of public and private initiatives, with the central government playing a minimal health policy creation and implementation role until the 19th century.

The monarchy's example of supporting health-care institutions did stimulate English aristocracy and set a pattern of philanthropic activity pursued up until the 1946 nationalization of hospitals. Unlike many European nations, England possessed a large wealthy aristocracy and later a bourgeoisie that emulated aristocratic philanthropic activities. These classes acted independently of the government to establish charitable, "voluntary" hospitals to care for the poor. Anderson (1972) comments:

"Both the Swedish and the English hospitals grew out of a paternalistic concept of welfare, but the Swedish concept was a product of a paternalistic state (lacking a strong aristocracy in the first place) while the English concept was a product of an aristocratic kind of class structured society where state intrusion was minimal and most likely not even regarded as an appropriate function." (Anderson: 45)

England's Poor Laws required parishes to provide for the medical needs of the deserving poor, strictly determining who was deserving and who was not. Persons not qualifying for the rudimentary Poor Law medical relief were treated at London's Royal hospitals and later in the 19th century at philanthropic institutions modeled on Henry VIII's endowment of confiscated church facilities. Thus, early in English history one can discover the pattern of a two-tier system of hospital care: one provided by the local parishes and later counties for the "deserving" poor, and the other funded by Royal, aristocratic, and later bourgeois philanthropists, for those unable to qualify for poor relief. Further, this historically-determined pattern will shape the terms of reforms in the 19th and 20th centuries.

Psychiatric care in the early modern period. The very rudimentary "psychiatric" care provided during the early stages of industrialization and urbanization was also characterized by the combination of public and private initiatives. Royal Bethlem, originally founded as priory of the Order of St. Mary of Bethlehem in 1247, was seized by the Crown in 1375, and in 1377 was converted for use as an institution for the mentally disordered. Comparatively,

Bethlem was a relatively wealthy institution since its board of governors had invested their donations and bequests in a rapidly increasing London housing market. However, the care offered the inmates, even in this most prosperous of institutions, was harsh, even brutal, and the object of public criticism and debate.

Royal Bethlem operated free from outside interference, until a series of scandals triggered Parliamentary inquiries and surveillance. Though its charter was unique, Bethlem was not alone in the mistreatment of the mentally ill unfortunate enough to be confined to a madhouse.[6] England and America of the 18th and 19th centuries abounded with private, profit-making facilities claiming to treat and even to cure physical and mental disorders (Larson, 1977: 19-39). Entrepreneurship in psychiatry became the focus of the first lobbying of Parliament on behalf of the mentally ill.

Poor relief treatment of the insane. In England the vast majority of mentally disordered persons were not confined for treatment in Bethlem or in London and other municipalities' private madhouses. Most persons languished in the prisons or suffered at the hands of the estimated between 10,000 and 15,000 parishes and townships operating their poor relief programs. The treatment of the poor, including the insane among them, was widely variable:

> "In some of the smaller parishes, the poorhouse was primarily an almshouse for the infirm and aged of respectable character; but in the large cities, the organized workhouse had superceded the poor house, and the succor of the impotent was at best only a secondary aim." (Jones, 1972: 19)

Thus, England's Poor Law facilities were as indifferent in their treatment of the mentally ill as were private madhouses. There are a few exceptional accounts of specialized treatment, and even these reinforce the grim picture of the incarceration of the mentally disordered: floggings, bloodlettings, starvation, physical restraint, purgings, and illegal detention were the rule, not the exception, in private and public facilities alike. An alarmed Parliament only gradually began meager efforts to remedy the conditions in those institutions where their limited, upper-class constituency was most likely to be residing--private madhouses. But these initial efforts, though precedent-setting, were feeble and ineffectual (cf. Parry-Jones, 1972).

The expansion of the scope of governmental operations. Thus, following the initial stage in the nation-building process, one of the consequences of governmental involvement in the lives of the insane was to increase the likelihood that a person would be imprisoned or experience the deprivation of confinement in an almshouse. This unanticipated build-up in the 18th and 19th centuries of the population of mentally disordered in prisons and poor houses was to inspire English mental health reformers. Campaigns were launched to liberate the insane from their bondage and to bring to these persons more humane modes of treatment. And, the consequence of the reform efforts was to be the further expansion of governmental activities.[7]

The Socio-Historical Context of Swedish Health Care Systems

Sweden's emergence as a modern, nation state in the late Middle Ages was initiated by a free peasantry's revolt against Danish donimation in 1434. Over the next 100 years Sweden expanded its territory, at the expense of Denmark, and secured for inself a role as a leading Protestant kingdom in Northern Europe. In the Thirty Years War Sweden played a military role all out of proportion to its natural or human resources (Hancock, 1972: 17-19; Samualsson, 1968; Scott, 1977: 118-206).[8]

War, nation-building, and the welfare state: preview of an argument. Sweden provides an example of a developing nation-state whose governmental operations grew out of the requirements of prosecuting far-flung military campaigns. The revolt of Swedish peasants ironically lead to the consolidation of political power in the hands of a Protestant monarch; the monarchy in turn established a centralized, partimonial bureaucracy to administer a growing Baltic kingdom.

59

Another factor gave rise to Sweden's civil service. Compared with her many European rivals Sweden was unevenly endowed with the major natural resources (e.g., rich in iron and lumber, but poor in coal); as a result Sweden was not a major commercial and manufacturing power in the early phases of industrialization and was late in emerging from the confines of economic feudalism. Further, Sweden lacked a good strategic position from which to conduct military campaigns from the Rhine to the Volga in order to maintain her holdings; the prosecution of protracted military campaigns of the Thirty Years War, over such great distances, and for such long periods of time, could only have been accomplished with a high degree of national consensus or coersion.

This national consensus alone could not overcome Sweden's disadvantages. Yet popular sentiment when mobilized by a well organized, centralized administration could enable the Swedes to conduct their far-flung military operations. The Swedes, like the Prussians, had developed a marvelous bureaucratic machine—first patrimonial, later rational-legal—to husband scarce resources, e.g., to collect the taxes and then disburse the monies to purchase the ships, armaments, and foodstuffs; to hire mercenaries; and to maintain the extensive lines of communication and supply.

And, once a bureaucracy is in place, it can be an instrument for organizing not only military, but also civilian enterprises. Following Wilensky (1975), this study will show that modern warfare greatly increases bureaucratic control and expands the scope of all governmental operations. It is in the early history of Sweden and Prussia that this pattern of expansion of bureaucratic control is most evident.[9]

The roots of liberal democratic government. The roots of liberal-democratic political institutions in both England and Sweden are deep. Yet there are some important differences in the developmental pattern of each nation's Representative institutions. In England, the landed aristocracy led the struggles beginning with the Magna Carta to limit monarchial power; in Sweden, an alliance between a free peasantry and the monarchy insured that arbitrary power was not exercised by the landed gentry. In particular, the early emergence of Swedish countervailing powers made possible the later development of formal, competitive electoral forms of political governance. With the aristocracy checked, consolidation of Swedish national political institutions could proceed.

The costs of the Swedish imperial wars were borne by the peasantry, in both taxes and manpower. In contrast to most of Europe, the peculiar Swedish form of feudalism did not entail the enserfment of peasants, and these ethno-linguistically homogeneous, free farmers were a counter-balance to monarchial or aristocratic domination. This balance of power of Swedish social classes led to a relatively orderly transition from feudalism to a modern democratic nation state (Hancock: 13-35). Anderson (1972) concurs with Hancock's characterization of Sweden saying:

> "The evolution of the Swedish society and economy is thus a fascinating case study in the juxtaposition of adequate, but not abundant resources, a talented administrative corps, a pervasive work ethic in the general population, and a liberal-democratic framework embodied in the written constitution of 1809." (Anderson: 41)

Health and welfare in an emerging nation-state. Like England and other European nations, Sweden faced the problem of how to manage the growing population of displaced persons, the casualties of agricultural revolution and rising birth rates. Swedish monarchs instituted Poor Laws, as did their counterparts in England, France and other countries, but it was Poor Laws with a difference; Sweden's Poor Laws distinguished between the rights of citizens to government subsidized health care and right to expect relief from poverty. The role of government as provider of health care for all has its roots in the early 17th-century mandates of Swedish monarchs.

Importantly, for the future development of health care services, the Swedish hospital was not saddled with the Poor Law odium of the tax-supported Poor Law hospitals of England (Anderson, 1972: 39). Queen Christina's promulgation of what has come to be called the "Beggar Regulation" in 1642, freed the hospitals from the specific task of caring only for the poor. Thus, the Swedish public hospital was established as an institution serving the entire community. This early creation of a universal public hospital service partially explains the hospital domination of medical care in Sweden. This precedent also explains why public hospitals have never been a second-class health care delivery system, as they have often been in England and the U.S.

This pattern of hospital domination in medical care was reenforced by the requirements of prosecuting military campaigns against the continental Catholic powers, the Russians, and the Danes. The Crown, by means of its civil service corps, established a series of Crown hospitals to care for the casualties of the extensive military adventures. In addition to Poor Law hospitals, this network of specialized hospitals and clinics was constructed and staffed to care for the numerous cases of venereal disease; these hospitals were supported by "cure house" taxes levied by the central government. The war veterans also placed a special burden on the län (parish) hospital, straining the meager resources of those few primitive facilities. The Crown agreed to assist the län in maintaining these hospitals and agreed to subsidize local parish hospitals from the mid-1600s.

Thus, early in the nation-building process the Swedish government was involved in providing for the medical care of its citizenry. More importantly, this governmental hospital care was separated from Poor Law relief programs at an earlier date than other European nations.

Anderson (1972) reports that though län hospitals were open to all citizens after 1642, the destitute continued to be the main users of these facilities and services. Physician services were meant to be provided at the hospitals, but those who could afford to do so (i.e., the bourgeoisie and nobility) chose to be treated privately at home. Parallel with these hospital-based services, the state also developed an embryonic public health service whose function was to provide medical treatment in rural areas and in outlying towns and villages as well as to assist in the management of epidemic diseases.

62

In sum, the Swedes freed health care from the Poor Laws by Queen Christina's 1642 proclamation, while the English Poor Laws (which stipulated the local parish hospital's role) continued to stigmatize the patients treated in these facilities. Further, the Swedish government's non-Poor Law mode of providing health care paved the way for the 1862 reorganization of governmental services. This nationalization process which included health care pre-dated by eighty years England's nationalization of health and mental health services.

Mental health services in Sweden since the Reformation. As in England, the Swedish Reformation meant the confiscation of convents and monastaries that had been providing shelter and care for the sick and poor. The Reformation also marked the expansion of state services. King Gustav Vasa was personally concerned with their plight and established Danvik Madhouse in 1551 after the expropriation of Stockholm's Franciscan monastary. For many years this madhouse, an annex to Danvik hospital, was the sole specialized hospital for the mentally ill in Sweden.

It was not until 1775 that the Crown hospitals (krono-hospitaler) were charged with the responsibility for admitting lunatics as well as the physically ill. The Lutheran Order of the Seraphim was given the task of governing these hospitals which had begun their institutional careers as Catholic convents. In the post-Reformation era these facilities were gradually assuming a new role, functioning as mental hospitals. However, as in England, these hospitals were criticized as expectations for the standards of treatment were raised by 19th century mental health performers.

The Origins of American Health and Welfare Services

The establishment of political institutions followed a different pattern in North America. Huntington (1968) notes that in America the Tudor constitutional form that England abandoned was transplanted in the colonial representative institutions and later in the United States constitution.

Differentiation in political structures and functions has resulted in the current differences between American, English and European continental political systems. The U.S. Constitution formally enshrined the separation of functions (and diffusion of power) in separate institutional structures—executive, legislative and judicial—though the practice of government today is only remotely related to the Founding Fathers' ideals. In England, power has increasingly been concentrated in one branch of government, Parliament's House of Commons, which has taken on an increased number of functions, legislative, executive, and even judicial (Huntington, 1968:109-122).

Poor relief under the American Constitution. The 1787 American Constitution left to the states the responsibilities for the poor and sick's care which they had been assuming since colonial times. The new federated states maintained discretion to do as little or as much as they desired to relieve poverty and treat illness. Colonial and later state laws pertaining to the mentally ill among the poor followed the English statues:

"The English principle that society had a corporate responsibility for the poor and dependent was reflected in early colonial legislation. As in England, most of the colonies require local communities to make provision for a wider variety of different groups of dependents." (Grob, 1973: 7)

Local residence and deserving status were criteria which qualified one for relief; non-local persons were moved on to another community. Yet, Rothman (1971) concludes that the colonists did not completely transplant English Poor Laws:

"Although American statutes were firmly based on English precedent, they did not mechanically repeat every stipulation and faithfully duplicate the system. Rather, assemblies selected from the English corpus those sections that they found most consistent with their own attitudes and most relevant to their needs, and in doing so gave a discernable American quality to the result." (Rothman: 20)

Thirteen different colonial assemblies, dealing with widely different economic and social conditions, did not exactly transplant English Poor Law statutes; still, the English model of local relief responsibility was a powerful one, and though it was adopted to local needs, its principle was more or less universally accepted. The proof of this is found in the legacy of the Poor Laws; currently the bewildering array of welfare and health benefits that defy reform (Steiner, 1971; cf. Aaron, 1973 and Moynihan, 1973).

U.S. national health care: a limited beginning. The U.S. federal government has been involved in the direct delivery of health care since 1793. In that year, the U.S. Congress passed the Marine Hospital Service Act, establishing a network of hospitals to provide care for the merchant seamen of an emergent maritime power. This hospital and health care service was financed by a tax paid by each merchant seaman. Falk (1977) comments on the tax:

> "It was in effect a compulsory contributary
> national health insurance program for a
> particular category of employed persons."
> (Falk: 162)

Along with federal and state veterans relief and hospital programs, the Marine Hospital Service (MHS) was the only federal health care service provided until the late 19th century. The MHS was the precedent for the establishment of a United States Public Health Service and the ever-expanding federal role in health care.

The mentally ill in America. The United States is unique among modern nation-states because of the conscious calculation involved in the creation of its political institutions. The American Republic was a bold social experiment, predicated on the conceptions of human nature, natural law, and civil society of Locke (Hartz, 1955). And once the conductors of this nation-building experiment had finished framing a national constitution, they turned their attention to internal domestic concerns of illiteracy, disease, criminality, and mental illness. The mentally ill were not "liberated" by the revolution. Dependency and degradation were the lot of persons so unfortunate as to lose their senses in Colonial times and in the new United States of America.

Mental illness was and is a cause of dependency. Colonial legislatures enacted laws to deal with the consequences of the insane's incapacity to conduct their own affairs or manage their estates. Massachusetts enacted legislation in 1641 and New York, Connecticut, and the other colonies followed the lead of Massachusetts; in 1665 laws were also enacted in New York to provide public care for "distracted persons;" in 1694 and in 1699, respectively, Massachusettes and Connecticut followed New York.

As early as 1662, alms houses were being established in Boston and other colonial cities; later in the 18th-century work houses were opened. In both institutions a heterogeneous population of poor, disabled, diseased, and mentally disturbed persons resided. This pattern of intervention was unplanned and spontaneous.

> "When a number of sick and dependent persons reached a critical size, the community moved toward the adoption of a more organized system. In the initial stage specialized institutions were not characteristic; most urban welfare institutions remained indifferentiated in both structure and function." (Grob, 1973: 14)

The general pattern of undifferentiated care has a number of exceptions: in 1770 a facility for the insane was opened in Williamsburg, Virginia, but it was the only such state-supported facility in America until 1810; and, Philadelphia's Pennsylvania Hospital was founded in 1752, after the Pennsylvania State Assembly had endorsed the concept of a hospital for the physically and mentally ill. Boston and Charleston were less successful in establishing separate hospitals; petitions were presented but not acted upon.[10]

In sum, in England, Sweden, and the U.S., the Protestant Reformation reduced the role played by the church in the relief of the poor and ill; the inter-related agricultural

agricultural, industrial, and demographic revolutions were providing more people who were at greater risk of unemployment, illness, and mental disease. The new national governments perceived the rise in these numbers of poor and ill persons with alarm and took measures to cope with them, because the traditional, religious institutional means of care had been diminished. And, philanthropically-minded citizens began to organize aid to the poor, sick and mentally ill, casualties of these social changes, especially in England and the U.S. where the scope of individual social reform was greater than in Sweden.

Moral Treatment of the Mentally Ill: A Model for Social Reformers

The French Revolution was ignited in 1789 by the spontaneous liberation of the prisoners of the Bastille. This transformation of France's old regime was also accompanied by the drastic reshaping of the patterns of patient care at the insane asylums of Bicêtre and Salpêtière in 1793. The director of this psychiatric revolution was a physician, Philippe Pinel.

Pinel was one of the outstanding examples of the embodiment of 18th-century ideals of rationalism and enlightenment. As an empiricist and humanist, Pinel found bleeding, corporal punishment, and imprisonment inadequate and ineffective means of managing mental disease. Mechanic (1969) observes:

"Pinel's program was based on his belief that
psychological factors were important causes of
emotional disturbances, as were social factors
and an inadequate education." (Mechanic: 52)

Descriptions of his treatment programs, coupled with his treatises on insanity, were widely published; translated into English in 1806, Pinel's work influenced both English, European, and North American practitioners and theorists. In America, Benjamin Rush's pioneering psychiatric writings, published in 1812, show the influence of Pinel and reflects the widespread influence of the humanistic mode of treating mental disorders (Mora, 1975: 24-50).[11]

Pinel was not the sole innovator of new modes of managing mental disorders. In 1792, William Tuke, a York, England tea and coffee merchant, persuaded his Quaker community to open a Retreat for the Quakers community as an alternative to the notorious private asylums and public facilities. He founded the Retreat not as a medical treatment center, but rather as a supportive environment in which the mentally disturbed might find comfort and relief from their symptoms. Patients were assumed to be rational and controllable, hence the absence of cruel and violent methods of confinement and treatment. Religious meetings were held in order to spiritually assist patient recovery, and visitors were encouraged (Jones, 1972: 25-54; cf. Foucault, 1965: 242-255).

The York Retreat was thus another model of an intentional, community-based effort to alleviate the mentally ill's suffering. The Quaker community sought to aid fellow Quakers regain their full mental faculties. Like Pinel's reforms at Bicêtre, York Retreats served as an example of how the insane could be managed in an intentional, therapeutic community dedicated to the rediction of psychiatric symptomatology by non-violent means. As such, moral treatment was represented in the late-18th century as a breakthrough and improvement in the treatment of the mentally ill. As treatment innovators and moral crusaders, Pinel and Tuke inspired individuals and politicians dedicated to the humane treatment of the insane.

The diffusion of treatment innovations. The intellectual and scientific interchanges between North America and Europe can be measured by the spread of Pinel's writings and accounts of the York Retreat treatment model to North America. Public spirited and concerned citizens took the lead in adopting the moral treatment mode of care to the American environment. For example, Grob (1973) notes that the Pennsylvania Friends established their own Retreat in 1813; Quaker philanthropist Thomas Eddy played a vital role in New York, helping found in 1821 Bloomingdale Asylum, a separate institution from the New York public mental hospital.[12] This pattern of diffusion of treatment innovations came to characterize psychiatry as it moved out of the asylum and into the field of medicine. New psychiatric knowledge was to serve an important intelligence function in reform politics.

The King's madness alters public policy. In very different way the national crisis posed by the progressive mental deterioration of George III called into question both the humanity, the medical bases, and the effectiveness of current methods of treating mental disorders.[14] The "treatments" of the King's madness by Francis Willis, clergyman-turned-proprietor of Lincolnshire madhouse failed to cure the ailing monarch. Despite the use of social isolation, physical restraint, starvation, bleedings, purging, and beatings, the King was not cured, and Willis was disgraced.[13]

In 1789, a Parliamentary committee was appointed to consider the likelihood of the King's recovery and to recommend the appointment of a regent. In the politicized environment, debates raged over the appropriateness of the treatments inflicted upon the Royal victim of insanity. Though political crises passed when the Prince of Wales, the future George IV, was appointed Regent in 1811, the public discussion of insanity (its causes and cures) continued to raise questions about the current conceptions of mental illness. In Jones' (1972) opinion, this debate contributed to a reform climate.

"The effects on lunacy reform of this first attack suffered by the King are intangible, but nevertheless, real. The sympathies of the nation were with the sufferer, and the note of moral condemnation which had previously characterized all approaches to the subject was entirely lacking." (Jones: 37)[14]

The "discovery" of the insane. The end of the 18th century found psychiatry to be one of the most underdeveloped of the developing sciences of medicine. The attempts to "cure" King George III were to reveal not only how unscientific psychiatry was, but also how cruel and inhumane its practice could be. The spectacular failure to cure the King further called into question the model of mental illness under which most persons were then treated.

The King's physician had employed the techniques used in his and other madhouses—purgings, physical restraint, isolation, and the like. Thus, as an alternative mode of treatment, the York Retreat gained a reputation it might not otherwise have obtained had it not been for the publicity surrounding George III's illness and the failures to treat the King using methods employed in London's notorious madhouses catering to the well-to-do of English society.

England's constitutional crisis created by the King's mental disability also focused attention on the adequacy of the policy methods devised for dealing with the insane. By the late-18th and early-19th century, alternatives to the coercive vagrancy laws and madhouse regulations were being contemplated. The English Vagrancy Laws of 1744 had made special provision for the confinement of dangerous lunatics; it was yet another attempt by Parliament to manage by coercive penal sanctions the dislocated and dispossessed, the human casualties of the depopulation of rural England and the growth of an urban-industrial economy. Parliament also acted in 1774 to regulate private madhouses, in order to prevent abuses, involuntary confinement, and to permit public inspection. Eleven years earlier, scandals involving involuntary confinement in these madhouses had prompted an investigation by a select committee into these enterprises. The final legislation enpowered a commissioner to license madhouses and required them to accept visitors and prevent wrongful detention, but did little else to insure that treatment provided by these private establishments was humane; discretion in madhouse operation remained largely with their entrepreneural operators. As in the new federal American Republic, alternatives to these public programs to aid the insane were now contemplated.

The Foundations of National Reform Campaigns

Thus, by the end of the 18th century, the English Parliamentarians and American legislators created measures that confined the insane and sub-normal (along with all the poverty stricken, criminal, vagabond, and other social casualties of urbanization and modernization) in workhouses, almshouses, or in this case, special institutions for the lunatics and idiots. For persons who could afford to pay for private treatment of mental diseases, profit-making facilities were created to treat and "cure" the afflictions of the mind. However, whether public or private, the care provided was custodial at best, and usually consisted of physical abuse which compounded the mental anguish of these unfortunates.

In contrast to this pattern of intervention, a number of late-18th century enlightened humanitarians, convinced of the potential perfectability of man, began to offer alternative theories of mental diseases and to propose new treatments. Treatment innovators like Pinel, Tuke, Rush and their followers, with their works and writings, proposed an alternative conception of mental processes, one which conflicted with the dominant, unenlightened view of human mental disability. The new theories lead to new treatment for the insane. And, these individual efforts to adopt new modes of treatment ultimately were to alter the policies of the governments in these three countries. The therapeutic models of Pinel and Tuke provided the inspiration for a 19th-century generation of mental health reformers. The next chapter traces the emergence of these reform campaigns and assesses the attempts of reformers to convince governments to adopt enlightened policies to guide the treatment of the mentally disordered.

1. There have been many studies that describe and explain the inter-related processes involved in nation-building. My own understanding of urbanization-industrialization process has been enhanced by Wilensky and Lebeaux (1958: 3-133); Bendix (1963: 1-116; 198-253); Moore (1966: 3-155; 414-508); Polyani (1957); and Schumpeter (1962).

2. Bendix (1964) examines these trends from medieval to modern societies with a view towards demonstrating that:

> "...authority and association constitute inter-dependent but autonomous spheres of thought and action which coexist in one form or another in all societies." (Bendix: 21).

Bendix goes on to note that the central fact of nation-building is the exercise of a nationwide, public authority which replaces medieval political order. Of this pre-modern form, Bendix says:

> "...medieval political life depends on the link between hereditary or spiritual rank in society, control over land as the principal economic resource, and the exercise of public authority. All those whose rank or status excludes them from access to control over the land are thereby excluded from any direct participation in public affairs." (Bendix: 66).

This system is broken by the twin revolutions, industrial and political, which results in the recognition of citizenship rights for all adults (Bendix: 67).

T. H. Marshall's (1964) analysis takes the problem of the inequities inherent in the economic system of any modern, industrial society and seeks to understand if such inequities can be tolerated, if an equality of citizenship is insured. In Marshall's view, citizenship --in its social, civil, and political forms--thus is seen as the source of conflict, even war.

3. Erikson (1966) notes the difficulties the Puritans encountered in North America in founding socio-political institutions upon the Bible. The problems which resulted stemmed from the contradictions between the received English common law tradition and the interpretation of scripturally-based law. The corporation settling Massachusetts also faced a problem in that their charter specifically forbade them from enacting statues which conflicted with English law; yet the intent of the Puritan magistrates was just that. Further conflicts arose because in this community self-consciously sought to define the boundaries of legal and illegal behavior, (e.g., case of witches).

4. The consolidated Tudor Poor Laws (the Poor Law Act, 1601; 43 Elizabeth c. 2) were a logical assumption by the state of responsibilities hitherto held by the church. Yet, expansion of state control was not the only motivations for their ecclesiastical relations with Rome; the dissolved English monastic holdings and profits were turned over to ambitious economic entrepreneurs, municipal corporations, court favorites, and the Crown itself; in all, one-sixth of all cultivatable land in England was placed on the market (Rowse, 1950).

    Paralleling the dissolution process was the enclosing of common lands and the resulting displacement of tenant farmers. The enormous human suffering necessarily entailed in this socio-economic upheavel cannot be underestimated; the rise of the numbers of beggars and vagabonds and the increased rural violence can be traced to these dislocations (Bindoff, 1950; 22-23; 75-76; cf. Hobsbawn, 1968: 100-108).

    The Poor Laws were social welfare end-products of these developments--national unification, the state's assumption of new powers, the establishment of a state church, dissolution of monastic holdings, and the enclosures of common lands. Hill (1969) comments that the emergence of capitalism is another factor to be added into an explanation:

> "Wage labour and the Poor Law rise together and complement one another. The harsh penalties imposed on sturdy beggars from the fifteen-thirties were intended to force the idle to work; later provision for the important poor was a delayed recognition of the fact that landless families starve if they have not an employed wage-earner." (Hill: 45).

In his analysis of this modernization process, Polyani (1957) argues that the Tudor and Stuart monarchs' efforts at Poor Relief sprang from a desire to slow down the transformation and to cushion those victims of common land enclosures, monastic dissolutions, and the rise of wage labor. He interprets the Poor Law strategy of relief in these terms:

> "England withstood without great damage the calamity of the enclosures only because the Tudors and the early Stuarts used the power of the Crown to slow down the process of economic improvement until it became socially bearable—employing the power of the central government to relieve the victims of the transformation, and attempting to canalize the process of change so as to make its course less devestating." (Polyani: 38)

5. Rimlinger (1971) observed that social protection under the old regime was in marked contrast to the medieval charity provided by clergy, local parishes, and the monastaries. The rise in beggars and vagabonds in England and the continent posed painful social decisions for the emerging national governments. The able-bodied poor was a focus of European relief policies; detering

these persons from seeking public relief was attempted through coercion and education. Rimlinger says:

> "In England, France, and other European countries, governments became initially concerned with the lot of the poor, not for the purposes of relieving suffering, but for the maintenance of law and order. The legislation relating to the poor began with measures to punish beggars and kept its repressive character until recent times." (Rimlinger: 19)

Thus, the Poor Laws were partially social control measures (cf. Piven and Cloward, 1971 and Polyani, 1957).

6. Allegations of patient abuse were fixed as "facts" in the public imagination by documentary novels and sensationalized newspaper accounts; visits to Bethlem gave concerned citizens the opportunity to directly observe the spectacle of patient mistreatment; and, the wandering beggars, the "Toms O'Bedlam," mentally disordered persons certified as Bethlem lunatics, testified to the inadequacy of an institution whose inmates had to beg for a living. If well-endowed Bethlem treated inmates in this fashion, what was the level of treatment in the work-houses, poorhouses, and county asylums? One can only infer from the meager impressionistic data that the conditions of the insane and feeble-minded constituted little more than imprisonment.

7. Beginning in 1763, public opinion was mobilized by the issuance of two writs of Habeas Corpus involving the illegal confinement at Miles Madhouse in Hoxton and the Turlington Madhouse in Chelsea. Parliament's House of Commons appointed an investigative committee, but eleven years elapsed prior to the enactment of the Act for Regulating Private Madhouses, 1774 (14 Geo. III c.9). This was a first, though feeble attempt to restrain the madhouse managers from abusing patients and to prevent

the illegal admission and detention of patients (Jones, 1972: 31-32). The weakness of the act was its inability to close an institution violating the law's detention provisions. Yet, despite this shortcoming, the importance of the law lay in the legal precedent it established: requirement of licensing of private, profit-making institutions and rights to inspect institutions by commissioners elected by Fellows of the Royal College of Physicians.

8. The Swedish peasant uprising in 1434 was transformed into a broad-based social revolution when it was joined by the Swedish nobility and led to the convocation of the first Riksdag (Estates-General) in 1435. Later a successful military alliance, 1521-23, with the Hanseatic League against Denmark resulted in Sweden gaining full independence from Denmark. In 1523 the Riksdag elected Gustaf Vasa as king; in 1527 Vasa, as King Gustav I, proclaimed the Reformation in Sweden, thereby aligning himself with the continental Protestant princes and kings for the next two centuries of Europe's religious wars.

The emergence of Peter the Great's Imperial Russia and Fredrick the Great's garrison-state Prussia as rivals for control of Central Europe, eliminated Sweden's hegemony. In a series of wars, Peter the Great's "westernizing" Russia wrested from Swedish control much of Finland, Estonia and Latvia, while Frederick the Great's Prussia defeated Sweden in Central Europe, thus eliminating Sweden forever as a major military and policital power (Hancock, 1972: 17-19; Samuelsson, 1968; Scott, 1977: 118-206).

9. Heclo (1975: 9-33) notes that Sweden moved from an agricultural economy to an industrial one about 70 to 90 years later than England, beginning in about 1870, compared with England's 1790 or so; Sweden also compressed the industrialization which took England about 200 years to accomplish, into less than 100.

Helco further notes that Sweden led England in the development of a civil service. The basic framework remained the same, despite the waxing and waning of royal power. Large administrative boards established first in 1634 under King Gustavus Adolphus II, carried out the policies developed by the much smaller department heads and their staff (Helco: 41-46). Chapman (1959) points to the striking survival of Sweden's 17th-century administrative state, with the early interdependence of the boards maintained throughout the centuries. The five original administrative boards now number over sixty, with a ministry having more than one board under its direction, e.g., the Ministry of Social Affairs contains the Royal Boards for social insurance, child welfare, and poor relief (Chapman: 18-19; 49-51).

10. Neither the Williamsburg Asylum nor the Pennsylvania Hospital represented a significant breakthrough in the early treatment of the insane. Both facilities were miniscule and could hardly have served a small fraction of populated American colonies: the Williamsburg Asylum could only treat between 25 and 30 patients. Between 1752-54 Philadelphia's Pennsylvania Hospital treated 18 persons for mental illness out of 117 persons treated for physical diseases in this the largest city in Colonial America (Grob, 1873: 13-34). The mentally disordered languished in the prisons and poorhouses when they were not confined to the homes of families and friends. This pattern of confinement and abuse was not broken until the new models of treating mental disorders were seized by policy-makers anxious to solve this pressing social problem.

11. Pinel's influence extended not only to America. The moral treatment ideology and practice initiated in England by the Tukes, took on a revolutionary case as a result of Pinel's liberation of mental patients. An Italian counterpart to Pinel--Vicenzio Chiarugi of Florence--also took up the cause of the enlightened treatment of the mentally ill and instituted sweeping reforms throughout Florentine asylums. And in post-

Revolutionary America, Benjamin Rush fought for similar improvements in Pennsylvania's hospital for the insane, inspired by Pinel's work. This late-18th and early-19th century internationalism in mental health care is reflected most vividly in the publication within six years of the English version of Pinel's treatise (1806), of Samuel Tuke's Description of a Retreat (1813), and Benjamin Rush's 1812 treatise on insanity which clearly showed his knowledge of and debt to Pinel's work (Grob, 1973: 39-48).

12. Many of Eddy's notions were drawn from Samual Tuke's account of his family's work and are expressed in Eddy's testimony, letters and petitions.

> "...Thomas Eddy presented to the governors of the New York Hospital a series of far-reaching recommendations that were intended to transform the character of the asylum. Influenced particularly by the York Retreat, Eddy summarized in lucid terms Samuel Tuke's Description of the Retreat. He emphasized the moderate and judicious use of the principle of fear; the necessity of treating the patient as a rational being, and the importance of promoting self-restraint by utilizing the precepts of medicine." (Grob: 62-63)

The creation of a therapeutic environment, suitable for the "moral treatment" and management of a person's symptoms, was the goal of Tuke's North American followers.

13. Up until 1770, the curious and the pleasure seekers could pay to view the spectacle of Bethlem inmates suffering the agonies of their mental afflictions. These scenes of Bethlem hospital appear in Hogarth's eighth episode of The Rake's Progress, including the 1773 engraving depicting the pitiable Rake manacled, head shaved, being viewed by two disdainful fashionable ladies; similar horrific descriptions of patient mal-

treatment occur in Harrison Aimsworth's novel, <u>Jack Sheppard</u>.

Various actual scandals in the 1770s attest to the essential truthfulness of these fictionalized accounts of the continuing inhumane treatment of Bethlem inmates: a 1752 pamphlet accused keepers of stealing food and inmates' personal property; in 1772 the House governor was dismissed for personal appropriation of food stuffs. A report on the institution's dubious medical treatment, as given to a House of Commons' Select Committee in 1815 by Bethlem's head Dr. Thomas Morro, gives further evidence of the appalling medieval treatment provided in this most lushly funded of institutions operated exclusively for the mentally ill:

> "Patients are ordered bled about the latter end of May of the end of June, according to the weather, and after they have bled, they take vomits once a week for a certain number of weeks; after that, we purge the patients. That has been the practice invariably, long before my time. It was handed down to me by my father, and I do not know any better practice." (Jones, 1972: 16)

Thus, even in the early days of policy-making, a kind of rudimentary intelligence was employed to aid policy makers.

14. The "madness" of King George III has now been posthumously diagnosed as variegated purphyria, a rare inherited metabolic disorder producing schizophrenic-like symptomatology; the madness symptoms are highly variable; at times a person can be lucid and normal when the disease is in remission; at other times incapacating madness grips the victim (Macalpine and Hunter, 1969). In 1788, the King's disease could no longer be hidden from Parliament and the public. This mental incapacity of an activist, constitutional monarch politicized the madness question.

CHAPTER IV

THE MENTAL HOSPITAL:
THE PRODUCT OF THE MENTAL HEALTH
REFORM MOVEMENT

By the early-19th century, English, Swedish, and American political elites all faced the task of managing the growing populations of poor, indigent, mentally disturbed, criminal, and handicapped persons. These casualties of urbanization, industrialization, and related processes, required assistance from the relief-giving institutions inherited from the late-medieval, early-modern period of nation-building and religious reformation. The institutional means of managing these persons were increasingly inadequate to the task. As noted in Chapter Three, new approaches to the treatment of the mentally disordered were initiated in Europe and North America. This seeming revolution in psychiatric care meant to reformers that the untreatable insane could now be treated, even cured, according to therapeutic innovators like Pinel and Tuke. Thus, there arose in England, Sweden, the United States, and other nations a group of persons dedicated to the translation of Pinel's and Tuke's achievements into national treatment programs for the mentally disordered.

The first goal in this chapter is to describe and explain the emergence of the 19th-century mental health reform movements in the United States, England, and Sweden. These reformers and their organizations demanded that governments change their pattern of intervention into the lives of the mentally disordered, specifically, the Poor Law mode of confinement and the scandal-tainted private hospital.

The policy reform proposed at this stage was this: the mentally ill should be separated from the physically ill, the convicts, the unemployed, and be provided appropriate care. The optimistic, often charismatic, 19th-century social reformers had attained a heightened awareness of social problems; these reformers were to play a key part in the public policy identification of the mentally ill as a population requiring specialized care. As noted, characteristic of 19th-century reforms in all three countries was the assumption that mental diseases were mutable, that improvements in the lives of the mentally ill could be effected by new methods of treatment. I will trace this first phase in the history of the reformers and reform movements. In this cycle of mental health reform policy actors sought to convince political elites of the need to adopt new modes of care for the mentally disordered.

In order to do this, I will map the cycles of mental health policy adoption in all three countries, describing the process whereby the care and treatment of the mentally ill was perceived to be not the responsibility of Poor Law institutions; and, then I will trace the translation of that perception into the initiation of a policy adoption process in all three countries. Finally, in this chapter I will explore the roots of disillusionment with the reforms accomplished by the often charismatic reformers of the 19th-century.

Moral Management Model of Treatment

The late-medieval, early-modern modes of managing mental illnesses were not predicated on verified etiological theories. Rather, the mentally ill were just one of many groups subjected to incarceration and physical abuse for condition. The era of moral treatment was marked by its confidence in the effectiveness of the asylum mode of treatment, yet this mode of care could not meet today's standards of scientific validity. Rather, the 19th-century reformer viewed mental disorders as treatable and that the asylum was the institution to provide that care. The reformers came to view government as the only agent capable of making new treatments widely available; government alone had the financial resources to construct and staff a network of institutions to care for the mentally disordered. Thus, governments, national and local, became the targets of intense lobbying campaigns mounted by mental health reformers. In this way, the reformers, acting to realize their own objectives, contributed to the expansion of the state. Thus, an unanticipated consequence of reform activities was an increase in the scope of governmental responsibilities, an extention of the rationalization of authority.

Intellectual foundations of reform: innovation and dissemenation of policy-relevant intelligence. There were a number of both theoretical treatises and actual treatment programs that served as templates for the 19th-century institution builders. In terms of our analytic typology (see Figure 1) the writings of late-18th century psychiatrists represented a body of policy-relevant intelligence, albeit, intelligence that was ideological and impressionistic, not scientific. For example, the reports on the York Retreat gave encouragement to reformers who viewed this unique program as a model of the implementation of the moral management that could cure mental diseases.[1] Tuke's treatment regime was predicated on the amenability of mental disorders to humane treatment. Samuel Tuke, William's grandson, wrote of assumptions upon which the Retreat was founded:

> "'Insane persons generally possess a degree of
> control over their wayward propensities.
> Their intellectual active, and moral powers,
> are usually rather perverted than obliterated;
> and it happens, not unfrequently, that one
> faculty only is affected.'" (Tuke as quoted in
> Skultans, 1975: 136)

The York Retreat served as a model; its theory and practice were disseminated on a world-wide scale. The founder of American psychiatry, Benjamin Rush, was influenced by the Tukes' work. The Tuke family and Rush were in turn influenced by Philippe Pinel, medical doctor, professor of Hygiene and Internal Medicine at the University of Paris, and director of Bicêtre Asylum and the Woman's Asylum, la Salpêtière. By his liberation of the shackled inmates, Pinel gained world-wide fame. The publication in 1801 of his Traite medico-philosophique sur l'alientaion mentale secured an intellectual influence more long-lasting than the news of his liberation of patients. Dain (1964) says of Pinel:

"By unchaining the insane in 1793, Pinel helped
to inaugurate the era of modern psychiatry.
With his contemporary, the English Quaker
William Tuke, Pinel replaced prevailing medical
and lay practices with a psychological and
humanitarian approach." (Dain: 4-5)

During the first quarter of the 19th century this professional optimism had become a widespread belief; the "facts"
about success of Pinel, et al. served the social reformers
seeking to translate the moral treatment mode of care into a
governmental-support system of care for all insane and
mentally defective persons.

The U.S. Establishes State Mental Hospitals

The opening of the Worchester State Hospital in Massachusetts marked the beginning of an era, the "institutional"
solution to the problem of mental illnesses. Today's state
and county are institutional heirs to hospitals founded by
reformers convinced of the humanity of institutional modes
of care. These reformers believed that the society that
created a new political order could, in turn, create specialized institutions which would eliminate dependence,
ill-health, unemployment, and illiteracy. Rothman (1971)
demonstrates the linkages between the campaigns for state
asylums for the mentally disordered with the reforms that
created public schools, prisons, poorhouses, reformatories,
and orphanages. The leaders of the brave social and political experiment had been alarmed by a number of developments: rapid population growth and the concomitant rise in
the numbers of unskilled, uneducated, under-employed, and
criminals.

The alms houses and prisons were proving to be inadequate to cope with the rising numbers of mentally disordered
and deviant persons; and, Poor Laws were not effective in
containing poverty. Rothman (1971) says of the early-19th
century social reformers:

"The response in the Jacksonian period to the
deviant and the dependent was first and fore-

most a vigorous attempt to promote the stability of the society at a moment when traditional ideas and practices appeared to be
outmoded, constricted, and ineffective."
(Rothman: xviii)

The asylum could restore the Republic's balance while eliminating these social ills.[2]

"There was a utopian flavor to this first venture,
one that looked to reform the deviant and dependent and to serve as a model for others. The
well-ordered asylum would exemplify the proper
principles of social organization and insure the
republic and promote its glory." (Rothman: xix)

Grob (1973) concurs with Rothman's view of the comprehensive
aims of social reformers:

"In general, most of the institutions founded
during the first half of the 19th century were
neither narrow nor singular in their purpose.
Almshouses, for example, were intended to provide work for the able-bodied as well as shelter and refuge for the aged and helpless poor.
Houses of refuge which cared for homeless
orphans and other juveniles, were supposed to
inculcate in young inmates proper behavioral
attributes as well as a trade... Penitentiaries
were intended both to punish and to reform law-
breakers. And mental hospitals would serve
both the community and the individual by providing care and treatment of mentally ill
persons." (Grob: 94)

Thus, the mental hospital was an instrument for solving, or
at least controlling an identifiable social problem: the
increasing numbers of mentally disordered persons.

The institutional antecedents of 19th-century reform.
As noted, there were antecedents to the asylum.   Americans
had been experimenting, albeit in limited and unsystematic
fashion, with alternative modes of treating mental diseases.

These experiments in some cases involved colonial or municipal governments as sponsors of asylum construction and
operation. Often these were joint ventures with public
spirited citizens, e.g., Pennsylvania's colonial legislature
had appropriated money in 1751 to build a hospital; in 1769
colonial Virginia founded America's first institution exclusively for the insane; Eastern Kentucky Lunatic Asylum for
the pauper insane opened in 1822.

Private asylums had shown limited successes with a new
technique of managing the mentally ill—moral management.
Adapted from Pinel's pioneering hospital work and the Tuke's
York Asylum, the Hartford Retreat and other facilities
testified to the benefits of a humane approach to managing
madness. However, only when this moral management model was
adopted by the 19th-century social reformers did the asylum
become an instrument of social change. That is, there was
no widespread participation by federal, state, and local
governments in the treatment of mental diseases, or in the
financial support of the mentally ill, until moral management became the ideology of the mental health reformers
committed to involving governments treating the mentally
ill.

There were several stages in this campaign to construct
state asylums: first, the early 1800s was a period of
philanthropy during which a number of new, city-based facilities were constructed; second, the campaign to construct a
separate state-supported mental hospital was successfully
completed in Massachusetts in 1833; finally, the diffusion
of the concept of a state hospital for the insane was conducted by Dorothea Lynn Dix (Trattner, 1979: 43-66; cf.
Caplan, 1969: 3-44).

The health needs of a growing urban population motivated
America's philanthropic community to finance new facilities.
Among the hospitals opening were a number of mental illness
treatment facilities. Between 1811 and 1822 McLean Asylum
in Massachusetts, the Friends Philadelphia Asylum, the
Hartford Retreat, and the Bloomingdale Asylum were opened.
The Bloomingdale facility was separated from New York's
Hospital, giving mental patients their own specialized
institution. Though the state had authority to appoint the

trustees of these hospitals, construction funding was provided by citizens' contributions; fees paid by patients covered the cost of operation and treatments. (Bloomingdale differed from the rest because is was state subsidized.) (Grob, 1973: 35–36; cf. Deutsch, 1949: 132–157; and, Rothman, 1971: 130–154).

The Worcester Hospital template of reform. A new era in mental treatment began when Massachusetts opened the doors of the Worcester State Hospital. Following Massachusetts' lead, New York opened state mental institutions. (Vermont, Ohio, Tennessee, and Georgia continued the trend.) On the eve of the Civil War, 28 of 33 states had built asylums.

The Worcester Hospital was not the creation of public-spirited citizens nor of an exclusive, sectarian facility. Rather, Worcester was the product of a self-conscious attempt by Massachusetts reformers and their state legislative allies to alleviate the suffering of a growing, dependent population. Thus, the opening of Worcester marked the beginning of a cycle of mental health reform. What were the factors which explain the opening of Worcester Mental Hospital in Massachusetts? What factors explain the timing of the hospital's opening?

The Rise of the Charismatic Reformer

A partial explanation for establishment of Worcester Hospital must include the role played by a charismatic social reformer. The Massachusetts state legislature of the 1920's possessed a humanitarian reformer who was concerned by the allegations of increases in the numbers of illiterates, mentally ill, sick, unemployed, and criminals in society and was committed to developing state policies to deal with these problems. This person was Horace Mann.[3] Mann, as a lawyer and then state legislator, was strategically placed for the realization of his reform goals. Whereas 18th-century mental health reformers were physicians, directors of asylums, and theoreticians, the new 19th century reformers were not necessarily specialists. A new type of humanitarian reformer, a generalist, now appeared on the policy-making scene.

In 1828, Massachusetts legislators had been investigating the conditions in and effectiveness of its jails. The committee of inquiry urged the state to make illegal the confinement of the mentally ill in prisons and to provide alternative treatments. The recommendation was not acted upon until Horace Mann took up this issue, and in 1830 legislation for the construction of Worcester was enacted (cf. Grob, 1966). Worcester opened in 1833 under the direction of Samuel B. Woodward, an administrator committed to moral treatment. Between 1833 and 1845 the average daily population rose from 107 to 359, and successful cures were claimed to range from 82 to 91 percent! Mann's role was a crucial one for Worcester's initial success and fame. His intellectual talents, coupled with his moral commitment to reformers, made him a powerful force for change when he occupied his legislative seat. Not only could he act as a policy initiator, but also he could continue to maintain and insure the actualization of his policies by overseeing the appropriation of funds, initiating further investigations, and seeking passage of new legislation (cf. Bardach, 1979).

The transfer of charismatic authority in reform. Mann's reform interests were wide-ranging. His strategic role as a legislator permitted him to pursue other reform objectives. Educational reform, specifically, the establishment of property tax supported, compulsory, public schools became the next legislative goal on his agenda. As he concerned himself with schools, the mantle of mental health reform was passed on to others in the Massachusetts network of humanitarian reformers.

The heir to Mann's reform work was Dorothea Lynn Dix, a retired Boston spinster school teacher who stayed at the Tuke's York Retreat. A protegee of humanitarian reformer William Ellery Channing, Dix began her crusade for the mentally ill after her ministry to prison inmates lead her to ask why the East Cambridge jail house confined both mentally ill and convicts in one facility. The neglect and confinement of the insane in the jail sparked Dix's curiosity and concern. She was moved to conduct single-handedly a survey of the conditions of jails and almshouses throughout Massachusetts to assess the uniqueness of the East Cambridge conditions.

Since the state had opened the Worcester Hospital, many had assumed the public had made sufficient provisions for the mentally ill. Yet, Dix's impressionistic evidence, her policy-relevant intelligence, raised new doubts. True, the hospital's policy of providing moral management under Woodward's direction had been established, Dix's policy-relevant data posed the questions: was the intent of the legislators being met? Were the mentally ill still being confined in almshouses and jails? Was Worcester able to provide moral management?

Impressionistic data in the service of reform. Dix discovered the answers to the questions when she volunteered her service as a teacher in the East Cambridge jail. She learned that Worcester lacked enough beds to treat the pauper insane; jails had to continue to house these persons. With the support of Mann, and the network of other humanitarian reformers, she launched an investigation of the physical conditions of and types of inmates confined in all of the state's jails and Poor Law facilities. Her presentation of reform-relevant evidence enumerated the confined mentally ill by form of institution. It documented the need for an expansion of Worcester and the need for an increase in the level of state support.

Dix carried her reform work to every U.S. state in an effort to duplicate her Massachusetts triumph. Her single-woman investigations and lobbying campaigns mobilized supporters of separate services for the mentally disordered.

The impact of the U.S. constructional form on mental health reform. By the 1850's a network of state mental hospitals testified to the success of the state-by-state work of Dorothea Dix and her assistants in the service of social reform. The state hospitals also pointed to the minimal role played by the federal government in the public management of psychiatric disorders. To remedy this, Dix began a campaign for a federal role in the care and treatment of the mentally ill. In 1853, as a result of her lobbying, Congress passed legislation establishing a federal hospital for the insane in the District of Columbia. This hospital, now called St. Elizabeth's, was opened in 1855 under the administration of the Department of the Interior.

Initially, the first patients receiving treatment were mili-tary personnel and residents of the District of Columbia (Deutsch, 1949: 184).

Though the founding of a national mental hospital marked another success for Dix, the hospital opening coincided with a major defeat for the reformers. In 1854, Congress was again impressed by Dix's arguments for the need for a direct, federal government role in financially supporting the pauper insane. Congress passed legislation providing that the proceeds from the sale of 12,225,000 acres go to maintain the needy insane population. President Franklin Pierce did not agree. In his veto message he said:

> "'(Should Congress) make provision for such ob-jects, the fountains of charity will be dried up at home, and the several states, instead of be-stowing their own means on the social wants of their own people, may themselves through the strong temptation, which appeals to states as to individuals, become supplicants for the bounty of the Federal Government, reversing their true relation to this union.'" (Pierce quoted in Piven and Cloward, 1971: 47)

Pierce's veto represented a major reversal of the mental hospital reformers; Dix was personally devastated and retired from the reform movement.

President Pierce's statement was a clear expression of the minimalist, states-right stance that opposed a federal role in promoting welfare. It served for nearly a hundred years as a support for those opposed to a federal role in health care. The minimalist approach took the form of the limited, direct provision of services for specific groups to whom the nation owed an obligation for services rendered— e.g., veterans and merchant seamen. Only very gradually did the federal government take on the burden of treating other "dependent client groups," lagging behind Sweden, England, and other countries in the public provision of health and welfare services.

Routinization of reform and the decline of the asylums.
Dix's departure from the mental health reform campaigns left
the field of reform to administrators and doctors in the
public asylums of the United States. Not until the emergence of Clifford Beers in the early 20th century did a
concerted mental health reform effort once again gain direction and momemtum. Although isolated dedicated practitioners of moral management (e.g., Pliny Earle) continued to
apply its techniques, the state mental hospital administrators were increasingly incapable of meeting expectations for
patient care. The hospitals--their staffs and environment--
were really not to blame for these shortcomings. Recall
that the private and public mental institutions of the early
1800's had never served many people; it is estimated that no
more than 500 persons, often ethically and economically
homogeneous, were treated in America's private asylums inspired by the Tuke's Retreat (Rothman, 1971: 130). A method
was required to bring the asylum treatment mode to a heterogeneous population. The mentally ill were still languishing
in prisons and almshouses. The persons who launched the
campaign for asylum construction were both aware of the
moral treatment's promise and the inadequacy of current
facilities and treatment programs.

Further, the York Retreat mode of treatment was not
feasible in the physically-isolated state asylums housing
hundreds of heterogeneous inmates. Though Dix's therapeutic
goals were broadly similar to Tuke and Pinel, her theories
of mental illness were not systematically developed and
could not and did not serve as a model for the routine operation of the hospitals she helped found.[4] Thus, the
directors of state asylums were not professionally prepared
to cope with the unanticipated consequences of the success
of Dix's crusade: overcrowding and understaffing. This
deterioration in the quality of care was most pronounced in
insane asylums, in contrast to the prisons, reformatories,
and other institutional by-products of the social reconstruction campaigns (Caplan, 1969: 47-175). Rothman (1971)
observes:

"...the insane asylum suffered the most dramatic
decline from a reform to a custodial operation.
By 1870 both the reality of institutional care and

the rhetoric of psychiatrists made clear that the optimism of reformers had been unfounded, that the expectation of eradicating insanity in the new world had been unfounded." (Rothman: 265)

Therefore, the vision of reformers, Dorothea Dix, Horace Mann, and others was not realized because of this paradox: by their very orderliness mental hospitals were designed to eliminate the social disorder thought to cause mental illnesses; yet, the translation of moral treatment in large, bureaucratically-run institutions, subsisting on inadequate state budgets, created the 19th-century "snake pits." Grob (1973) concurs with Rothman, saying:

"The apparent success of early mental hospitals rested upon a series of circumstances: the small number and homogeneous nature of patients; the internal therapeutic atmosphere that arose from the enthusiasm and sometimes charismatic personality of superintendents; and close interpersonal relationships, to cite only some of the factors." (Grob: 186)

The error in measuring the asylum's success. One of the sources of policy-relevant intelligence used by Dix and others in their lobbying campaigns was high rates of cure claims by the administrators of model asylums. The abject failure of the 19th-century asylum coincided with the criticism of these estimates of the effectiveness of the institutional model of care. One of Dix's cadre of charismatic reformers, an original mental hospital administrator (and a founder of America's psychiatric profession), Pliny Earle attacked the "recovery rate" data presented by his colleague, Samuel Woodward, director of Worcester State Hospital. In his 1887 work, The Curability of Insanity: A Series of Studies, Earle assailed the 80 percent recovery rates Woodward claimed he achieved at the Worcester State Hospital. Yet Earle's criticism, however well-founded, ignored an important legitimation function of these claimed cure rates (Grob, 1973: 182-186; cf. Rothman, 1971: 263-269 and Caplan, 1969: 88ff).[5]

For example, whatever the accuracy of Woordard's claim of 80 percent cure rate, his alledged successes lent credibility to his claims. Further, Woodward was engaging in a practice common to private asylum directors in England and the U.S. The rates advertized by the proprietors of private, corporate asylums were designed to lure wealthy patients. And patients--and more importantly, their families--were not capable of evaluating the truthfulness of these claims. The paucity of reliable consumer information, coupled with the primitiveness of psychiatry, contributed to the inability to judge the effectiveness of treatment programs.

Likewise, in the U.S. and England, state legislators and Parliamentarians were not themselves capable of evaluating these claims. They lacked both the training, time, and inclination to determine the effectiveness of moral treatment. They relied on "experts" like Dix, depending upon their assessment of the successfulness of curability methods. Dix and her fellow reformers were the contemporary experts who had evaluated the evidence and were in a position to argue for a policy of asylum construction. Mid-19th century state legislators did not have in their service legislative analysts and research staffs. The underdeveloped practice of psychiatry had not generated a significant cumulative body of evidence to support the claims of reformers. Thus, the gap between the high hopes of the moral treatment advocates and the mental asylum lobbyists were shattered by the hard realities of implementing a treatment ideology. Neither the nascent profession of psychiatry, nor the methods of patient care were developed sufficiently so that the lofty goals of moral management for the masses could be realized. Attempts to offer moral treatment on a large scale would have to await the mid-20th century and its community care programs. The positive consequences of this first cycle of mental health reform was the boost it gave to the extention of governmental services and the base it created for a psychiatric profession.

The Consolidation and Rationalization of U.S. Mental Health Care

In the wake of President Franklin Pierce's veto of the land-grants support for the poor mentally ill, the reform movement halted its activities. Always dependent upon Dix's charismatic personality and her cadre of supporters, the campaign for federal governmental finance of the mentally ill halted. Dix took leave from her U.S. reform burdens. She traveled to England to recover her health, and once rested she continued her investigations of conditions in English and Scottish asylums, ultimately making recommendations to Parliament for improving British mental hospital services. Upon her return to the U.S., Dix's final public service was to head the U.S. Army's Nursing Corps during the Civil War.

With Dix's retirement the 19th-century U.S. mental health movement had reached its zenith; the years following Pierce's veto were characterized by a consolidation of the gains won and defensive actions to stem the erosion in state financial support and administrative reorganization. Notwithstanding these efforts, the almshouses, poorhouses, and prisons still contained far too many of the pauper insane who deserved to be properly housed and treated in asylums. Despite the best efforts of asylum administrators and mental hospital lobbyists to facilitate their transfer, reports consistently showed that the insane were not being segregated for proper treatment. Further, asylum managers experienced continuing difficulties in estimating the need and demand for asylum care, with the result that newly opened facilities, specifically constructed to relieve over-crowding in almshouses and hospitals, were soon themselves overcrowded (Caplan, 1969: 154-189).

Need for administrative rationalization. Dix and other reformers, in their rush to create new institutional modes of care, left the U.S. with a mixture of private and public institutions. The proliferation of institutions and asylums --public and semi-public--resulted in difficulties in patient supervision and hospital management. And the private institutions were not subject to any state control at all. Officials saw the solution increasingly as a greater role of government in the monitoring of these institutions' operations and controlling of their costs.

The legislature of the leading reform state, Massachusetts, had selected a committee for the investigation of all charitable organizations, (public and private) in order to determine the extent of impropriety in their operation, as well as to develop proposals for the improvement of their operation. The main committee recommendation was to empower a permanent board of charities to monitor the operation of asylums and other institutions. The 1863 legislative adoption was the first of several such adoptions by other states (Deutsch, 1949: 246-249). Some state legislatures did not respond favorably to recommendations of their charity boards. For example:

"...North Carolina Board of Public Charities, in its first annual report to the General Assembly (1865), not only vigorously protested against the abominable treatment of dependent insane in public institutions, but arraigned the prevailing system of poor relief in toto." (Deutsch: 250-251)

Though Pliny Earle and a few other treatment innovators persisted in the application of moral management, most hospitals had abandoned those techniques and had lapsed into custodialism. Under such conditions there was renewed public concern over illegal confinement in mental institutions. The "solution" to this recurring problem was to create a separate ombudsman to oversee the management of the mental institutions. For example, the New York State Commissioner in Lunacy was charged with the powers of inspection of all facilities. The extension of government control is also exemplified by New York state's landmark 1890 legislation, viewed as the solution to the problem of overcrowding. The 1890 act placed the state in full control of all asylums. The act further abolished the distinction between acute and chronic care institutions; it divided the state into hospital districts and required a hospital be constructed for each catchment district. New York City, with its network of facilities, was exempt from this requirement. The law further required the speed-up of the transfer of the insane to the new asylums from the almshouses; and, it mandated that the state would now bear the whole cost of the care and treatment, previously charged to the counties of the inmates' origins (Deutsch, 1949: 260).

New York's centralization solution was not the only method adopted by states to cope with the breakdown in the treatment of the mentally ill. Wisconsin's rationalization took the form of decentralization of control by giving county government responsibility for mental hospitals. Yet, the Wisconsin State Board of Charities encountered the same problems which confronted New York: increasing the capacity of state asylums was not reducing the numbers confined in almshouses and jails. The pathways to the county institutions lay through the state hospitals; new cases were admitted to the state hospital first, and then transferred to the county if they were determined to be chronic.[6]

Whether decentralized or centralized, a much more rationalized mental hospital services system was gradually established, integrating public-sponsored private facilities and public hospitals into a network of state asylums. This rationalization process also occurred in England and Sweden. The initial European attempts to provide alternatives to prisons and poorhouse confinement of the mentally disordered were to also degenerate; new, humane institutions reverted to pre-reform custodial care.

Thus, in the U.S. the overcrowded, understaffed state hospitals mocked the ideal of moral treatment. Frugal state legislatures, overwhelmed initially by charismatic Dix's arguments, were now more sophisticated in coping with hospital manager's claims of success in curing the insane. And, bureaucratization of mental hospital services limited the chances of treatment innovations. Examinating the English experience with mental health reform can shed further light on these processes. By comparing U.S. and English experiences and deepening the analogies between developments in each country, the most important determinants of the success or failure of mental health reform can be revealed.

English Mental Health Reform in an Age of Optimism

The task of mental health reform was complicated by the U.S. federal system of government. Reformers had to convince individual state legislatures and governors of the need for asylums because interpretations of the Constitution did not provide for the legal means whereby the federal government could direct the states to construct mental hospitals (e.g., President Franklin Pierce's sustained veto of the land-grants for the mentally ill). In contrast, in the more centralized English political system, mental health reform movement was more successful in realizing its goals. In England, because the institutional and procedural barriers to the adoption of a national policy were fewer than in the U.S., the mental health reform movement's chances of initial success were increased. That is, in the 19th-century English political system, well-organized, strategically-placed reform movements could be much more effective than in a system like the U.S. where it was much more difficult to secure strategic placement.

The initial national success of the English reformers. In England a national mental health reform movement achieved its first success with the foundation of county asylums following Parliament's passage of the County Asylums Act of 1808. Prior to the 1808 Act, Parliament had relied on the Vagrancy Laws of 1714 and 1744 to manage the growth in population of persons labelled "rogues" and "vagabonds" the casualties of common land enclosures, agricultural unemployment, and urbanization. These regulatory acts were essentially extensions of the 1601 Poor Laws; that is, they were measures designed to control an undesirable group rather than treat the causes of their disruptive behavior. The 1744 Act contained specific provisions pertaining to lunatics. Under this vagrancy legislation at least two justices of the peace were required to detain lunatics and to either maintain or attempt to cure them; in addition, the management of the estates of the insane was given to the justices of the peace. Further amendments to these acts made provisions for the detention of criminal lunatics.

The Parliamentary base for a reform movement. In contrast to the United States Congress in 1808, the British

Parliament was prepared to consider reports on the plight of the mentally ill and to learn of the attempts to treat mental diseases.

Parliament could consider a national investment in new mental illness treatment facilities because there was a succession of dedicated humanitarian legislators prepared to direct bills through the sole national legislative body. In contrast, there were no mental health reformers in the 19th-century U.S. Congress, something which was to change dramatically in the 20th century. Leading Parliament's deliberations on the appropriate mental health governmental action was Charles Williams-Wynn. Williams-Wynn, then Under-Secretary of State for the Home Department, directed the passage of the County Asylum Act of 1808, an act implementing the recommendations of the 1807 Select Committee Report. The plight of criminal and pauper lunatics under provisions of the Poor Laws was of deep concern to Williams-Wynn. As both a member of the government as a Home Office official and as a member of Parliament, Williams-Wynn employed his dual positions to further his personal goal of improving services for the mentally ill. When Parliament called for an inquiry into the conditions of lunatics and the insane, Williams-Wynn was able to secure for himself the chairmanship of that investigative committee. He then went on to spearhead the campaign to pass legislation embodying his recommendation, and finally, as a Home Office official, was able to preside over the implementation of the legislation. In contrast to Dorothea Dix, Williams-Wynn had an opportunity to play multiple roles in policy making, thereby furthering the reform movement's aims. Thus, the case of Williams-Wynn illustrates how the strategic placement of committed reformers permits policy enactment and the monitoring of the implementation (Jones, 1972: 59).

The impact of constitutional form on reform proposals. Further, this English legislation of 1808 demonstrates the importance of other factors which distinguish 19th-century U.S. and English mental health policy making. For example, while the Massachusetts legislature possessed a Horace Mann committed to social reconstruction, the English Parliament had as one of its members for at least twelve years earlier, a reformer interested in not only gathering evidence on the conditions in the nation's institutions, but also proposing implementing specific legislation.

Given the fusion of powers and functions in the English Parliament, the social reformer and Parliamentarian was able to monitor his legislation and suggest amendments in light of information gathered in the cabinet administration of these programs. The 1808 County Asylum Act authorized parish justices of the peace to raise property taxes to build and maintain asylums. Patients were to be admitted who were deemed to be dangerous or criminal by two justices. The parish paid charges laid down by the justices, and patients were discharged after having been certified by a committee of justices as having recovered. In 1811, Nottingham opened the first of these county asylums authorized under the County Asylums Act:

> "The asylum was built to accommodate 76-80
> patients and yet this accommodation was found
> at once to be inadequate. By the terms of the
> Act, there was no way in which the asylum
> staff could exercise their discretion in
> admitting patients." (Jones, 1972: 62)

Williams-Wynn's amendments to the 1808 Act in 1815 and 1819 sought to remedy the problem of overcrowding by requiring medical certification of insanity or lunacy to be produced by the parish overseers of the poor. The 1819 Act permitted justices of the peace to directly admit patients, without the concurrence of the parish overseer, thereby weakening the control of the mentally ill by Poor Law authorities.

Despite the best efforts of Williams-Wynn, county asylums did not instantly spring forth across the English contryside. In the first twenty years of the act only nine hospitals were constructed. But a precedent had been set; English public treatment of the insane was now being provided by county governments that levied taxes to pay hospital construction and staffing. The important policy differentiation process had begun: national government now recognized the need for separate facilities for the specialized treatment of the mentally ill.

Private madhouses and their regulation. In constrast, controversies continued over private institutions and Royal Bethlem Hospital. Allegations of mistreatment, abuse, and illegal detention in madhouses continued to spur investigations. The proprietors of notorious private profit-making madhouses, licensed under the Act for Regulating Private Madhouses of 1774, operated under the not-so-thorough annual scrutiny of so-called Lunacy Commissioners, selected from among members of the Royal College of Physicians. Williams-Wynn and other 19th-century reformers were critical of the commissioners performance and disturbed by the statutory limitations on their scope of operation. Facilities outside London, Bethlem, and the Poor Law facilities were all exempt from an annual examination. Despite the success of the Parliamentary Reformers in enacting the County Asylums Act, their attempts to pass legislation to strengthen the surveillance powers of the commission were thwarted. Though the House of Commons passed Williams-Wynn's bills, the House of Lords vetoed them in 1816, 1817, and 1819. This failure of the first reform attempts led to the disillusionment of the Parliamentary reformers and their ultimate disbandment (Jones, 1972: 54-63).

In sum, the results of reform were highly variable. Successfully enacted reform policies were poorly implemented. Bethlem remained outside the purview of the five Lunacy Commissioners and continued to be the site of scandals. Poor Law workhouses, prisons, and almshouses continued to be the place of incarceration of the mentally retarded, psychologically disordered, and the aged.

Toward a rationalization of services. Thus, early 19th-century England's institutions to confine, manage, and cure the growing population of mentally disordered persons were an uncoordinated, ad hoc collection of facilities, laws and regulations, subject to the continued review and tinkering by concerned, public-spirited parliamentarians and interested citizens. Only gradually were attempts made to systematically organize and rationalize these facilities and services.[7] The process of bureaucratization, whereby the conflicting laws were consolidated, the administration and finance of state-supported facilities clarified, and the regulation of private institutions tightened, took the next fifty years.

Lord Ashley and the Humanistic Reform Movement

The U.S. reform movement had witnessed the transfer of charismatic reform leadership from Horace Mann to Dorothea Dix. In England, the mental health reform movement also witnessed a change in the leadership and institutional supports for reform. After Williams-Wynn withdrew from a leadership role, the chief humanitarian-social reformer became Lord Ashley, later the 7th Earl of Shaftesbury, whose interests ran from working conditions in coal mines and factories to private manhouses and asylums.[8] Of Lord Ashley, Briggs (1959) says:

> "He believed in the unremitting exposure of social evils, and was driven by a fierce evangelical energy that never left his conscience quiet or allowed him to stay still." (Briggs: 335)

Like his American counterpart, Dorothea Dix, Lord Ashley was religiously devout, thoroughly committed to the view that governments must intervene to alleviate suffering and improve the quality of life. This vision of the positive benefits of governmental social welfare policy was to conflict with the limited government views exposed by the followers of Jeremy Bentham. Throughout the 19th century the Benthamite utilitarians clashed with the evangelical humanism of the Earl of Shaftesbury. Within and without Parliament, these conceptions of society and government were in constant conflict, ever seeking to gain dominance over the other.

> "Evangelical humanism stemmed from an emotional appreciation of the plight of the poor and oppressed. It may be said to have started with the Wesleys, and to have reached its fruition in the person of the seventh Earl of Shaftesbury; but Radicalism came from cold reason: from a fundamental love of order, a hatred of administrative confusion. Its dominant figure was Jeremy Bentham, whose thought was to have so much influence on Chadwick and J.S. Hill." (Jones, 1972: 55)

Reformed Poor Law and Public Health: Expansion of Governmental Health Operations

Though they sought to reduce relief and halt the rise in welfare costs, the Benthamites were unwittingly the initiators of public health care in England.[9] One of the chief social atomists, Edwin Chadwick, whose reforms insured the workhouse incarceration of the poor, believed the sick did not bear personal responsibility for their disease. Disease was costly--laborers were unemployed, deaths resulted, and disease created paupers out of the survivors. Benthamite economics dictated a positive, governmental role in the elimination of diseases responsible for unemployment. More importantly, the Benthamites were aware that epidemics which swept London and other industrializing cities did not heed class lines.

> "Good economics was an irresistable argument to the bourgeois Benthamite. It was public parsimony which led to the first public investigation into the sanitary conditions in the towns-management of Doctors Arnott, Kay, and Smith in 1838 to investigate the typhus epidemic which was causing so much destitution throughout London." (Eckstein, 1958: 13)

As a Poor Law Commissioner, Chadwick himself authored the 1842 report on the causes of unsanitary and unhealthy conditions in England's sprawling industrial cities. By using data compiled by the newly created Registrar General, (England's public records office) and provided by the Poor Law medical officers and relief workers, Chadwick identified the correlates of typhus, typhoid, smallpox, cholera, and tuberculosis--the unsanitary, crowded, and polluted living conditions of England's sprawling cities. In response to the report's call for action Parliament passed the Public Health Act (1848), creating a local and a national board of health responsible for the elimination of the causes of epidemic diseases and for combatting their periodic outbreak. The significance of the 1848 Act lay in Parliament's permanent commitment to the struggle against disease. Governmental involvement in public health deepened. In 1875 further legislation was passed, codifying the law and regulations growing up around the 1848 Act, stipulating the central and local governments' powers and responsibilities for sewage, drainage, water, housing, food, and public hospitals.

"In the last quarter of the nineteenth century the situation improved dramatically, and although the causes of this improvement are likely to have been complex and multiple, substantial credit at least must go to the system of sanitary control embodied in--though not, as has been said, inaugurated by--the Act of 1875." (Watkin, 1975: 49)

Thus, the unanticipated consequence of Benthamite social policy was the initiation of a public health service in Britain.

Reformed Poor Laws and Mental Treatment: The Chadwick-Ashley Rivalry

Chadwick served as a Poor Law Commissioner, implementing the 1834 legislation he co-authored with Nassau Senior. He was thus fulfilling a number of key roles in the policy process: policy designer, enactor, and implementor. In the process of carrying out his reforms, Chadwick confronted another policy giver who also played a number of policy roles, Lord Ashley.

The County Asylum Act and Madhouse Act of 1828 had charged commissioners with the task of inspecting the condition in London's infamous profit-making madhouses as well as the new county asylums. However, the plight of the pauper lunatics in parish poorhouses was not to be the concern of the lunacy commissions. Rather, Chadwick's new Poor Law Commissioners concerned themselves with the fate of the thousands of mentally ill persons who formed a significant number of the dependents of the Benthamite welfare state (Jones, 1972: 108-114). Chadwick's ruthless, socially-reductive, 19th-century economic views of the causes and cures of poverty led him to adopt policy measures to root out the less-eligible, and able-bodied who shunned work, insuring that they did not receive public support. This same relief legislation was applied in all its stringency to some thousands of people who were totally "unable to support themselves, and who were in some cases subject to coercion" (Jones, 1972: 124). In its operation, the 1834 Poor Law Commissioners sought to weed out the seemingly dangerous insane residing in the workhouses and to secure their transfer to county asylums.

The conflicting goals of parliamentary-based reformers. Chadwick's hostility toward evangelical, humanitarian-inspired relief efforts, coupled with his antipathy for the medical profession, made him a likely foe of Lord Ashley. Ashley's efforts attempted to ease the suffering of the insane, to insure that they were decently housed, and to prevent involuntary and arbitrary confinement. Chadwick's concern was in saving money, and he opposed lunatic asylums costing more money to operate than the bleak workhouses. To maintain cost controls, the Benthamites sought to gain complete control over the facilities treating the mentally disordered. Thus, in the 1838 hearings on the operation of the new Poor Law, Chadwick's aide, Edward Gulson, as assistant Poor Law Commissioner, advocated the transfer of the control of the lunatic asylums to poor commissions (Jones, 1972: 127-128).

In contrast to Chadwick's parsimonious approach, Ashley took the view that the quality of treatment in private and county asylums had raised their operating costs. Taking up the leadership of the mental health reformers, Lord Ashley began to work for the passage of legislation expanding the powers and the scope of the lunacy commissioners. Ultimately, Chadwick lost in his efforts to consolidate and unify relief and care for the insane, though this loss did not result in a clean administrative separation of the two forms of care. Unlike the Swedes, the English were unable to fully remove the Poor Law stigma from public health and mental health care. Under the Poor Law, the sick in hospitals did not necessarily lose their right to vote, the pauper sick who became residents of these institutions did. The Poor Law odium inhered in public health care until 1946.

Mental Health Legislation in the New Poor Law Era

The framers of the 1828 Madhouse Act intended that annual inspections would identify abuses of patients. Yet, the popular concern over illegal detention did not abate and reports of cursory inspections and illegal detentions persisted. Parliament responded to the organized, focused concern of the champions of the mentally disordered by passing the 1842 Lunatic Asylum Act.

The 1842 Lunatic Asylum Act gave the Metropolitan Commissioners in Lunacy power to inspect all private madhouses and county asylums twice a year, for a three-year period. Lord Ashley was chairman of the commission consisting of lawyers, medical doctors, and public-spirited citizens. The inspections of commissioners were designed to gather data on the plight of persons in insane asylums and to make recommendations for future legislation. Their tours were intended to both insure compliance with detention laws and assess the conditions in county asylums, public lunatic asylums, and licensed private madhouses.

Ashley presented the final commission report to Parliament in 1844. Like his U.S. counterparts, Horace Mann and Dorothea Dix, and his English predecessors, he argued that England ought to follow the lead of the initiators of moral management and transform the custodial mental institutions into enlightened, moral treatment facilities.

> "The commissioners argued for legislation to make
> the building of county asylums mandatory instead
> of permissive, and for a uniform system of inspec-
> tion by a statutory authority. Reforms were
> called for in the system of certification so as to
> prevent collusion between the certifying doctor
> and relatives of the patient." (Watkin, 1975:358)

Parliament concurred in the Lunatic Act, 1845, and set up full-time lunacy commissions, with the broad powers Ashley envisioned necessary to realize his goal of bringing enlightened treatment to all the insane.

A separate lunatic and pauper Asylum Act in 1845 mandated the counties and boroughs to provide asylums for the pauper lunatics—a clear repudiation of the Chadwick goal of deterrent-type confinement facilities. Lord Ashley was appointed to head the new lunacy commission.

After his father's death in 1851, Ashley assumed the hereditary title of the 7th Earl of Shaftesbury, yet his succession to a peerage did not diminish his social reform work. Under his charismatic leadership, concern for the mentally ill became institutionalized; psychiatry began its emergence as a ligitimate branch of the medical profession at the same time. The forerunner to the Royal Medico-Psychological Association was founded in 1865 and pioneered the establishment of nation-wide standards for training and certifying mental health nurses. And, progressive doctors like John Conolly at Harwell Asylum abolished physical methods of restraint, continuing the humanitarian approach of the Tukes.

The recurring public concern over illegal detention. Despite the lunacy reform acts, public indignation over illegal detention could still be aroused by the rumors, allegations, and reports of patient ill-treatment, illegal confinement, and difficulties in obtaining patient releases. Ironically, public concern over illegal detention, or the questionable legal commitment, occurred after the 1845 Act.

"Ashley (Shaftesbury) and his small band of parliamentary reformers had done their work too well. They had aroused public indignation in order to press for legal control over the private madhouses." (Jones, 1972: 154)

When allegations and findings of illegal detention were reported in the press, in popular novels, court cases, and Parliament, the reformers were placed on the defensive. Though they had secured their legislative goal of a system of inspection and monitoring of mental institutions, the legislation's implementation was, by Shaftesbury's own admission, imperfect. By subsequent acts of Parliament in 1853 and 1862, Shaftesbury sought to remedy defects in the detention-monitoring machinery, but these incremental improvements did not quell public agitation.

Yet, another Parliamentary inquiry was called in 1877. As Lunacy Commission head, Shaftesbury gave evidence, yet he despaired at having to defend his hard-won (much-maligned) reforms of 1845 as well as his tenure as head of the enforcement commission. Still, his authoritative testimony, coupled with his prestige, was enough to convince the inquiry committee of adequacy of the needed safeguards and the Parliamentary Comittee of Inquiry determined there was no need for further legislation.

By the 1880s, however, with Shaftesbury in ill health, the proponents of codification of mental detention laws again introduced legislation which Shaftesbury opposed. Again, public concern had been whipped up by allegations, and Parliamentarians responded to the call for new legislation. In this final 19th-century Parliamentary struggle, "legalism" triumphed. The 1885 death of Shaftesbury removed the main barrier to the codification of a detention law which was to be finally approved in 1890.

> "From the medical point of view, the Lunacy Act of 1890 was out of date before it was passed. It represented the legal view of mental illness --that there was a condition which made it necessary in certain circumstances to deprive a man of his personal liberty, and that every possible device must be used to limit these circumstances." (Jones, 1972: 226)

While guarding against unwarranted detention, the 1890 Act reduced mental institutions to a purely custodial-care role in the treatment of the mentally ill because only the most extreme cases of mental disability could qualify for placement in asylums. Any potential therapeutic role of these institutions was drastically reduced. As a result, doctors were reluctant to use asylums as the primary site of care, instead choosing more hopeful settings for their patients' treatment.

Thus, the efforts of the creators of the 1890 Act had the unanticipated consequence of transforming asylums into the "dumping-grounds" for the most hopelessly insane of patients. The moral therapeutic goals of formerly innovative institutions were no longer realizable with a patient population of the hopelessly demented and institutionally adapted. In a word, the 1890 triumph of legalism doomed the moral treatment programmatic goals of asylums. Custodial mental institutions were less likely to be the site of the development of new etiological theories and their concomitant treatment modalities. Thus, the original vision of the therapeutic community was lost partly because psychiatric legalism was enshrined. Not until 1959 were the last vestiges of legalism removed.

Nineteenth Century Social Legislation in the Sweden

England and Sweden both faced a crisis in the management of poor relief in the 1830s. The 1830s' economic depression increased the number of paupers demanding assistance from local, parish Poor Law authorities. These countries differed in the methods selected to cope with the inadequate methods of poor relief programs. In part these differences were a reflection of the political institutions of these two countries. During the 19th-century, both countries were formally constitutional monarchies, the power enjoyed by the Swedish Parliament, the Riksdag was less than that of England's Parliament. After an attempt to sustain a limited monarchical form of government failed, the Swedish crown regained control of machinery of state in 1775. Only in the late-19th century did the popular representative institutions regain their dominance. From the standpoint of reform, the dominance by the monarchy meant that the royal civil service played a key role in formulating and implementing new policies.

Bureaucratic hegemony on the governmental form. If Sweden was characterized by the late development of competitive party politics and the persistence of monarchial power, it was also remarkable for its administrative bureaucratic elite (Heclo, 1974: 39). As previously noted this administrative corps had its origins in warfare. This patrimonial bureaucracy was to evolve into a modern rational-legal civil service, characterized by its political neutrality and accountability to the civil service code. The royal civil service exercised its control through five central government boards, with corresponding regional (län) units appointed by the governor (landsovding).

A parliamentary-ministerial system of government was instituted early in the 1840s, yet Swedish ministries did not take administrative control of the state. Then as now, the ministries served chiefly as policy-making units. The monarchy's administrative boards continued to direct the implementation of policies developed by the political ministries' departments. Heclo (1972) observes that:

"To this day the Swedish central government retains the division between the small departments (usually less than 100 emplyees, including office and janitorial staff) designed to develop policy and the fairly independent boards handling the bulk of the administrative business." (Heclo: 41)

In contrast, the evolution of English parliamentary system had streamlined and fused the legislative and administrative function in the ministers of state. Further in constrast to Sweden, the English were early in developing parliamentary parties; yet, the English were late in the establishment of a fully elaborated, professional corps of public servants, approximating Weber's ideal-typical model of the bureaucracy. The U.S. system is yet a third example of how a Western liberal democracy can be organized, though it naturally shares many more features with England than Sweden.

Poor Relief in Sweden in the 19th Century

Up to the early-19th century, governmentally-provided poor relief in Sweden was characterized by state control, at both local and national levels. This control was designed to insure that poor relief was not an attractive alternative to work. Like England, Sweden experienced the demographic changes—rising birth rates, falling death rates—associated with the revolution in agricultural technology. These developments had the effect of dislocating the free peasantry. Unable to find work on the land, the former peasant was forced to wander from village to town in search of a means of subsistence. Later, in the 19th century, the acceleration of developments of these trends resulted in massive peasant immigration to the United States.[10]

Legislative precedents for a national assistance law can be detected as early as 1764. Royal edicts were issued which stipulated that every parish was responsible for its poor. Having fixed the principle of local responsibility, this royal decree also required that local taxes be levied for the construction of children's homes and for hospitals.

The lack of a Poor Law stigma in the state health care system. Swedish public hospitals, in constrast to their English counterparts, were not tainted with the Poor Law stigma. The Crown's central administrative boards had already set up veneral disease treatment facilities and appointed county medical officers to deal with the casualties of war (Heclo, 1972: 51; cf. Anderson, 1973: 39–42). In the 1700s, with the construction of the first county hospital, the principle of access to medical care as a citizen's right was established. This "free-access" principle was to distinguish Sweden from England and the U.S. for the next two hundred years. For example, English Parliamentary struggles waged between Chadwick and Ashley for control of the mental institutions could not have taken place in Sweden, where the demarcation between Poor Law relief and medical care was clear. The Swedish government's separate provision of hospital care outside the Poor Laws is also illustrative of the early power enjoyed by Sweden's administrative Royal Boards.

"Nowhere was the importance of Swedish central administration better demonstrated than in hospital care. Late in the 1600s, the first county medical officer was appointed under the authority of the national administration and during the next century their numbers grew considerably." (Heclo, 1972: 51)

There is another important distinction between England and Sweden: in Sweden the workhouse never played as central a role in the relief, management, and deterrence of the poor as it did in England. In part, the workhouses' smaller role was a function of Sweden's relatively lower levels of industrialization and urbanization; as the first new nation-state, England was first in experiencing the difficulties of managing the social casualties of the fairly haphazard and prolonged movement from rural agricultural to urban-industrial society. But the evidence is also clear that Benthamism never gained such hegemony in Sweden as it did in England.

Swedish Poor Law Reforms in the 1830's

The 1830s' economic depression forced thousands onto the already swollen parish poor relief rolls. In England, the relief crisis had created demands for reform, demands which Nassau Senior and Edwin Chadwick headed. Sweden's parish (län) poor relief officials also demanded that the central government respond to the crisis and reduce the län's relief burden. England's response to this crisis had been to end what Heclo terms "medieval parochialism" in welfare and to adopt new "scientific" laws of economics and administration in the management of the poor; the Benthamite 1834 "reforms" instituted placed a heavy emphasis on the cost-saving, deterring workhouse system of relief. In constrast, Swedish political elites responded to the economic crises by not adopting as coercive relief systems as England enacted. Swedish relief efforts did not swing between the extreme of outdoor relief and the workhouse. And gradually, vagrancy itself ceased to require punishment. Swedish social policy began to adjust to the new economic reality of a free labor force and abandoned the incarceration of the unemployed who wandered from town to town seeking work.

In 1837 a national, comprehensive investigation of the Poor Laws examined various reform options; Swedish ruling elite did want to institute that form of welfare reform. The importation of the English workhouse was considered, but officials determined that not enough facilities could be built to house the growing numbers of paupers and that these institutions could not be effectively administered. Sweden's administrative corps was more thorough and deliberate than they were partisan and dogmatic in their examination of the problem of poverty and its solutions. This more complete examination led the Swedish to reject Benthamism. Rather than impose the coercive workhouse system, Sweden's ruling elites decided to strengthen its restrictions on the migration of bad welfare risks from one parish to another. Also, employers whose migrating workers became welfare dependents were held responsible for these new cases, hence creating incentives for employers to insure their workers did not become burdens (Heclo, 1972:59-60).

Bureaucratically-Led Health Reforms of 1862

In 1818 the state levied a tax to finance the "cure houses" designed to combat veneral disease. But this public health measure was only an initial health reform initiated by the civil service. The central government's role also expanded in the 19th century with the subsidy of parish (län) hospitals and the direction of the deployment of teams of public health service personnel in both the growing urban centers as well as in rural regions. Most important of all, the 1862 reorganization of local government was to have the greatest impact on health service delivery. Anderson (1972) notes Crown's bureaucracy, stripped of its Baltic Empire, had turned its attention and energies to Sweden's domestic problems. The product of this examination of local affairs was a proposal for the restructuring of local government.

Yet, bureaucratic zeal to rationalize local government was not the only source of this reorganization plan. The mid-19th century was a period marked by renewed demands for greater citizen participation in governmental affairs. The proposals for local government reforms were an attempt by the ruling oligarchy to satisfy these demands of farmers and the growing ranks of bourgeois professionals, proprietors, and industrialists for greater participation while at the same time maintaining the oligarchy's grip on the central government.

The county councils were given the task of electing the new Upper Chamber in a reformed Riksdag. The new tier of government—the county council—was given responsibility for education and training programs, economic and agricultural development and, most importantly, health and medical care. As a result, since 1862 the county councils have become the major authority in public health (Anderson, 1968: 210-213; 224-227).

The rise of the county hospital network. The county council (landsting), was the vehicle for devolving governmental responsibilities as well as rationalizing health and welfare services. Before 1862, a län had had a governor appointed directly by the Crown; under the consolidation of läns into twenty-five counties and four municipalities, local political power was to be vested in directly elected representatives which formed the county councils. All county councils in turn were to elect representatives to a newly created Upper House of the Riskdag. This reorganization of local government did have the consequence of increasing the representatives of government, but without much thought as to what the functions of the county councils would be. Anderson (1972) found that:

> "Up to this time the state (central government) had been subsidizing the general hospitals, even though they were owned by local parishes, and had been completely responsible for mental asylums. It was also fully responsible for the public health officers scattered throughout the country. Furthermore, the state had from the very beginning assumed responsibility, both financial and administrative, for the medical schools." (Anderson: 42)

Under the governmental reorganization plan the counties now assumed control of all the hospitals and hospital-based care. The funds to support this new hospital-based system were to be originally one-fifth of the retail liquor tax collected in each county. Additional patient fees were levied to support these services, but as income and property taxing power was granted to the counties, the need for patient fees as a source of funding decreased. The conse-

112

quences of governmental reorganization was this: expenditures on hospitals increased. From 1861 to 1904 the number of hospitals increased 63 percent, from 46 to 75; the number of beds increased 165 percent, from 2960 to 7856. Sweden thus embarked on a hospital construction campaign because the 1862 reforms created a unit of government whose sole mission was health.[11]

Swedish Mental Hospitals in the 19th Century

It was not until October 19, 1775 that Crown hospitals (Kronohospitaler), originally Catholic convents in the post-reformation period, were charged with the task of admitting lunatics and the seriously ill. The Order of the Seraphim was placed in charge of these hospitals. The order exercised its responsibilities with dubious effectiveness and much criticism until 1876. For example, an 1822 report characterized these institutions as "storerooms for these unfortunate lunatics." As in England, a visit to these "storerooms" was considered a public amusement. The spectacle of the insane's agony had a popular appeal in Stockholm as well as in London, and only gradually did an alternative, more hopeful conception of mental illnesses take hold in Sweden.

Professionally-led mental hospital reform. C.V. Sonden, the reform-minded head of Danvik Hospital, was largely responsible for bringing to the attention of concerned government officials the plight of the mentally ill. A commission was formed whose assessment of the need for improved care facilities prompted the central government's Board of Medicine to relieve the Order of the Seraphim of their responsibility for the mental hospitals in 1876. The mental hospital reform proposals presented a survey of the Crown hospitals and estimated that 1200 beds were required to relieve overcrowding and enhance the quality of the treatment of the mentally ill. Further, persons not treated in the mental hospitals could be treated at home. By the mid-19th century, the estimated accommodation was for 0.4 beds per 1000 persons to meet the requirements (Retterstol, 1975: 207-255).

Höjer's (1938) overview of the Swedish mental hospital system at the end of the 19th century sums up the situation:

"In the 1880s one thousand beds were available to the state for this (psychiatric) care. At the turn of the century, this number had risen to five thousand." (Höjer, 1938: 110)

From 1876 on, the central government assumed command over the meager facilities then available for the insane; the focus of control remained with the Board of Health until the administrative responsibility for mental hospitals was trasferred to the counties. In contrast to the U.S. state system and the Parliamentary monitored English system, the Swedish mental hospital remained under the direction of the national Medical Board, while health care was devolved to the county governments. This dominance by medical administrators was to have important consequences for future Swedish reforms.

The Rationalization and Consolidation of Mental Health Care in Three Nations

The wave of mental hospital construction was sparked by the desire to bring the moral treatment for mental diseases to all people. Asylum construction was a specific manifestation of the broad-based, norm-oriented, social reform movement seeking to define and manage the new social problems of insanity, juvenile delinquency, illiteracy, poverty, and criminality. The assumption in all these 19th-century campaigns was that these social evils were soluable by purposive governmental action. In the case of mental illness, the asylum was the instrument for this social reconstruction of disordered persons.

By the mid-19th century, reformers in Sweden, England, and the U.S. had all succeeded in establishing separate care facilities for the mentally ill. At least in England and the U.S., the horrors of almshouse, workhouse, and prison confinement of the mentally ill and retarded had moved Parliament and the U.S. state legislatures to increasingly assume direct responsibility for the mentally ill's treatment. These legislative bodies also responded to the appeals of reformers by enacting detention legislation that attempted to strike a balance between the rights of the mentally disordered, their need for humane treatment, and the demands that society be protected from the dangerous among the psychologically disturbed.

Yet, in both England and the U.S., the sheer pressure of increasing numbers of inmates and the meager financial support, coupled with the inexperience of the institutional staffs and the primitiveness of the treatment modalities, subverted the intent of the reformers. The very success of reformers like Horace Mann and Dorothea Dix, Charles Williams-Wynn, and the 7th Earl of Shaftesbury unintentionally helped create new, horrific conditions that present-day reformers are still attempting to eliminate. In England, the county asylums, the variously constituted lunacy commissions, and the tightening of legal admission requirements had the effect of making the goal of moral treatment ultimately unattainable. In the U.S. the new state mental hospitals, while initially providing humane alternatives to prisons, workhouses, and the like, degenerated into custodial institutions, unable to provide inmates with individual, supportive care and treatment as envisioned by Dix and Mann. In contrast, in Sweden, the influence of inspired, charismatic reformers was minimal; a biomedical model of mental illness was to predominate: Sonden believed mental disorders required medical solutions (Retterstol, 1975: 219). Yet, this 19th century commitment to a medical model of mental disorders was to limit the terms of policy developments in the 20th century. Only reforms that fit this medical (hospital-dominated) model were given serious consideration.

Rationalization and centralization. Sweden's 1877 centralization of mental hospital services contrasts sharply with the decentralized U.S. state and local efforts and the eclectic British network of private, county, and sponsored facilities. In the U.S. expanding national programs for the mentally ill were blocked for nearly a hundred years partially by President Franklin Pierce's veto of Congressional legislation setting up land-grant funding for state mental hospitals; yet even in this funding proposal for the federal government was limited: there was no national board of health or lunacy commission either administering or investigating on a national basis.

In a highly-centralized and bureaucratic-political system like Sweden's, health and mental health services were much more likely to be placed at a much earlier date under national control than in a decentralized, federal system like the U.S. The constrast between England and the U.S. reveals that though the 19th-century English central government played a much more activist, interventionist role in mental health care, such a role did not prevent the decay and corruption of the goals and dreams of mental health reformers. Even with central-government inspectors directly investigating allegations of patient mistreatment and false confinement, the decline of county asylums into merely custodial institutions occurred. Thus, critics observing the lack of any central government role in the U.S. until 1946 should note the failure of moral treatment programs occurred even when central government reformers (like Shaftesbury) were monitoring the implementation of reform legislation.

The general principle one can glean from these data is this: centralized politics can more easily assume responsibility for health and welfare programs. Yet, the bureaucratically-dominated Swedish administration of mental hospitals left less scope for the therapeutic innovation and reform initiatives. In the more institutionally decentralized U.S. and England, the treatment innovators could more easily experiment with new treatment modalities even though the public care had generally degenerated into custodialism. The opportunities for reformers to expose maltreatment, arouse public indignation, and persuade legislators to enact new legislation was greater where more than one approach to the problem of mental disorders existed. Where Sweden's medical approach to mental illness provided certain opportunities for research and treatment, it precluded others. In a more "open" environment, where there were strong traditions of citizen initiated reforms, there was a greater chance for the "new" discoveries of the next generation of reformers to become the basis of policy initiatives.

The next chapter traces the developments of the late-19th and early-20th century that were to have a profound impact on the renewal prospects for reform. There were a number of advances that altered the social and political climate in which reform options were considered. These further cycles of mental health reform will be analyzed with the aid of our analytical framework.

1. The 19th century common belief was that the stimulation
   and excitations of economic and social life brought
   about mental breakdowns; thus, by removing persons from
   these over-stimulating environments, one could reduce
   the course of suffering. And, in this controlled
   environment, social reformers believed it was possible
   to apply the moral treatment methods claimed to be so
   successful.

   Further, the theory of mental illness prevalant at the
   time held that the person could assist the recovery of
   their sanity and hence full control of their minds by
   the force of a normative climate in which the social
   expectations were clearly delineated and continually
   reenforced. For a review of the moral management theories and techniques of Pinel and Tuke, see K. Jones
   (1971), Caplan (1969, Dain (1964), Skultans (1975). For
   a critical evaluation of moral management, see Foucault
   (1965).

2. Rothman's study (1971) shows the asylum mode of treatment was merely one of many similar innovative institutional modes of education, treatment, management, and
   resocialization being adopted during the optimistic,
   Jacksonian-era social reformers. In this period
   American states embarked on their experiments in public
   schooling, poverty management, delinquency control,
   criminal rehabilitation, and the curing of insanity.
   The bold, new institutions and the experiments conducted
   therein were viewed with interest by Europeans, e.g.,
   tourist Alexis de Toqueville arrived in May, 1831, along
   with Gustave de Beaumont, to study the revolutionary
   U.S. penal system.

3. Horace Mann and fellow New England social reformers
   demonstrate that individuals can and do occupy multiple
   roles, as governmental officials or legislators and also

as representatives of special interests. In the case of Mann, et al., their official actions in promoting mental hospital construction sparked interest in reform and launched the career of one of the most successful 19th century social reformers-lobbyists, Dorothea Lynn Dix.

As educator, legislator, lawyer and mental health reformer, Horace Mann was only one of the many prominent Massachusetts citizens who contributed to the cultural richness and political texture of American society. Other prominent citizens included Senator Daniel Webster; slavery abolitionist William Lloyd Garrison; philosophers Henry David Thoreau and Ralph Waldo Emerson; Presidents John Adams and John Quincy Adams; man of letters Henry Adams; and Dorothea Lynn Dix, mental health reformer, to name a few.

Dix's first calling to reform work led her at the age of fourteen to open a primary school. The school failed, due to the harsh regime she sought to impose on her young charges, but she was not discouraged and moved to Boston where she continued in her single-minded pursuit of educating the young. Up until the age of forty she pursued this career with her total energy, acquiring a reputation as a successful teacher. Her achievements brought her into contact with the humanitarian reformer William Ellery Channing. He asked her to assume tutorial responsibility for his children and the relationship which grew out of that association left a deep impression on Dix; her commitment to social reform was broadened after establishing a relationship with one of the foremost of the enlightened 19th century New England intellectuals.

Yet Dix's move from education to mental health reform was affected by the deterioration of her own health, not just by Channing's suggestion. It was only after her physical collapse in 1836 and subsequent recuperation that Miss Dix began her crusade for the pauper insane. Dix took an eighteen month trip to England to recuperate at the Tuke's Retreat and returned to America with a new career goal in mind. She was freed of financial worries due to a generous bequest, and so left teaching and began a new career.

4. Dix's conception of mental illnesses were not markedly at variance with her contemporaries in the medical profession, though her specific views are hard to glean from polemical statements to state legislatures. Dain (1964) does analyze her psychiatric views and reveals her opinion that insanity sprang from civilization; cure could be affected prior to formation of brain lesions; social and physical isolation was the most effective way to treat insanity; the foreign born were viewed as more difficult to cure; mechanical restraint should be reduced to a minimum; physical violence only increased the patient's suffering; and, the normal characteristics of the insane ought to be strengthened in the treatment programs so as to enhance recovery (Dain: 186-172). Dix was respected by her fellow reformers and by trained doctors like Pliny Earle and Samuel B. Woodward. The Association of Medical Superintendents of American Institutions commended her numerous times. And, Abraham Lincoln thought highly enough of her layman's medical knowledge, organizational abilities, and dedication to appoint her head of the U.S. Army Nursing Corps during the Civil War.

5. There were several reasons for disappointing results with moral treatment employed on a large scale. The first asylums, private and public, were small facilities, serving fewer than 100 patients (e.g., Massachusetts' McLean Asylum for the Insane averaged only 61 patients per year between 1818 and 1830). This mode of treatment had never been tested in large residential facilities. Compounding the unproved adaptability of moral management to large-scale treatment was the fact that moral treatment had been used on patients who were fairly homogeneous, socio-economically, ethnically, and religiously. The York Retreat was opened for Quakers only, and New World Retreats followed the similar restrictive admission policies, only admitting private, well-to-do patients. Further, the selectivity in admissions also applied to the symptomatology patients could exhibit and still be admitted for treatment. Chronically-disabled persons were not subjected to moral treatment on a large enough basis to demonstrate its

effectiveness.   Thus, when translated into the large-scale state asylum, moral management was found wanting.

Dain (1964) reports that a 1956 reanalysis of Pliny Earle's report, critical of the cure rates, concludes that Earle was overly pessimistic in his criticism of Woodward's claims.   J. Sanbourne Bockoven's analysis suggested to him that 40% of the patients admitted in any given year to Worcester Hospital were cured, ten times the number suggested by Earle (Dain: 20-21).

Earle's estimates may have been wrong, but the nature of the problem of overestimation was not; private, profit-making asylums clearly used inflated cure rates in competition for wealthy patients. The post-Civil War years experience in both private and public facilities were definitely showing that patients were not getting better quickly.   Increases in the numbers and rates of chronic patients in residence led to doubts about moral treatment's effectiveness.

6. Deutsch (1949) examines the administrative consolidation and rationalization process in several states. The North Carolina board was terminated, as was the board in Ohio in 1871, for revealing the plight of the pauper insane. This early example of the variability in states' willingness to reform welfare institutions demonstrates the origins of the difficulty of carrying out social welfare reform within a decentralized political system.

Deutsch points to New York State as best exemplifying the successful implementation of the separation of the treatment of the mentally ill as well as the administrative consolidation and rationalization of mental hospitals.   New York's initial attempt in 1865 was embodied in the Willard Act which required that all new cases be treated at the Utica Asylum and the chronics be housed at the Willard Asylum, thereby avoiding confinement in poorhouses and prisons.   By 1869 the Willard Asylum, the largest facility in the U.S., housing 1500 persons, was overcrowded. Officials were surprised when the numbers of chronic persons had increased such that

the New York State's institutional capacity was outstripped. The poorhouse horrors of overcrowding
capacity were now evidenced in an insane asylum.

There was opposition to separate treatment for the
insane. Dr. John B. Gray, superintendent of the Utica
State Asylum, held the view that a separate treatment
was inimical to the mentally ill. Gray believed mental
institutions would eventually be inhabited by chronic
incurables, resulting in reduced standards of care and
patient abuses (Deutsch, 1949: 236-239; 252ff.).

7. Tentative steps were being taken towards a centralized
   administration of mental health services as early as the
   1828 Madhouse Act, regulating both private and public
   facilities, in metropolitan London and the provinces.
   The number of inspectors of conditions in these facilities was expanded, so that there were up to fifteen
   inspectors at one time. Under this act, the inspection
   of private and subscription hospitals was removed from
   the Royal College of Physicians; all commissioners were
   now appointed by the Home office. This tentative link
   with the Home office was the first step towards inte-
   grating all mental treatment facilities into one comprehensive service. A further 1845 increase in the
   bureaucratic mode of managing mental institutions was
   due to the passage of the Lunatics Act of 1845 (Jones,
   1972: 145-147; cf. Watkin, 1975: 357-359).

8. In 1834, the Benthamites succeeded in obtaining policy
   hegemony by their capture of the Poor Law reforms. The
   post-Napoleonic War period witnessed the acceleration of
   urbanization and industrialization. The English political elites, temporarily freed from foreign concerns,
   turned their attention to the welfare administrative
   problems.

   Alarmed by growth of relief costs and dependent populations, Parliament ordered an investigation. The
   investigative committee was captured by Bentham's
   personal secretary, Edwin Chadwick, and by economist

Nassau Senior. Their recommendations were harsh: termination of outdoor relief; stigmatizing of the poor by means of confinement in workhouses; applying the standard of least eligibility centralization of the Poor Law administration; and, reducing the level of expenditures. This "reform" worked, at least temporarily. Poor relief expenditures fell from seven million pounds in 1832 to four million in 1837. That workhouses' harsh regimentation functioned as the deterrent that Senior and Chadwick, as good Benthamites, envisioned. Widows, children, aged poor, and unemployed workers would rather suffer almost any amount of privation rather than submit themselves to regulation by the Poor Law authorities (Briggs, 1961; Marshall, 1970; Rimlinger, 1971; Furniss and Tilton, 1977; cf. Piven and Cloward, 1971).

Exceptions from this reform were made for the sick. Under the Poor Laws, a sick person was not necessarily regarded as a pauper. Given the shortage of treatment facilities, Poor Law infirmaries ended up treating not only paupers, but also ordinary, self-supporting citizens who required medical attention. The receipt of such treatment by non-paupers did not necessarily result in their disenfranchisement, and hence, stigmatization (Marshall, 1970: 19-20).

Marshall goes on to argue that England has suffered in the 19th century more than other modern, industrial nations from the Benthamite reforms of poor relief programs:

> "Nowhere else could you find quite the same combination of harsh deterrent principles, centralized policy control, and administration by an isolated authority, detached from the normal organs of local government, specializing in the treatment of paupers, and nothing by paupers, and functioning in regions peculiar to itself." (Marshall:34)

Only with the 1945 triumph of the Labour Party were the last vestiges of Benthamite Poor Law administration abolished.

9. The 1834 reform of the Poor Laws did combine the parishes into larger units administered by Boards of Guardians. These Boards were charged with the care of the destitute ill. The voluntary hospitals, endowed by philanthropists and maintained by private subscriptions, treated all poor persons, irrespective of whether they were "deserving," according to the Poor Law eligibility rules. These hospitals achieved some prestige primarily because they became the designated teaching hospitals and centers for medical research. The Royal Colleges for the Medical Sciences and Practices (e.g., surgeons) certified these voluntary hospitals as suitable for teaching and research, and thereby further reenforced the two-tier nature of hospital care in England.

England did not establish a public health corps until after 1850; the health corps was the enforcer of health standards in sanitation, food production, and housing, and did not provide health care in remote and sparsely populated regions of the country (cf. Cartwright, 1977: 109-113).

10. The transformation was accompanied by what Polyani (1944) has called the "discovery of society." A new sense of an enlarged social community gave rise, says Polyani, to a sense of collective responsibility. This new social responsibility is seen in the first efforts to relieve the poor. As noted, the establishment of state churches in reformed England and Sweden and other emerging Northern European nation-states, and the disestablishment and dissolution of the monastic holdings, created a social vacuum, a vacuum filled by the state.

11. Swedish private practice has always played a secondary role in the delivery of health care of publicly-provided hospital-based physician services. Still, private practice has existed, and continues to meet needs not filled or inadequately filled by the public sector. County hospitals have not expanded fast enough to provide jobs for all doctors, so some have been forced to "choose" private practice. Anderson notes:

"Hospitals and public health posts were more
desirable because they provided a base income. Private practice must have been
economically hazardous, but even so, it
expanded along with the rest of the health
service." (Anderson, 1972: 43)

Economic risk-taking by entrepreneurial physicians was
rewarded because the hospital-based, "free-at-the-time
-of-access" service was not and still cannot meet all
medical needs. With the expansion of the Swedish
industrial sector in the late 1800s and the concomitant
growth in affluence of an urban, middle class, a new
client group was created which was willing to pay for
the comfort and convenience of home treatment. The
trade unions also formed voluntary medical societies to
insure workers against the loss of pay due to illness
and the costs of out-patient care; standards were set
for the solvancy and administration of these insurance
groups, thus expanding the private sector client group.

Ironically, the development of county hospitals and
private insurance meant the model social democratic
nation did not pass legislation enacting universal
health insurance until 1947, and this legislation was
not fully implemented until 1955. The provision of care
for catastrophic illness by means of the hospital
service, coupled with the government regulated, private
insurance for private out-patient care, delayed the
adoption of a central government universal health
insurance (Anderson: 42-44).

CHAPTER V

THE ENVIRONMENT FOR REFORM:
THE RATIONALIZATION PROCESSES IN PSYCHIATRY,
REFORM MOVEMENTS, AND THE WELFARE STATE

The origins of the contemporary reforms of national mental health policy can be discovered not only in the seemingly remote events of the 18th and 19th centuries, but also in the more recent developments in psychiatric nosology, in the growth of the professional mental health organizations, in the development of fully organized mental health association, in the expansion of national health and welfare services, and in the prosecution of modern total warfare. As I suggested in Figure 2 in Chapter Two these factors shaped an environment favorable to policy reform in England, Sweden and the United States. This chapter presents these developments and demonstrates how they contributed to the policy breakthroughs achieved by mental health reformers in the 20th centiry in the United States, England, and Sweden.

Advances in Psychiatric Theory, Research and Practice

The late-19th and early-20th centuries were marked by significant advances in psychiatric theory, research and practice. The developments created an environment in which new proposals were formulated and put forth by reformers and their movements in the U.S., England, and Sweden. Specifically, the work of Emil Kraepelin, Sigmund Freud, Jean Martin Charcot, Hippolyte Bernheim, Pierre Janet, Eugen Bleuler, Adolf Meyer, Harry Stack Sullivan, Carl Jung, Melanie Klein, to name a few, brought psychiatry out of the asylum and placed it (and branches of psychology as well) in university departments and research institutes, thereby giving respectability to a profession that had heretofore largely been associated with the madhouse (Mechanic, 1978: 95-115; Mora, 1975; Redlich and Freedman, 1966).[1]

The theoretical and applied work of these founding figures of modern psychiatry and psychology did not result

126

in the consolidation of research and treatment under a dominant scientific paradigm. Because of the continuing competition among theoretical orientations and traditions, psychiatry remains at a preparadigm stage of development. The lack of a paradigm is symptomatic of a discipline in the process of adopting one or another dominant theoretical orientation under which normal scientific activity can take place (Mora, 1975; cf. Kuhn, 1962).

> "A great variety of contrasting trends and assumptions are at the base of psychiatry's theoretical and practical foundations. The current proliferation of psychiatric concepts and methods of treatment bears witness to this fact." (Mora, 1975: 1)

The mental health professions of England, Sweden and the U.S. were not all equally enthusiastic about all of these conceptual and therapeutic advances. Swedish psychiatry was much more receptive to the Germanic organic-orientation (Landfeldt, 1961; cf. Fischer-Hamberger, 1975). The United States and England partook of the psychodynamic as well as organic orientations (Mora, 1974; Lewis, 1961).

The Policy Implications of the Diffusion of Psychiatric Orientations

The policy impact of the psychoanalytic movement was quite limited even in the United States where psychoanalysis—in its various permutations—enjoyed the greatest popularity (though the emergence of psychoanalysis is significant as one of many indications of a more optimistic approach to the treatment of mental disorders). Thus, various neo-Freudian psychotherapies became more widely accepted and employed by psychiatrists, clinical psychologists and psychiatric social workers, and   Freud's work became symbolic of a conceptual breakthrough in the management of mental disorders (cf. Frank, 1963).[2]
The Kraepelin's taxonomy marked the beginning of the work attempt of psychiatrists to approximate the standards of other medical specialties. And, advances in physiological psychology provided a renewed sense of confidence in a profession that had experienced a period of disillusionment with mid-19th-century theories and research.

The policy-making relevance of the advances of psychiatric orientators is this: for mental health reformers and policy makers, the developments in psychiatric theory and practice were to provide a justification for new policies designed to have an impact on the persistent problem of mental disorders. Further, the emergence of psychiatry and psychology was tied to the formation and development of the associations and organizations in each nation that sought to further the cause of mental health reform and up-grade the standards of the mental health professions. These developments mark an end to the era of mental health reform that was dominated by the solo-charismatic reformer and a beginning of a period noted for formation of associations and government bureaus dedicated to the cause of improving the treatment of the mentally ill.

Given the national variation in these developments in psychiatric therapy and research, there were variations in the policy-relevant-intelligence uses to which these developments were put. By examining the developments in England, Sweden and the United States, the linkage between reform movements and psychiatric advances can be made clear.

The Formation of a Formal Reform Movement in the United States

The meeting of the National Committee for Mental Hygiene (NCMH) on February 19, 1909 marks the birth of the modern U.S. reform movement. Psychologist William James, psychiatrist Adolf Meyer, William Welch of Johns Hopkins University, the remarkable Clifford Beers, and others concerned about the plight of the mentally disordered, assembled to create a voluntary, lay and professional organization. Though there had been short-lived organizational predecessors to the NCMH, the cause of mentally ill was never effectively assumed by a national organization.

Associational antecedents of NCMH. In several states and cities anti-poverty societies concerned themselves with the mental ill in addition to their other concerns. In 1972, the New York State Charities Aid Association (SCAA), was both critical of the operation of New York's asylums and

creative in its role as one of the framers of New York's
1890 mental health legislation. The SCAA's founder Luisa
Lee Schuyler worked in conjunction with Dr. Stephen Smith to
realize their mutual reform goals: the centralization and
rationalization of state psychiatric service.   Smith also
participated in the short-lived, New York-based National
Association for the Protection of the Insane and Prevention
of Insanity (NAPIPI).   Founded in 1880, disbanded in 1886,
the National Association had a brief, yet influential exis-
tence (Deutsch, 1949: 310-314).   While it contributed to the
climate of reform in New York and furthered the SCAA's work,
the NAPIPI expired because of internal conflicts between
neurologists and psychiatrists and external antagonism from
the Association of Medical Superintendents of American
Institutions for the Insane (AMSAII) that resented hospital
investigative activities (cf. Mora, 1975).

   A charismatic leader founds a citizens reform movement.
The National Committee for Mental Hygiene differed from its
predecessors in a number of important respects.   First, the
NCMH was created by Beers out of a deep, personal commitment
to eradicating mental disorders.   He had been hospitalized
for the treatment of delusions and paranoia.   His direct
experiences of the brutal methods of control employed by
mental hospital staffs—beatings, solitary confinement, physical restraints—and his ultimate triumph over his symptoms, lent enormous credibility to his critique of current
treatment modalities, hie plea for enlightened, humane care
of the mentally ill, and his proposal for the formation of a
new mental health association.   Above all, his lucid autobiography, A Mind that Found Itself (1908) transcended the
exposes, historical novels, and popular fictionalized (and
often titillating) accounts of life in asylums and experiences of mental illnesses.   Because Beers had secured
professional endorsements, and had Harvard psychologist
William James write the introduction, his autobiography
possessed credibility and had an impact in academic, professional, and governmental circles (Deutsch, 1949:300-310; cf.
Clausen, 1961; Ridenour, 1963).   Second, Beers intended his
movement to attract the concerned citizen.   Because layman
Beers was the founder and director, he insured the mixture
of professionals and laypersons that became an integral
feature of the organization.   Third, Beers himself was

another chief reason for the success of the NCMH. As a charismatic figure, he attracted attention to the enhanced acceptance of the committee's message. Beers' physical energy and financial resources initially sustained the new society: up until 1912, Beers borrowed money to operate the society and served as its principal staff; in 1912 mental health philanthropist Henry Phipps began to underwrite the association. Finally, Beers was able to attract an important psychiatrist and former member of the Public Health Service, Dr. Thomas W. Salmon. Salmon served as the first medical director and was to play a crucial role in increasing the NCMH's impact.

In a move that enhanced the NCMH's influence, Beers and Salmon were able to develop a cooperative, working arrangement with the American Medico-Psychological Association (later the American Psychiatric Association). Rather than the adversary relationship between early reform associations and the professional hospital administrators, the NCMH sought to build alliances between different elements in the mental disease treatment community to further the cause of reform. Finally, the NCMH gathered intelligence for its reform activities when it worked cooperatively with the federal government by gathering data on mental hospital resident populations (Ridenour, 1963).

The intelligence form of associational reform movements. As the NCMH's director, Salmon conducted tours of jails, nursing homes, hospitals, state asylums, and other facilities to determine the conditions of psychiatric patients in these diverse institutions. Like Dorothea Dix or the Earl of Shaftesbury, Salmon began again the process of "re-discovering" the insane (cf. Matza, 1966). More importantly, the data gathered served the intelligence needs of the reform movement. These surveys became one of the main functions fulfilled by the Committee's Division of Hospital Services in the absence of a national mental hygiene data gathering agency. Salmon also performed a vital service in World War I. Unlike others, he identified the need for specialized services to cope with the psychiatric casualties of war. As a consultant and later chief psychiatrist to the American Expeditionary Force, he designed and implemented a rudimentary screening procedure for

130

inductees and treatment programs for psychiatric casualties. In a future war, the results of screening tests would serve as evidence that supported the reform movements' call for a national mental health reform effort (Deutsch, 1944a: 360-361; cf. Bond, 1950).

In sum, the creation of a professional staff at NCMH meant that charismatic reform advocate Beers was freed to perform the needed public relations and fund raising work necessary to sustain the fledgling movement. Further, Salmon's professional credentials and his previous association with the U.S. Public Health Service helped cement the cooperative alliances between the federal government and the NCMH that both furthered the committee's goals and enhanced its prestige.

The proliferation of associations and professionalization of reform. The late-19th and early-20th centuries witnessed the formation of a number of professional and voluntary associations. In the 19th century the National Association for the Protection of the Insane and the Prevention of Insanity (NAPIPI) was founded during the same decade as the National Conference of Social Work (1872), the American Public Health Association (1872), and the Charity Organization Society (1877 et seq.). The linkages between the personalities and themes of these movements are reflected in the fact that the NAPIPI was organized at an 1880 meeting at a special session on lunacy at a meeting of the Confer-ence of Charities and Correction held in Cleveland. Members of the Conference of Charities had been debating the merits and planning the formation of a specialized mental health association throughout the late 1870s, culminating in the 1880 success (Deutsch, 1944a: 338-339; cf. Trattner, 1979: 67ff).

In the 20th century, the interconnections of the voluntary reform associations were evident and continued to develop as social reform became professionalized. A measure of this professionalization of reform is the founding in 1918 of the nation's first graduate school of social work at Smith College. One of the specializations in this program focused on mental health. Another illustration of both the professionalization of reform and the interconnections of reform organizations is the fact that Julian Lathrop, a leading social worker, was a founding member of the NCMH. Also, the National Conference of Social Work held its 1919 convention on the topic of mental hygiene (Deutsch, 1949: 318-323; cf. Ridenour, 1963; Wilensky and Lebeaux, 1958).

Further, the linkages between the emerging child guidance movement and the NCMH reflect the perception of and convergence on the cause of mental disorders. Beginning in 1909 with Dr. William Healy's Chicago Juvenile Psychopathic Institute, and continuing with Healy's tenure as head of Boston's Judge Baker Foundation in 1917, the study and treatment of juvenile deliquents was begin. Among the youth treated mentally disturbed youth received special attention. The NCMH became involved in the child guidance movement in 1922 with the creation of its Division on Deliquency and its Prevention (Ridenour, 1963).

Beers and the NCMH staff also worked to inspire states and localities to establish mental hygiene committees modeled along the national committee's lines. Deutsch (1949: 328-331) estimates that there were over fifty state and local mental health associations, though some were convened only periodically to deal with a specific issue or problem. And in 1919 Beers formed the International Committee for Mental Hygiene (later the World Federation for Mental Health). In 1930, the First International Congress on Mental Hygiene was held; a second meeting was assembled in Paris in 1937. The convening of both congresses was one measure of the internationalization of the psychiatric profession and the reform movement. Besides illustrating the diffusion of mental health reform ideology, these meetings also testified to Beers' charisma.

The organizational density of reform movement in the U.S. Thus, the NCMH relationships with other reform associations in child guidance, international mental hygiene, social work, and psychiatry, created an increasingly denser network of organizations dedicated to monitoring governmental facilities, protecting patients' civil liberties, furthering psychiatric research, encouraging early-disease detection, increasing the public's awareness, and expanding federal and state mental health programs. Yet, the focused efforts of these associations was to have a significant impact on the policy deliberations at the federal level only after the Second World War placed members of the mental health reform movement in key positions in the federal health bureaucracy and after members of the U.S. Congress became convinced of the need to expand the national government's role in psychiatry.

The Development of English Reform Movements: The Impact of the Governmental Form

In England, the establishment and development of associations to aid the mentally ill and retarded was linked to the expansion of psychiatric services. The connection was much tighter because of England's more centralized polity (Yardley, 1974; 27ff). In such a political system, with its fusion of executive and legislative powers, the groups seeking to influence the outcome of the policy deliberations take on organizational characteristics that reflect the political system these associations are attempting to influence. In the case of mental health, the English reform societies developed into centralized, London-based associations focusing their attention on the legislative policy-making and governmental implementation.

Routinization of reform charisma. England's first mental health association was formed in 1842. The Society for Improving the Condition of the Insane had a direct connection with Parliament and its Metropolitan Lunacy Commission. Lord Ashley (later the 7th Earl of Shaftesbury) served as its first head and Dr. Daniel Hack Tuke, heir to the English moral treatment movement, was an ardent member. Dr. Tuke linked the society with the association of asylum administrators and the developing psychiatric profession. This first English mental health association did not survive, but Shaftesbury and his associates formed another organization in the late-19th century that did survive to the present day.[3]

The modern reform association dates from the founding in 1879 of the Mental After-Care Association (MACA). The organizers of the MACA were inspired by the articles of

Colney Hatch, Chaplin of the Middlesex Asylum, published in the Medico-Psychological Association's Journal of Mental Science. Among the organizers of MACA was Daniel Hack Tuke, the direct hier to 18th-century mental health reformer, William Tuke.

In the next year, the linkages were forged between the original Society for Improving the Condition of the Insane, the official administrative apparatus for monitoring asylums, and the Parliamentary leadership of the mental health reform movement. The seemingly omnipresent humanitarian, the 7th Earl of Shaftesbury, was elected to the MACA's presidency. Thus, this new association consisted of elements that pre-figured England's national mental health reform establishment.

The MACA provides a policy template. Despite its formidable leadership, the MACA did not press for new national policy initiatives. The activities of the society were limited to providing post-hospital care, reflecting the view of its members that no further reform legislation was required:

> "The propaganda of this small society was very
> gentle, and its work in community care pro-
> ceeded patiently and slowly in the early years
> of the twentieth century." (Rooff; 1967:95)

The tiny numbers of mentally ill provided care raised questions about how seriously one ought to consider this as a full-fledged reform society. In 1887, 41 people were cared for; that number rose to 670 in 1918. Given that there were approximately 50,000 residents in English county asylums in 1887 and 116,700 in such asylums and other mental illness treatment facilities in 1919, it would appear that the MACA was insignificant and ineffectual. Yet, in the small network of persons who administered Britain's health and mental health services, who passed legislation pertaining to those services, and who funded humanitarian reform projects, the MACA was not trivial. Like the small York Retreat of the previous century, the MACA served as a policy template for the London County Council in its attempts to develop services for the mentally disoriented. Further, by the year

1924, the association had nearly doubled the number of persons served to 1176. Though its activities were mainly confined to London, the MACA's work did provide the 1924-26 Royal Commission on Lunacy and Mental Disorder with a workable model of patient care that could be incorporated in a national mental health service.

The diffusion of the Beers' concept of a reform association. English mental health reformers did create an association that was to have lasting policy relevance. Modeled on the U.S. National Council for Mental Hygiene, the English National Committee for Mental Hygiene was formed in 1919; its primary goals was the prevention of mental diseases and the education of officials and the citizenry. The NCMH also served as a link between the English lay and professional psychiatric communities and those of other nations. Participating in the World Congresses, the English NCMH provided linkages between reform-minded networks, enabling them to share information thereby increasing the diffusion of innovations in patient treatment modalities and the like.

The English NCMH shared interests with another, more specialized and older association that was a part of the English reform network, the National Association for the Care of the Feeble Minded. Founded in 1896, the NACFM was reconstituted in 1913 as the Central Association for Mental Care (CAMC) reflecting the advances in the understanding of mental retardation. The primary function of the CAMC was to assist local authorities in complying with the terms of the 1913 Mental Deficiency Act; specifically, the CAMC was designated the agency to provide housing, day-care, and rehabilitative services under the terms of the legislation (Jones, 1972: 211-215).

The linkages between reform movements and governments. The CAMC illustrates the cooperation and integration of governmental and voluntary services. As implementation agent of national policy, the CAMC received direct operating subsidies from local authorities. This was because many authorities were reluctant to expand their staffs and were willing to support the community care work already being conducted by the CAMC under the terms of the 1913 legislation. This policy continues today. Presently, the English National Association for Mental Health receives operating subsidies from the Department of Health and Social Security; local chapters providing direct services receive such grants from local authorities.

Summary Observations on Mental Health Reform Movements

Though data on the history of early 20th-century mental health reform movements in Sweden is lacking, the information on English and U.S. movements in the late-19th and early 20th-centuries does suggest some generalizations. First, the formation of mental health reform movements in the late-19th and early-20th centuries eliminated the source of instability in the reform campaigns. That is, these associations provided continuity to reform work (e.g., the campaigns to improve conditions in mental hospitals). Prior to the formation of these associations, reform campaigns were usually the product of one individual or group of persons who may or may not have been successful in arousing the interest of the general population, let alone elected officials. With the advent of these associations, the instability and fragility of such solo reform efforts was reduced. As in other forms of authority, routinization in reform makes possible more predictable and sustainable social action.

Second, the first mental health reformers did not always have the advantages of alliances with professional associations and the branches of governments (administrative or legislative). With the formation of permanent associations, such linkages could be forged. These formal and informal connections increased the generation and flow of policy-relevant intelligence, made possible reciprocal relationships between persons sharing common goals, and forged alliances for concented reform work. Further, with the increase in the number of organizations having similar or overlapping concerns, a network of reform movements was formed in England and the U.S. Such a network was more difficult for elected officials to ignore.

Finally, the formation of permanent associations and their proliferations made possible the circulation of the key members of these organizations, thereby building linkages between elements of a growing network of mental health reformers. In order to make the assessment of the relative impact of these associations, it is necessary to further trace the development of the health and welfare services in which reformers operated in these three nations. As suggested above, linkages between the reform associations and governmental institutions would be crucial for the future successes of the reform campaigns.

The Welfare State: Organizational Environments for Mental Health Reform

The advances in psychiatric theory, research, and treatment methods and the development of the mental health reform movements occurred in differing national, organizational environments created by the welfare states of United States, England, and Sweden.

In the United States, localities have had continuing responsibility for the health care of the poor. This public provision of in-patient care had its roots in English Poor Law institutions. Yet, in contrast to Sweden, these U.S. tax-supported hospitals rarely occupied the central role as the primary site for the delivery of health care. In the post-Civil War era, the voluntary hospital benefited from public-spirited philanthrophy, with the result of reinforcing the secondary-role of public medical care.

Like their English voluntary hospital counterparts, the U.S. private hospital played a central role in the education, training and certification of medical personnel. The pure-type of this system can be seen in Johns Hopkins' 1893 endowment of a university and medical school. The Johns Hopkins University's Medical School served as the model of health care education and delivery and was replicated by other private hospitals and later by state university systems (Anderson, 1972: 39ff).

Thus, by the early-20th century, the private sector dominated the U.S. health care industry. In contrast, in England the public and private sectors were comparative equals, though the private sector was held in higher social esteem. In Sweden, the dominance of the county-based hospital service was in striking contrast to the under developed U.S. public sector.

The early-20th century mental health services of all three nations reveals greater convergence: all nations had adopted the model of the governmentally-funded and administered hospital-based mode of treatment, the scope of psychiatric private practice was greater in the U.S. than in England or Sweden. The 20th-century reforms in psychiatric care occurred within an organizational environ-ment created by the expansion of health and welfare services in each nation. The development of their organizational forms of health and welfare services will be traced to demonstrate how such services contribute to variation in the mental health policies.

The Expansion and Rationalization of U.S. Health Services

The underdevelopment of national health and welfare services was to be gradually reversed as the United States, like other modernizing societies, began to attack the health problems associated with urbanization and industrialization (Wilensky and Lekeaux, 1958).

In 1902 U.S. Congress passed legislation forming a new federal health service—the Public Health and Marine Hospital Service (PHMHS). As heir to the Marine Hospital Service, the new agency assumed administrative responsibility for the merchant marine hospitals as well as new public health functions taken on by the federal government. In 1912 the PHMHS charter was revised again. In this administrative rationalization of the marine hospitals were integrated into the federal bureau now called the Public Health Service (PHS). The PHS had as its goals and responsibilities the preservation of the nation's health, the imposition and regulation of interstate and international quarantines, the undertaking of basic health research, and related activities (cf. Straus, 1950). Until 1939, PHS was a branch of the U.S. Treasury Department; administrative reorganization resulted in its transferal to the Federal Security Agency; and, in 1953, the FSA was finally absorbed into the newly created omnibus, Department of Health Education and Welfare.

The PHS served as one model of how the federal government could expand its role in the health industry dominated by entrepreneurship. More importantly, the PHS served as a bureaucratic base for health reform, formulating and implementing federal governmental health and mental health policy. By training of health personnel, supporting basic and applied research, and providing direct services, the PHS thus was both an organizational template and an agent of socialization for a generation of reform-minded public servants, convinced of the capacity of the government to improve the U.S. population's somatic and psychic well-being.

Governmental form and structural interests block health reforms. Anderson (1972) and Marmor (1973) report that agitation in the U.S. for health insurance followed closely on England's 1911 legislation. The American Association for Labor Legislation (AALL) proposed coverage for both hospital and physician services, to be financed by employer, employee and state governmental contributions. Betwen 1915 and 1918, ten state legislatures charged commissions with the task of providing estimates of the need for, and the actual costs of, health insurance and in sixteen states health legislation was deemed necessary and bills introduced. In the social policy trend-setting states (e.g., New York and California), intensive lobbying campaigns were mounted by pro-health insurance proponents.

The failure of the pro-health insurance movement to secure passage in any of the sixteen states illustrates the difficulty in initiating national reforms in a federal system (cf. Wilensky, 1975). The American Medical Association (AMA) perceived such legislation as a threat to the fee-for-service, private practice enjoyed by the bulk of the nation's doctors. However, as a structural-interest group, the AMA was willing to negotiate, bargain, and thereby gain some control over the outcome of the reform process. The AMA simply did not block all reform initiatives. The AMA set up, at the behest of its more liberal members, a task force to study the insurance proposals in cooperation with the AALL. When the AMA could not co-opt the reform process, its cooperation turned to opposition. The AMA's reform-minded, academic doctors withdrew to their teaching and research interests and left the professional politics in the hand of the practitioners who opposed any governmental role in health care financing and administration (cf. Marmor, 1973).

Internal professional reforms. The medical profession was not only resisting public health reforms, it was also initiating internal professional reforms that would strengthen medical practitioners as a structural interest group. The adoption of the 1911 Flexner Report recommendations reduced the number of degree-granting medical schools from 135 to 66 because state legislatures approved AMA and American Medical Colleges doctor certification standards for physicians . These reforms increased both the standards for training and certification and the medical profession's social prestige and political power. Post-World War I health reform struggles saw a more powerful AMA, allied professional associations, and private health insurance companies able to resist a renewed campaign for comprehensive health insurance (cf. Larson, 1977).

The Committee on the Cost of Medical Care and the AMA. Failure of the campaigns for federal or state health insurance forced government insurance advocates to adopt an alternative strategy. A group called the Committee on the Cost of Medical Care (CCMC), formed in 1927 by public spirited, pro-health insurance advocates and supported by eight foundations, conducted a five-year study into the economics of health care and illness prevention. In four years CCMC published twenty-seven reports. Its final report recommended: (1) better organization of health care, especially by means of group practice; (2) improved public health services; (3) group payment of costs, as a non-profit insurance or taxation, (4) coordination of services; and (5) improved medical education, with an emphasis on preventive medicine (Falk, 1977: 165-167; cf. Anderson, 1972; 66-73).

As with the AALL proposals, the AMA attacked the CCMC's recommendations as a threat to the solo practice, and to the fee-for-service payment system. While views differed within the AMA, the majority of the AMA membership, as well as the American Hospital Association membership, felt that governmentally-sponsored group payment of costs and coordination of health services was an anathema.

The Social Security Act: reform via incrementalism. President Roosevelt's Committee on Economic Security considered not only social insurance proposals to attack the economic crisis of the 1930s, but also entertained the concept of national health insurance. The Committee, however gave low priority to health insurance since other Depression-era needs seemed much more pressing and funds were limited. Further, AMA lobbying ultimately succeeded in the striking of a national insurance proposal from the Social Security Bill (Anderson, 1972: 69). Still, the CES policy proposals and the Social Security Act of 1935 created another important policy precedent that expanded the opportunities for health reforms. One of the Social Security Act's creators, I.S. Falk says:

> "Nevertheless, we did achieve in the Social Security Act of August, 1935, federal grants-in-aid to the states for maternal and child health and for crippled children's health services (Title V), and the first permanent authorization to the Public Health Week and the authorization of funds for OHS investigation of disease and problems of sanitation." (Falk, 1977: 168)

As with mental health, the U.S. somatic health policy adoption process was an incremental one. Only gradual and minimal advances were made by the public health insurance advocates.

Incremental mental health reforms. The piecemeal process of policy adoption is illustrated by national mental health policy initiatives. The passage of the 1914 Harrison Narcotics Act stemmed from a public concern over drug abuse. By levying taxes on pharmacological substances considered socially undesireable, the U.S. Congress hoped to reduce the public's consumption of these drugs; therefore, the Treasury Department was charged with the implementation of the Act's provisions. The Treasury Department also housed the PHS. This organizational coincidence created conditions for the collaboration of the Treasury Narcotics Bureau and the PHS in the management of drug addiction.

In 1919, Congress increased the formal cooperation of PHS and the Narcotics Bureau by authorizing the construction of two federal hospitals intended to treat drug addicts, one in Lexington, Kentucky, and the second in Fort Worth, Texas. The Public Health Service was given administrative responsibility for these hospitals, and a Narcotics Division was created within the PHS to manage these facilities. The PHS already was experienced in hospital management; it had been operating the maritime hospitals, and so logically assumed responsibility for this new federal venture in the direct treatment of a newly identified population of dependent persons—drug abusers.

An administrative reorganization and concomitant redefinition of agency goals took place after the PHS took on this new policy mandate. The PHS staff realized that drug addiction could be a manifestation of character disorders. The name as well as the mission of the PHS Narcotics Division ought to be altered, reflecting the possible multiple causes of drug addiction. In 1930, PHS staff received authorization to change the Narcotics Division's name to the Division of Mental Hygiene. In this same year, the PHS Mental Hygiene Division also assumed responsibility for the somatic and psychiatric services provided by all federal prisons. Thus, by the 1930s, U.S. federal government provided mental and physical health services through the PHS and the Veterans Hospitals. In the process, a policy precedent had been established by the PHS management of federal hospitals, making it much less likely that a 20th-century President would veto legislation expanding the federal government's health services.

The embryonic bureaucratically-based mental health reform movement. The appointment of Dr. Lawrence Kolb, the first Chief Administrator of Lexington Hospital, as head of the PHS Mental Hygiene Division marked a move toward the creation of a separate national institute for mental health. This development created a potential base for the campaign to directly involve the U.S. federal government in the provision of mental health services. Kolb believed in the need for a federal agency designed explicitly to support psychiatric research and training as well as to provide care and treatment. The precedent for an institute was provided by Congressional action in 1937 creating a National Cancer Institute. With the support of the American Psychiatric Association, American Neurological Association, and the National Committee for Mental Hygiene, Kolb directed the drafting of a proposal for a mental health institute, but World War II intervened. The national emergency required the full attention of the mental health professions, and the creation of a national institute for mental health would await the Allied victory in 1945 (Deutsch, 1949: 512; Felix, 1967: 40-46).

Nevertheless, the foundations had been laid for a national mental health institute. A federal-level coalition was being formed that could build policy-creating alliances with Congress, and later the White House, in the design, passage, and implementation of a series of innovative mental health legislative mandates.

Thus, the U.S. mental health reform on the eve of World War II was poised for a campaign to convince the federal government of the need to significantly expand its role in the provision of psychiatric services. At a minimum, the supporters of the Kolb proposal were expecting that mental health would begin to receive federal money for etiological and epidemiological research and personnel training. However, the involvement of the federal government in the provision of direct services could be contemplated only if the legal precedents for such a role had been established. It was World War II, and the concomitant increase in federal activities directed at improving health, that created a policy environment in which the mental health reform movement could succeed in obtaining Congressional and Presidential approval for the national mental health institute proposal. Once the U.S. National Institute of Mental Health was created, a new, more effective branch of the mental health reform movement was in place to work for increases in the federal government's contribution to the war against mental disorders. The subsequent chapters will trace the creation of NIMH and suggest how it enhanced the capacity of the U.S. mental health reform movement to obtain its objectives.

The English Health and Welfare State in an Era of Liberal Reform

By the late-19th and early-20th centuries, the English health and welfare state was being critically evaluated. New students of poverty and disease examined the abject failure of the Benthamite Poor Law reforms. Sidney and Beatrice Webb and others, infused with Fabian Socialist doctrine and prepared to support their policy recommendations with thorough social and economic research, worked to create a new social order by means of incremental reforms. Just as the psychiatric profession was establishing a more sound technical and scientific basis for their practice, so the social sciences were emerging from history and law, and the findings of the new social science research were being applied in the policy arena. It is no accident that Parliamentary lobbyists, like the Webbs, helped found the London School of Economics to place the social sciences and its applications in public administration on a sound academic footing. As noted, reform and experimentation in the mental health field was moving out from the asylum. As in the U.S. late-19th century therapeutic-innovations and advancements in the scientific understanding of neurological and psychological processes were being considered and adopted in sites outside the once innovative asylums. Further treatment of the mentally disordered was increasingly being shaped by growing health and welfare services instituted by the dominant Liberal Party and perpetuated by both the Conservative and Labour governments. Thus, to understand mental health policy adoption, one needs to comprehend the linkages between the growing array of governmental services. Increasingly, policy reforms in one sector of the welfare state could not be undertaken without affecting another branch.[4]

The diffusion and adaptation of health and welfare reforms. The Boer War and the social scientific documentation
of poverty were not the only factors which shaped the climate of reform. The Liberal Party's Poor Law reform and
1911 health care legislation were also tools for the
ambitious David Lloyd George, Chancellor of the Exchequer,
to further his own political fortunes while checking the
growth of the Labour Party.

Ironically, Imperial Germany's conservative Chancellor
Otto von Bismarck provided Lloyd George and other liberal-
democratic statemen with a model of policy innovation
designed to "capture" the oppositions' proposals and fore-
stall the overthrow of Prussian monarchy (Brigg, 1961: 62
ff). Like Bismarck, Lloyd George was impressed by two
English political "facts." One fact was the growing threat
to the Liberal Party by the nascent Labour Party supported
by the trade union and cooperative movements. If Lloyd
George could provide a Liberal Party social policy alternative, he could thwart the electoral advances of Labour.
Second, Lloyd George was impressed with the very real policy
innovations which the German welfare legislation represented. The marked departure from the Poor Law approach to
poverty and ill-health provided a model which was copied by
England and most other industrial nations (cf. Hay, 1975).

The Liberal Party's legislative program reflected this
determination to hold onto office while also engaging in
much needed social reforms by adapting the German social
welfare legislation to England's needs. The Labour Exchange
Act (1908) and Old Age Pension Scheme (1908) were legislative triumphs which marked the beginning of the dismantling
of the Poor Laws and reflected the German programs. The
health insurance scheme passed in 1911 was, however, not
modeled on German policy. Rather, Lloyd George's health
bill reflected his conception of what was required to meet
medical costs and what could be passed by Parliament and
accepted by the medical profession and health insurance
schemes.

The 1911 health insurance act constituted the Liberal
alternative to the Fabian socialist proposals for the whole
scale abolition of the Poor Laws. Yet, a war-weary elec-

torate rejected the welfare policy innovating the Liberal Party in the grim post-World War I years; the Liberals were defeated in the General Election of 1919, marking the beginning of their march into political oblivion. Further, Lloyd George's health insurance scheme also did not weather the post-World War I crises well: the implementation of health insurance created new criticisms, new complaints discrediting the concept of public health insurance in England (Eckstein, 1958: 19-29; Marshall, 1970: 24-39).

Consolidation and integration of mental health services. The 1919 establishment of the Ministry of Health, placed mental health services in a new organizational structure, and brought the ultimate coordination and integration of psychiatry and somatic services closer to reality. Public health--originally a creature of the local Poor Law administrators--was now also placed in the new ministry that:

> "...took over all the functions of the local government board, including responsibility for many matters only directly connected with health policy, such as Poor Law, Housing and Local Government." (Jones, 1972: 232)

In 1920, the new Ministry of Health assumed the management of the Lunacy Boards of Control--the inspectorate whose functions remained unchanged since 1890. The inter-war years were marked by administrative innovations in the mental health services. That is, the consolidation of health care functions under the Ministry of Health initiated a process of integrating mental health into health services. Whereas the 19th-century reforms had tended, often unwittingly, to place mental care services on the periphery, the 20th-century administrative reforms began the slow process of building institutional linkages between psychiatric and somatic services.

The Royal Commission of 1924-26: new foci of reform. This shift in attitude towards mental health services was also reflected in the report of yet another Royal Commission called by Parliament to investigate the state of mental health services. Public concern had mounted again about the quality of patient care and the adequacy of legal safeguards in the wake of an official 1922 inquiry into one hospital's conditions. Besides a national survey of the existing laws and of the operation of mental hospitals, the commission was also concerned with the coercive effect of the distinction between persons designated as paupers and all other persons certified for treatment.

In its recommendations, the commission called for an end of pauper status designation; the Commission advocated changes to the 1890 act to facilitate voluntary admission of patients to treatment and suggested that local authorities expand the scope of their community treatment services. Though legislation based on the commission's landmark recommendations was delayed, the individual mental hospitals and local health authorities were utilizing their institutional discretion to develop and implement innovative treatment regimes, for example, introducing occupational therapy. The Mental After Care Association also was demonstrating the viability of alternative modes of post-hospitalization treatment, though its actions were confined to London.

The Royal Commission's recommendations were finally taken up by Parliament in 1929, with legislation finally being passed into law in 1930.

> "The Mental Treatment Act did four things; it reorganized the Board of Control; it made provisions for voluntary treatment; it gave an official blessing to the establishment of psychiatric out-patient clinics and observation wards; and, in line with the Local Government Act of 1929, it abolished outmoded terminology and brought the official expressions used in connection with mental illness more into line with the modern approach to the subject." (Jones, 1972: 249-250)

Thus, reform of mental health laws was linked with 1929 reform of local governmental services, prefiguring the 1970's reorganization of local governmental social services and local authorities that necessitated a restructuring of the National Health Service. Further, the 1929 reform of local governments was significant because the stigmatizing terms "pauper" and "Poor Laws" were abolished, though the dismantling of the last vestiges of the Poor Laws-mode of management were not removed until the 1944 Labour Party victory (cf. Marshall, 1970).

The impact of the new reforms. Though the world-wide economic depression placed constraints on the expansion of governmental services, the 1930 legislation did have the salutory effect of increasing the numbers of persons voluntarily admitted for treatment. In 1932 only 7 percent of all admissions were voluntary; by 1938 this number had risen to 35 percent (Board of Control, 1932, 1938). This change meant that more persons were now presenting themselves for non-coercive psychiatric treatment that employed the lastest theories for managing mental diseases.

In addition to this welcome shift, there were a number of innovations in the delivery of mental health services. The physical additions to Royal Bethlem hospital emphasized the new, decentralized concept of psychiatric care, a contrast to the massive institutional concept adopted by the Victorian asylum builders. The Runwell hospital that opened in 1937 was the only hospital constructed entirely on the decentralized, villa-model of hospital construction. In terms of the delivery of services, the organization of the City of Oxford's mental health and child guidance services was to serve as a model for mental health services for the rest of England. The integrative, holistic approach to the treatment of mental diseases emphasized by Oxford stressed early detection, preventative treatment outpatient clinics, and post-hospitalization rehabilitation.

In sum, in England, as in the U.S., the governmental provision of mental health services was poised for further reforms and modifications. The innovations in treatment techniques, the development of new administrative means of managing the mentally ill, the advances in the development of the profession of psychiatry, the involvement of voluntary organizations—these all created a new environment in which reformers could mount their campaigns. The form these reform initiatives took was not to be set by the English mental health reformers themselves. Unlike the network of mental health reformers in the U.S., the English counterparts were not poised to campaign for a separate national mental health institute, nor for a separate categorical grant program designed exclusively to modernize facilities and encourage treatment innovation. Rather, English mental health reforms were to a take second place to the goal of restructuring the whole health care industry.

The Organizational Context of Swedish Reform

In contrast to England and the U.S., Sweden's 1860s health reforms had been initiated by a central government's professional civil service, intent on devising rational solutions to the health care delivery problems. This early, bureaucratic dominance of health policy making was to characterize the expansion of health policies in the 20th century. Health was not the sole concern of politicians and the bureaucrats.

Sweden's rapid industrialization, beginning in the 1870s, was also marked by innovations in social welfare legislation. Following Germany's lead, Sweden instituted its first occupational health and safety law in 1889; in 1901 a workmen's compensation law was enacted that began coverage for industrial accidents; an eight hour day law was passed in 1918. Further advances in social welfare legislation was marked by the enactment of child welfare legislation in 1902, and state old age pensions were authorized under the 1913 legislation. These laws were modeled on the conservative German and liberal English innovations in social welfare legislation and did not mark a fundamental breakthrough for a socialist-inspired public policy. These laws were based upon the insurance principle and were often viewed as instruments for social control, not social change (cf. Janowitz, 1976). Not until the 1930s' electoral triumphs of the Social Democratic movement did the modern, Swedish welfare state begin to emerge and take on its now familiar characteristics (Sidel and Sidel, 1977: 110-128; cf. Heclo, 1974: 211ff).

In the health policy arena, the process of devolution of responsibilities, begun with the 1860s reforms, continued with transfer of full budgetary to the county councils:

"In 1901, the twenty-five county councils were given full budgetary authority over hospitals, while the powers of the National Board of Health were limited to examining and approving building plans and stipulation qualifications for hospital physicians." (Heidenheimer, et al., 1975: 19)

A subsequent chapter will discuss the national crises that brought the Social Democrats to power and will note the health and welfare policy advances made possible by Social Democratic rule, and place the advances in mental health care within the context of these welfare developments.

1. For a survey of Freud's theories and research see Hall (1954); for a personal and intellectual biography of Freud see Jones (1953); Freud's own lectures provide an excellent overview of the wide-ranging empirical data, conceptual apparatus, and therapeutic techniques of psychoanalysis (Freud, 1968, 1964); for an example of the expansion and extension of Freud's theories, see Erikson (1950).

2. G. Stanley Hall had invited Freud in 1909 to conduct a symposium on the occasion of Clark University's twentieth anniversary. Freud's lectures created considerable attention in academic and therapeutic circles. The Journal of Abnormal Psychology published the transcripts of the symposium on psychoanalysis late in 1909; serious criticisms of Frued's work were also voiced by psychiatrist Theodore H. Kellogg, who viewed psychoanalysis as only an interesting phase in the history of experimental psychiatry. While Kellogg's skepticism was well-founded --psychoanalysis has not been found to be useful in treating chronic psychoses--he was incorrect in assessing the future popularity of Freud's concepts.

Freud's works were translated by A.A. Brill and others. American psychiatrist William A. White, along with C. Stanley Hall, Smith Ely Jelliffe, and James J. Putman, founded the New York Psychoanalytic Society (forerunner to the American Psychoanalytic Society) in 1911; in 1913 White and Jelliffee founded a journal, Psychoanalytic Review, which served as a model for the continuing dissemination of the Freudian concepts and competing psychodynamic research finding, and therapeutic results.

3. Dr. Henry Maudsley carried on the tradition of John Conolly with his writings on moral insanity: Body and Mind (1873), Responsibility in Mental Disease (1874), and Pathology of Mind (1879); and he wrote extensively

on heredity, character, and social and psychological Darwinism. Late-19th century psychiatry was convinced of the organic basis of insanity, and hence Maudsley was concerned with the understanding of the inheritance of madness (Skultans, 1975:23ff). Maudsley's chief contribution to English psychiatry was not his theories of mental disorders. Rather, his endowment of a new mental hospital in London. After World War I "the Maudsley", as it came to be called, served as England's first teaching hospital in psychiatry and provided model acute-care and out-patient treatment services (cf. Wing, 1978).

> "The theme of heredity and organization is espoused by one physician after another. The writer whose influence was, and remains, the greatest is, no doubt, Henry Maudsley. Throughout his writing, the term "heredity neurosis" recurs. This interest expresses itself in many dire warnings such as: 'No one can escape the tyranny of his organization; no one can escape the destiny that is innate in him.'" (Skultans, 1975: 23)

Daniel Hack Tuke, the grandson of the founder of the York Retreat, was espousing similar, popular views of the connection between heredity and insanity in his Manual of Psychological Medicine that otherwise anticipated many modern ideas (Mora, 1975).

4. In their 1910 study The State and the Doctor, Sidney and Beatrice Webb predicted that any attempt to institute a state-operated health insurance program would be defeated in Parliament by the doctors and their private insurance allies. Chancellor of the Exchequer, Lloyd George, proved the Webbs wrong: Parliament did enact his health insurance legislation, albeit in a modified form. But if the Webbs were wrong in their specific prediction about the outcome of the health insurance enactment struggles, they were correct in their prediction of which groups would be opposed to the

implementation of a comprehensive, national health insurance scheme. That is, the Webbs were right in identifying the Friendly Societies as one source of opposition to a governmental scheme.

The Friendly Societies were organized by trade unions, private insurance pools, or by panels of doctors and were already providing limited insurance to their members. A comprehensive nationalized insurance threatened these associations with extinction, and they resisted any administrative attempts to eliminate their role. Lloyd George, if he wanted his health insurance scheme at all, thus had to strike a deal with these powerful interest groups. Eckstein (1958: 9-98) analyzed the nature of the bargain and concluded that the compromise had doomed the chances of success of the national scheme. Thus, because of the 1911 legislation one half of the British population was insured and one half had nothing; the salaried middle classes, the self-employed were ineligible for any coverage. For the poor, the local authority health services and hospitals were available, though these were far from adequate; the Poor Law odium prevailed and continued to stigmatize those who had to submit to relief health care. By the 1940s, England's mix of public and private health services were increasingly viewed as unworkable and seemingly unreformable. A radical policy departure was gradually seen as the only means of bringing order out of administrative and financial chaos:

> "By 1946 it must have seemed a hopeless administrative mess, which could not be made workable. Simply by bringing the middle class and the dependents of the working class within its scope. This explains the remarkable general wartime agreement that the insurance method was improper for any future medical system." (Eckstein, 1958: 26)

CHAPTER VI

MODERN WARFARE, NATIONAL CRISES,

AND MENTAL HEALTH REFORM

The consensus of analysts and participants alike is that the economic crises of the 1930s and World War II created conditions favorable for policy innovation. The mobilization for combatting crises and prosecuting of total, modern war necessitates taking an inventory of a nation's resources, both physical and human. Such an inventory-taking process can result in the identification of gaps, inefficiencies, and inadequacies. It may prompt national elites to take measures to remedy these problems. In the case of physical plant and equipment, England's war mobilization in 1939 illustrates the consequences of evaluating hospital resources, judging them inadequate, and developing a national medical service to effect a complete reorganization of the hospitals to cope with the casualties of total, modern warfare. In the case of human resources, the large numbers of rejections of draftees due to mental disorders shaped the awareness of administrators and politicians in the U.S. and contributed to the enactment of the nation's first mental health legislation. In contrast, the case of Sweden illustrates how economic crises can create new political conditions that are favorable for the forces posed for health and welfare reform initiatives.

The impact of modern war is not only confined to health care. There is considerable evidence to suggest that modern, total wars had important egaliterian effects. President Lincoln's Emancipation Proclamation—an edict distasteful to the Great Liberator in the Civil War's early years—was a device to more fully mobilize support for the war effort. The Beveridge Plan for a new, post-war Britian was designed in part to strengthen the compact between the dominant Tory war leadership and the Labour Party trade unions. In both cases, a better tomorrow was promised to millions who had been excluded from the benefits of full citizenship (cf. Marshall, 1964).

154

The effects of war for social welfare programs, of which mental health services are a part, has been testified to by many observers. Wilensky (1975: 70-85) cites persuasive evidence to support the hypothesis that the mobilization for the prosecution of modern, total warfare is favorable for the development of the welfare state. An examination of World Wars I and II reveals that they can result in the full employment of human and physical capacity productive resources.[1]

English Mobilization and its Health and Welfare Policy Consequences

England in World War II illustrates how policy makers responded when faced with annihilation. The English had planned for modern war; the Spanish Civil War had given English planners a grim picture of the military and civilian casualties that could be expected from wide-scale, systematic bombardment of cities. The prospects of physical destruction, human casualties, and psychological damage—all these moved England's planners to consider how they would respond. Naturally part of their plans included the allocation of health personnel and hospital resources.

In the face of modern war, policies that had been unacceptable were now adopted by the medical profession and hospital boards. On the eve of World War II the medical profession had decided to consider accepting salaried service. At the August, 1939 meeting, a resolution was passed calling for renumeration by salary and pension for a regionally organized, hospital-based medical service and for regional administration of such a service (Abel-Smith, 1964: 422). The hospitals—a mixture of voluntary (e.g., privately endowed and operated philanthropic institutions), county (i.e., old Poor Law facilities), and municipal hospitals—were in many cases understaffed, and were looking to the central government for some provisions of funds.

The lessons of World War I for mental health services. The mobilization of hospital beds and medical personnel in anticipation of World War II did not bode well for England's psychiatric services. Previous experience with modern war-

fare gave the English some sense of what they might expect
from the stressful, demanding process of mobilization. The
First World War had placed England's county asylums at the
disposal of the War Ministry. The Ministry directed a
massive discharge of mental patients to accommodate the huge
casualties from the Western Front. The figures of patients
in residence reflect this wartime mobilization of every
available hospital bed: in 1914 there were 138,000 persons
in residence in mental institutions giving England a rate of
3.77 per 1,000; the resident population had declined to
116,700 with a corresponding decrease in the rate to 3.09
per 1,000 in 1919 (Board of Control, various years). The
wartime confiscation of psychiatric hospital beds not only
reduced the resident populations, but also contributed to a
deterioration in the quality of care in these essentially
custodial institutions: overcrowding increased while the
number of staff and their quality decreased.

Expansion of rationalized health administration. World
War I did have one salutory effect: the mismanagement of
this national medical crisis identified the need for a new
central government department to coordinate health services.
In 1919 the Ministry of Health was established. Thus,
modern warfare had already given England's policy planners
and medical community a sense of what was to come in a
second international confrontation and an administrative
machinery to more effictively cope with the crises. An
early 1939 survey of hospitals illustrates the impact that
an expanded administrative apparatus can have on a nation's
health services. In the survey the Ministry of Health discovered only 80,000 hospital beds suitable for prolonged
treatment of casualties. The decision was made to organize
an Emergency Medical Service (EMS) that grouped hospitals on
a regional basis and graded facilities on their suitability
for the reception of casualties. London itself was divided
into ten sectors, each with a teaching hospital. Hospital
beds were to be made available to the EMS by discharging
100,000 patients on the war's outbreak, thereby implementing
the plan.

Inventory-taking and mobilization. On September 1,
1939, the British emergency plans went into effect. This
plan required the evacuation of patients from voluntary

hospitals to local authority facilities or to the patients' families and friends. The plan required that all doctors, from consultants on down, were given military rank equivalences and required to serve in any region or any facility --voluntary, municipal, or local authority. ("Full-time service" meant the elimination of private practice, thus eliminating the two-tier system of treatment which prevailed in World War I.) Finally, mobilization meant doctors were now salaried. A major shift in the relationship between doctors and the government had occurred.

By the autumn of 1940, Britain was experiencing its most severe aerial bombardments. Yet the worst fears--based on projections from air raids in the Spanish Civil War--never materialized. This is not to say London and other urban-industrial-transportation centers were not severely damaged nor that persons were not killed and wounded. The scars of the Battle of Britain are evident in London today. What the data reveal is a pattern not anticipated by the wartime planners. Abel-Smith (1964) reports that on any one day there were never more than 7,380 air raid victims "in-hospital." The London hospital regions had at least 9,000 beds available for immediate occupation, with 25,000 beds in reserve in neighboring counties; in the whole country there were never less than 70,000 to 80,000 beds available for war casualties. True, there were local shortages; many hospital surgical teams were overworked while others were underemployed.

> "And throughout there was always reason to fear that the worst was still to come--from gas attacks, secret weapons, and the very real possibility of invasion. But the price of this constant readiness for the unknown was paid by the ordinary civilian sick who found it hard to be admitted to any type of hospital--particularly a voluntary hospital." (Abel-Smith, 1964: 430)

Thus, the most disasterous scenario never materialized. The hospitals--public and private--were able to make available more than enough beds in even one of the most critical battles of World War II, the Battle of Britain. Yet, the

successful mobilization of hospital resources had unanticipated disasterous consequences for the chronically ill--the
poor, aged, and mentally disordered.

   The chronically-ill casualties of mobilization.   The
aged, mentally ill, and other chronically ill were displaced
by the EMS mobilization of hospital beds for acute civilian
and military casualties.   The government was subsidizing
bed-vacancies in anticipation of their need during post-air
raid panics.   By creating a financial incentive to participate in the EMS, the government was insuring cooperation of
diverse medical institutions, brought together under one
unified administration during a national crisis.

   Hospitals were paid to keep beds empty in anticipation
of casualties.   A reduction in number of beds available
meant a reduction in the subsidy.   Cash-starved hospitals
could not be blamed for taking guaranteed money in lieu of
uncertain fees from civilian patients.   Gradually, the
Ministry of Health realized the problem it had created and
made efforts to induce hospitals to readmit civilians,
particularly in voluntary hospitals, and to decrease the
number of beds available to treat war casualties.   But the
hospitals, especially London's teaching and voluntary
hospitals, resisted, reporting that a maximum of only 600
beds could be free for civilian use.   A year-long dispute
between the Health Minister and the notable hospitals ensued
that was resolved by a Ministry of Health survey of beds.
This report revealed that 90 percent of the London council
hospitals (i.e., local authority) were occupied, while less
than 50 percent of voluntary and teaching hospital beds were
filled.   After this report, further discussions and negotiations were held, and in March, 1942 the voluntary hospitals
finally agreed to accept the original proposed reduction of
casualty beds and to make its beds available again to the
chronically ill (Abel-Smith, 1964: 424-39; Titmuss, 1950:
450-93).

   The unanticipated consequences of hospital subsidies.
The hospital of bed subsidies, the modernization of operating theaters and wards, the expansion and improvement of
the pathological and blood transfusion services, the addition of newly trained nursing staff, and the development of

an orthopedic and rehabilitation service all raised the level of quality of health services in England. The health care services had been improved in the process, contributing to the survival of a nation faced with annihilation. At the same time, the role and scope of central government financial and administrative control had been greatly expanded because of governmental administration of medicine. Though the Emergency Medical Service had taken great care to not violate the independence of the private hospitals it administered, by 1944 it was nevertheless clear that a major reorganization of health care delivery systems would occur when the war ended. The EMS had gone part of the way towards refinancing and reorganizing hospital services, but many of its arrangements had an effect only because of the national emergency atmosphere. The ad-hoc cooperative agreements, the allocation beds and personnel, the infusion of new funds --all these would be lost unless a plan for post-war hospital care was drawn up and adopted. As military victory seemed certain, Churchill's coalition government prepared plans for a revitalized English health service for a reconstructed post-war England (Titmuss, 1962: 81-87).

The impact of war on psychiatric services. Plans were made not only for the physical, but also for the psychiatric casualties of war. The War Ministry contemplated the dramatic rise in cases of neurosis and psychosis and pointed to the need for the management of psychiatric casualties. The professional community was also concerned. A psychiatric committee's October 11, 1938 expert report recommended the establishment of immediate care centers, out-patient clinics, special hospitals, camps, and work centers in safe areas, mobile teams of psychiatrists, and mobile child guidance clinics. The plan was never adopted. Instead, the Coalition Government decided that panic and loss of morale resulting from air raids was a number one problem. The government did not adopt the psychiatrists' proposals, but instead decided to employ the army, police, and other uniformed personnel to reassure the public, stiffen morale, and quell panic. The army had refused to commit its limited manpower to control civilian population under enemy attack, so maintenance of public order remained the responsibility of nonmilitary personnel. Neither did the Ministry of Health adopt the psychiatric experts' recommendations.

Investment plans for new out-patient centers and special hospitals were dropped in September, 1939. These facilities along with beds in other specialized facilities, were converted for use in the national emergency. A physical upgrading of mental hospital facilities under the Emergency Medical Service did occur; however, these improvements were made to bring these facilities up to the national standards of hospitals designated to receive civilian and military casualties (Titmuss, 1950: 70f).

The main effect of the war on psychiatric care in Britain was to lower the quality of care for persons remaining in mental hospitals.

> "It was decided that mental hospitals and mental deficiency institutions would have to make a considerable contribution to the (Emergency Medical Service's) scheme. Many of the hospitals in the country areas were to rearrange the accommodation for their ordinary patients by crowding-up to make room for casualties in one wing or block which could be fitted to receive them. Certain hospitals were to be completely cleared of their patients. (Titmuss, 1950: 74f).

The implementation of this plan meant that 25,000 beds in England and Wales were given to EMS and the armed forces and additional numbers of beds were reserved for military psychiatric patients. Bomb damage and the evacuation of facilities in coastal cities further reduced the supply of beds for civilian psychiatric patients. Therefore, the overcrowding of mental hospitals is not surprising.

> "...overcrowding in mental hospitals, which amounted to 2.3 percent in 1938, rose to 14.4 percent in 1939, and the peak of 16 percent in 1940. In other words, the mental hospitals in England and Wales were compelled to squeeze 116 patients into the space occupied originally by a hundred. (Titmuss, 1950: 487)

In terms of absolute numbers, in 1938 there was a deficiency of 2,993 beds in mental hospitals; in 1940 this had increased 505 percent to 18,117 (Titmuss, 1950: 297f).

The "rediscovery" of the neglected insane.   The 1945 inspections by the Boards of Control for English mental hospitals verified that a disaster had struck mental hospitals.   Poor ventilation, power-outages, poor nutrition, overcrowding, and inadequate medical care contributed to a higher death rate for mental patients, particularly from tuberculosis.   Patients also suffered uncalculable psychic damage because of the sheer physical crowding and decline in the quality of even minimal levels of custodial care. Though admissions to institutions declined during the war and discharges increased, the seemingly positive statistical trends reflected the implementation of the EMS beds policy. Every local health authority reported to the Board of Control the fact of long waiting-lists of patients in urgent need of institutional care (Titmuss, 1950: 497-498).   One possible benefit of war can be noted.   For some patients, release from mental hospital to make way for the war wounded was obviously beneficial.   Though the re-socialization of former mental patients could not be systematically undertaken during this national emergency, the ad hoc readjustment of many ex-mental patients to life outside the asylum meant that there were fewer persons unnecessarily in residence when hostilities ceased.

War created the demand for reforms.   Thus, one specific public branch of Britain's health services was clearly in need of reorganization and an increase in financial support. The pre-war, second-class status of psychiatric services-- especially for civilians--had meant that under the EMS mental patient treatment was reduced to even lower priority.   A post-war psychiatric service could only begin to treat the backlog of cases and admit new persons to treatment if the Ministry of Health insured that mental hospitals were going to receive their equitable share of health funds under some new form of national health service.   Reconstruction of mental health care was placed on the English national policy agenda along with the revamping of somatic hospital services.   In both cases, modern warfare had increased the degree of central governmental management of a welfare state services and had created expectations for greater govern-

161

mental direction and financial support in the future. A larger, not smaller, welfare state was thus seen as an inevitable product of the prosecution of modern, total warfare.

Warfare forges new reform movement associations. Prior to the war mental health reform associations had provided innovative services and filled gaps in the psychiatric services even as the hard-pressed public institutions failed to meet even the minimal levels of care for mental patients during the depression years. In anticipation of wartime psychiatric casualties, the voluntary associations banded together and agreed to form the Mental Health Emergency Committee (MHEC). MHEC consisted of the voluntary, reform-minded representatives of the Central Association for Central Welfare, Child Guidance Council, and the National Council for Mental Hygiene. The national emergency brought rival groups together in the common belief that their efforts were going to make a critical difference in both the management and care of military and civilian psychiatric casualties.

The MHEC assisted the EMS, providing services the government could not. Specifically, MHEC worked with the thirteen civilian defense regions. The evacuation of children from cities to rural "safe" areas was a major concern of MHEC personnel, and MHEC acted as a self-appointed monitor and critic of this massive relocation program. For example, MHEC noted the need to avoid stigmatizing children with the label "problem child". MHEC condemned the overcrowding of under-staffed evacuation centers. MHEC also noted the need for qualified psychiatric social workers. The identification of the underdevelopment of psychiatric social work was thus another "benefit" of war. The Ministry of Health was convinced to require the local authorities to appoint social workers, thereby marking the development of this profession.

Finally, wartime pressures resulted in the merger of the often competing English mental health associations. The formation of a broad-based, national mental health reform organization--able to better lobby for mental patient rights --was a direct product of the mobilization for war. The

Mental Health Emergency Committee served as the basis for the Provisional National Council for Mental Health, formed in late 1942. In the English tradition of central governmental patronage and guidance, the Ministry of Health had been heavily subsidizing these competing and overlapping organizations and had called for their amalgamation in the 1939 Feversham Committee Report. Wartime meant that the recommendations were postponed. Once victory in war was considered probable, these organizations turned to consider their obvious organizational problems. Merger was reconsidered, and a streamlined voluntary mental health association was created following a recognition of need for a united mental health reform movement. It was hoped that a new organization would be better able to lobby for improvements in psychiatric services treatment (Titmuss, 1950: 379-81; Jones, 1972: 270-72). An assessment of the effectiveness of the English National Association for Mental Health will be presented in subsequent chapters.

World War II's Impact on U.S. Health and Welfare Services

Though the U.S. was in a very different economic, social and geographic position when it was thrust into World War II, the national leadership had been planning for an eventual involvement in the world-wide struggle. These preparations included the development for methods to cope with the psychiatric as well as somatic casualties of war. The American mental health community and military and civilian leadership were aware of the new horrific potential of modern war machines. Given the terrible facts of modern war demonstrated by the Spanish Civil War, the U.S. leader contemplated how they would cope with the new reality of total warfare. In the process they would expand U.S. health and welfare services.

U.S. prepares psychological services for war. In preparation for a full U.S. combatant role, the psychiatry professionals were also contemplating the psychological consequences of total war. As early as the 1938 Munich crisis, far-sighted psychiatrists and mental hygienists had made several proposals for coping with the psychiatric consequences of war. One measure advocated was the psychiatric screening of all recruits, but this objective--along with recommendations for maintenance of civilian morale, treatment of military psychiatric casualties, and maintenance of minimum hospital standards--was only partially realized towards the war's end. In fact, on the war's eve the U.S. psychiatric leadership was timid; the civilian and military leaders were indifferent or ignorant; and the psychiatric professionals were few in number and ill-equipped in terms of knowledge of the etiology of mental illnesses and access to treatment and preventive techniques.

Civilian morale and mental health. In both the U.S. and England, there were widespread fears that civilian morale would collapse and that psychotic and neurotic ¡ episodes would increase under the tremendous demands and strains of total war. Ironically, the war planners failed to consider the beneficial psychological consequences of an end to unemployment and the real improvement in the standard of living experienced by the U.S. and British populations. Also, they overlooked the significance for mental health of participation in a common struggle against the personification of evil--Hitler and his minions. In this "just" war all persons could play a crucial role, however small, and thereby contribute to a final, total victory (cf. Durkheim, 1951).

Psychiatric screening of military personnel. If the British case illustrates the inventory-taking process as it pertains to hospital beds, the U.S. case illustrates this process as it applies to personnel. The British did not institute a psychiatric examination, but the U.S. did. There were pre-war calls for such pre-induction psychiatric examinations by the trustees of the William Alanson White Psychiatric Foundation in 1938, by Captain Dallas G. Sutton of the U.S. Medical Corps in a 1939 article in the foundation's journal, and by the Council of American Psychiatric Association in May, 1939. The William Alanson White Psychiatric Foundation published in October, 1940 an outline of a psychiatric screening test for draftees. However, the implementation of these proposals for screening awaited the U.S.'s involvement in the war: the psychiatric screening was viewed as a relatively low-proirity item by military leaders in the planning for possible U.S. troop deployment.

Once induction of draftees commenced, the very real shortage of psychiatrists and other mental health personnel became quickly evident. This lack of skilled personnel coupled with the extreme haste and confusion of the first months of the U.S. Selective Service's operation meant the assessment of psychiatric impairment of potential military personnel was extremely difficult. The hastily-assembled war-management machine was also unable to cope with what well-qualified psychiatric advice it did receive. For a brief period, Dr. Harry Stack Sullivan, head of the William Alanson White Foundation, served as consultant to the Selective Service Administration, but Sullivan resigned after his proposals for accurate examination procedures were ignored or poorly implemented by unsophisticated and ignorant personnel. Military chiefs—and their civilian superiors—were unable to appreciate Sullivan's plans, and only the high rates of psychiatric casualties among military personnel convinced the war leadership that screening tests might be an economical way to reveal the unsuitability and vulnerability of potential inductees. Further, as the war intensified and an increased number of men passed through the induction centers, shortages of psychiatric personnel in the U.S. were revealed (Deutsch, 1944c). To remedy these personnel shortages and to continue to attempt to identify the psychically unfit, social workers were employed to conduct a medical survey which included health, work, social, and educational histories of draftees. By fiscal year 1945, $1 million of federal funds were being spent to subsidize the medical and psychiatric survey being conducted in 39 states. In the U.S. as in England, mobilization for modern war began to deeply engage the psychiatric profession in the prosecution of war. The wartime use of psychiatry thus began to create conditions favorable for a post-war expansion of the government's role in the provision of mental health services.

An assessment of psychiatric impairment: policy-relevant intelligence. The U.S. screening (however rudimentary) did reveal a surprising number of psychiatrically-unfit men. Twenty-two and seven-tenths percent, or 1,091,000 of the 4,800,000 men rejected were rejected because of neuro-psychiatric unfitness. Approximately 235,000 of the psychiatrically unfit were rejected because of neurological (i.e., organic) conditions. But 856,000, were disqualified because of functional psychosis, neurosis, schizophrenia, and other conditions. This evidence of psychiatric impairment was presented by General Lewis B. Hershey in August, 1945 at a Congressional hearing and shocked and dismayed national leaders. These results of the psychiatric screening were some of the first bits of evidence (i.e., policy-relevant intelligence) to suggest possible levels and degrees of psychiatric disability in the country. This evidence formed part of the testimony which helped convince Congress of the necessity of establishing a national mental health program. However, later professional evaluations of the Selective Service data called into question the generalizability of these data.[2]

Wartime advances in psychiatry. In both the U.S. and England, the treatment of military psychiatric casualties provided an opportunity for innovative psychiatrists and psychotherapists to attempt to implement new treatment techniques. The development of occupational therapeutic techniques and other rehabilitation methods aided the psychiatric community in their post-war management of the mental casualties of war. In the United States Dr. William Menninger and his associates contributed to the upgrading of the quality of psychiatric care and improved effectiveness of treatment programs. New methods of care reversed the policy of discharging chronic psychiatric casualties:

> "...patients were concentrated in 28 specially designated general hospitals for the treatment of psychotic and severe neurotic reactions; neurological centers were established in 18 general hospitals. Elaborate treatment procedures developed at convalescent hospitals resulted in the return of from 15 to 25 percent of psychiatric casualties." (Deutsch, 1949: 468)

In 1942, 80 percent of the Army's psychiatric patients were transferred to veterans or state hospitals; by 1945 Menninger's program resulted in a return of 75 percent directly to their homes. Treatment at the front also contributed greatly to the return rate of the war's psycho-neurotic casualties and provided evidence of the mutability of mental disorders.

The implications of the Army's psychiatric services for civilians and non-war conditions were clear to Dr. William Menninger:

"The net result and lesson from this experience was that intensive, effective treatment could be and was instituted for a larger number of psychiatric patients... It served to prove the theory that psychiatric patients, if treated early, have an infinitely better chance to recover." (Menninger, 1946: 576)

The evidence of the success of early and prompt treatment persuaded Congress to appropriate $10 million in matching funds under the 1946 National Mental Health Act for aid to community psychiatric services.

World War II also resulted in modifications of psychiatric nomenclature. Kramer (1968) says of the first post-World War II classification:

"This classification took into account much of the experience that had been gained in dealing with many psychiatric casualties that occurred during World War II. Indeed, the rubrics in this classification were quite similar to those in the nomenclature of the Armed Forces of the United States." (Kramer, 1968: xiv)

The modified diagnostic classification was to be of great value in the post-war years in the development of both an American and an international classification of mental disorders (cf. Diagnostic and Statistical Manual-II, 1968).

The National Mental Health Foundation and the rediscovery of the mentally ill. The war also provided some very real and intensive training for a group that had little or no experience in the field of psychiatry: the conscientious objectors. One primary place of employment for the cadre of World War II objectors was state and county mental hospitals and VA facilities. These highly principled men found that American society permitted its mentally disordered, handicapped, and aged to reside in filthy, overcrowded, understaffed custodial institutions that provided little hope for humane care, let alone therapeutic treatment. In short, the mentally ill were again "discovered," and society's neglect of this population of dependents was again made manifest (Ridenour, 1963).

In 1947, conscientious objectors organized themselves into the National Mental Health Foundation (NMHF) to expose the mental hospitals for what they were and to renew the call for reform. Ironically, the NMHF's activities were to offend the organizational heirs of Clifford Beers. The National Committee for Mental Hygiene had lost much of its reforming zeal. The NCMH had become mainly an educational society and a means for the social advancement for persons primarily concerned with the appearance of conducting "good works" by joining voluntary organizations (cf. Davis, 1938). Thus, as in England the war provided an opportunity for the reform movement itself to be revitalized. The NMHF, composed of newly radicalized mental health reformers, attempted to alter American society and to reactivate a mental health movement that had grown complacent.

Cooroborative evidence of patient abuse. The activists of the NMHF were not alone in their discovery of the maltreatment of the mentally ill. Albert Deutsch, in addition to being a chronicler of the treatment of the mentally ill in the U.S., was an ardent crusader for the rights of mental patients and an advocate of new, humane treatment programs. He had toured state, county, and veterans mental hospitals during the 1940's as a staff columnist and feature writer for the New York Star. He had already completed the first edition of Mentally Ill in America (1937), a book he was encouraged to write by Clifford Beers.

From 1944 through 1947, Deutsch continued visiting mental hospitals and writing about conditions he observed. His articles were collected and published in The Shame of the States (1948). His volume corroborated reports of overcrowded, understaffed mental institutions; of patient abuse and physical disease; of the iatrogenic character of psychiatric treatment itself. Thus, in England and the U.S., the war resulted in overcrowding, high disease rates, premature deaths, early discharges, poor treatment, or no treatment in mental institutions. Deutsch's expose, along with that of the NMHF, provided further evidence that war had a detrimental effect on the quality of care of chronically ill. More importantly, the renewed reforming activities were to have the unanticipated policy impact of strengthening the arguments of the proponents of an expanded federal role in the treatment of the mentally ill.

Deutsch's findings were significant not only because they were supportive evidence of the detrimental impact of war on mental hospital services, but also they assisted the efforts to attempt to reform the Veterans Administration (VA). Deutsch (1949) reports that he was nearly imprisoned for an early version of his book published in the New York Star; he was cited for contempt of Congress by the head of the House Veterans' Legislation Committee for failure to reveal the names of Veterans Administration physicians who provided Duetsch with evidence of patient abuse. Yet the 1948 reforms of the VA by President Truman and the reorganization of its medical program by General Omar Bradley was in part due to Deutsch's testimony, newspaper articles, and publication of Shame of the States.

The formation of a bureaucratic-base for mental health reform activities. In the U.S., the war involved some of the nation's most highly qualified, innovative psychiatrists, psychologists, and sociologists in the administration and evaluation of psychiatric services. The direct experience in managing the national wartime psychiatric campaigns—both military and civilian—was to serve these public-spirited reformers well as they sought to establish a new national, federally-funded institute committed to advancing research, improving the training of personnel, increasing the numbers of such personnel, and providing new, innovative service to the civilian population. Members of the bureaucratically-based reform group were to play a crucial role in the campaign to persuade Congress of the need for a greatly expanded federal mental health role (Felix, 1967).

169

Of course, the war-trained officials were not alone; support for their position came from the enlivened mental health associations and organizations of psychiatric professionals. The following analysis show that the formation of this policy-making alliance, facilitated by the war, would be crucial for the U.S. reform movement's successes and explain the lead the U.S. took in mental health reform in the post-war era.

National Crises and the Welfare State: The Case of Sweden

The development of an elaborate and lushly-funded welfare state in Sweden, in the absence of mobilization for and prosecution of total, modern war, suggests the lack of a necessary, casual relationship between war and welfare. The triumph of the Social Democratic movement in the 1930's marked the opening of an era of innovative social reform. A series of national crises and the Swedish Match Trust Scandal, the strikes in Ådalen, the Great Depression—brought the socialists to power.[3]

Wilensky (1975) reviewed these Swedish crises and concluded that:

> "On close inspection, Sweden may not be an exception to the hypotheses that war crises promote equality... These events [f. 1931-32] constituted a national crises which brought the Social Democrats and Farmers Party (now the Center Party) to power and cast the die for the accelerated development of the most celebrated welfare state of our time." (Wilensky: 73)

Sweden's deliberate pace of health care reform. The economic and political crisis conditions that led to the forty-four year political, administrative, and ideological hegemony of the Social Democrats, did not result in crash programs to assess national resources or in the full-scale mobilization of these resources to meet the crises. The best one-word characterization of the Social Democratic pace and method of social welfare reform is "deliberate."[4]

This deliberate pace was adopted by the Social Democrats in the reform of the health services. The availability of relatively free hospital care for catastrophic illness under the system of county hospitals delayed, in Anderson's (1972) opinion, the "consideration of universal health insurance for out-of-hospital services until the 1940s. Such an act was passed in 1947 and put into effect in 1955" (Anderson: 44). The first majority Socialist government in Britain enacted a national health program within one year of assuming office; in contrast, the triumphant Swedish socialists did not begin to consider national health insurance until the late 1930s.

> "As seems characteristic of the Swedish style, the deliberations were hardly pervaded by a sense of crises. This was to be no crash program but a sober examination of the problems and issues, although it seemed clear that some form of univer- sal and compulsory health insurance would even- tually be recommended. The primary issues were out-of-hospital physicians' services and drugs. It is conceivable that World War II slowed down deliberations on important public issues (the Committee did not report until 1944), but govern- ment commissions in general appear to proceed with a certain logical, deliberate, and inevitable pace." (Anderson: 74-75)

Mental health reform had an even lower priority. Sweden did not address the question of mental health care and laws governing commitment to mental institutions until 1966, twenty years after the English legislation merged mental hospitals with somatic hospitals into a comprehensive health service and seven years after the English substantially revised laws governing admission to psychiatric facilities.

In other words, the hypothesis that war and national crisis create conditions conducive to social reform is not clearly supported by the Swedish case. As a major noncom- batant, Sweden still was involved in the war, the economy benefitting from increased demand from both Axis and Allied nations. Yet, the assumption of power by the socialists coupled with the war did not hasten the introduction of health care programs. The war may have even slowed consideration of national health insurance.

The Context for Post-World War II Reforms

Early-20th century advances in psychiatry had presented reformers with a personal sense of optimism: mental disorders seemed more manageable with the placement of psychiatry theories and research on a firmer footing. Still, many of the etiological mysteries of mental disorders remained. Mental health reformers could only hope that new discoveries would reduce the need for lengthy and costly hospitalization for mental diseases. From the policy-creation perspective, the development of organizations dedicated to mental health reform enhanced the predictability and durability of the reform movements. True, the energy of reform associations declined in the 1930's and 40's as other social issues and national crises consumed the public's attention. Warfare, however, with its mobilization of human and physical resources, did give a boost to reformers and their movements.

The war established the precedent for governmental involvement in health welfare services. This precedent was particularly important in the U.S. where such involvement was previously deemed illegitimate. Since Franklin Pierce's veto of legislation that would have funded services and provided support for the mentally ill, the U.S. federal government had lagged behind other nations in the provision of welfare services. The Great Depression, followed by World War II, had changed this policy environment so that the federal government could contemplate initiating new domestic social policies. In mental health this new initiative led to the creating of a national institute.

The World War II experiences of the English are also illustrative of war's impact on the physical and institutional resources of a nation. The Emergency Medical Service's primary responsibility was to mobilize hospital resources and medical personnel. In the process, the inadequacies of England's psychiatric facilities were revealed. The war also fostered the cooperation and coordination of voluntary organizations in the work of evacuating and caring for city children. The overcrowding of those mental hospital facilities which continued to provide psychiatric care throughout the war created appalling conditions that cried out for reform. Finally, a comprehensive national health service emerged as a solution to these inadequacies in both psychiatric and somatic services.

In contrast to the U.S. and England, Sweden, not having directly experienced warfare, did not undergo the wrenching and disruptive experiences associated with modern war's prosecution. Given the domination of the reformist Social Democrats, Sweden could proceed in a calculating fashion to adopt and implement new policies. For example, Sweden was not driven by events to confront conditions in their psychiatric hospitals, the shortages of trained personnel, or the limitations of psychiatry's diagnostic and treatment techniques. Lacking such experiences, Sweden did not hasten in 1946 to enact legislation designed to involve the national government in a new, dramatic, and direct way in solving the mental health problems identified by war.

In subsequent chapters, the variations in the post-World War II adoption process will be examined with a view toward determining the relative importance of the war, the advances in the development of psychiatry, the increases in the organization of mental health reform groups for the outcome of the policy deliberations. The explanation will not exclude one or another of these elements, but rather will attempt to fit them into a coherent model that gives these factors meaning.

1. Taylor (1965) cites evidence that shows that democra-
   cies were organized and mobilized earlier and more
   thoroughly in World War II than the model totalitarian
   state, Nazi Germany.

   Supportive of Taylor is Albert Speer's (1970) unique
   insider's account of Germany's economic resources not
   fully being employed in the mortal combat because of the
   irrationalities inherent in the charismatic-authorita-
   rian rule of the mentally imbalanced Austrian. The case
   of Nazi Germany reveals the irrationalities of charismatic authoritarian leadership can mean that full
   mobilization cannot be effected. The German's considerable industrial resources were not fully mobilized until
   1944, giving further support to Weber's (1946: 245ff)
   insight into the instability, unpredictability, and
   inconsistency of charismatic domination, even when that
   domination is of a highly bureaucratized state.

2. In a 1953 survey of the extent of psychiatric impairment, then NIMH director, Dr. Robert H. Felix and his
   director of biometrics, Dr. Morton Kramer, were cautious
   in their analysis of the screening test results. They
   noted that the sample of men examined by Selective
   Service was not representative, due to deferments, age
   of inductees, voluntary enlistments, and the exclusion
   from the examination of men obviously physically unfit.
   "Thus, the prevalency rates from Selective Service
   examination cannot be applied with any conviction to the
   entire male population aged 18-44 years" (Felix and
   Kramer, 1953: 9). Yet, the 17.8 percent rejected due to
   psychiatric disorders is remarkably within the range of
   psychiatric impairment uncovered by Srole et al. (1962:
   197-9). The psychiatric ratings of persons comprising
   stratified random samples drawn in mid-town Manhattan
   suggests that at any one time from 23.4 percent of the
   population is impaired, of which 10.2 percent are rated
   as having "severe symptom formation" or "incapacitated."

Thus, though the Selective Service screening results must be treated with caution, they are not a completely inaccurate impression of the degree of psychiatric impairment.

3. Swedish national crisis did result from the bribery scandal involving the multi-national tycoon, Ivar Kreuger, head of the Swedish Match Trust, and the Prime Minister, Carl Gustaf Ekman, of the prohibitionist wing (Frishnade Folkpatiet) of the Liberal Party. The revelations of the bribery drove Kreuger to suicide and Ekman from office at a time when Sweden was in the midst of the world-wide Great Depression.

Ekman's resignation only heightened the financial panic and increased the potential revolutionary action by Swedish workers. In 1933 Sweden was still recovering from the shock of the killing by government troops of striking workers at the Ådalen sawmills, in May, 1931 and the subsequent establishment of a "Soviet Republic" at Ådalen. The Social Democrats had charged the Liberal minority government with responsibility for the workers' deaths and helped organize massive demonstrations and sympathy strikes in Stockholm and other cities (Ander, 1958: 165-70; Oakley, 1966: 242-43).

Does the Swedish case constitute an exception to the hypothesis (Wilensky, 1975) that war crises promote equality? My view is that the Swedish case does not demonstrate a clear, direct relationship between national crises and the push for equality. No less severe economic crises, strikes, and political turmoil failed to launch an era of socialist rule in Britain. Ramsey MacDonald's second minority Labour government collapsed under the strain of speculation on the pound, and MacDonald felt forced to abandon socialist principles to form a government of national unity with the Tories. This move split the Parliamentary Labour Party and alienated the Trade Union Congress and rank-and-file Labour supporters. In nations with less developed liberal-democratic institutions, the post-World War I economic crises brought in Fascist governments, e.g., Mussolini in Italy, Hitler in Germany.

4. This deliberateness characterized the Social Democrats' approach to the nationalization of key sectors of the economy. The Social Democrats did not adopt a program of nationalization of industry until 1949, when the 27-point program drawn up and adopted by LO (the national trade union congress). This program declared the Social Democrats' intention to nationalize natural resources, industrial firms, credit and banking institutions and the means of transportation and communication (Hancock, 1972: 208-14). Yet, the pragmatic Swedish Socialists abandoned the program when electoral reverses in 1948 coincided with an expanding post-World War II economy and offered excuses to shelve a scheme that threatened to mobilize the divided opposition to Social Democratic rule. The deliberateness and pragmatism, combined with economic good fortune, in part accounts for the hegemony of Sweden's Socialists (cf. Wilensky, 1975).

CHAPTER VII

POST-WORLD WAR II MENTAL HEALTH POLICY ADOPTION:

THE FIRST CYCLE OF REFORM

In 1945 the United States was uniquely positioned to adopt a national mental health policy. The underdevelopment of federal mental illness treatment programs made possible the adoption of a national policy marked a new era for mental health services. In the absence of a federal institutional arrangement for the management of the mentally ill, a policy adoption opportunity was available to the mental health reformers who could draw on the latest modes of treatment.

In contrast, in England and Sweden, national decision-makers were not confronted in 1945 with a concerted mental health reform movement seeking to exploit a policy-creation opportunity, but rather with social reformers with broader concerns. The plight of the mentally disordered, though not ignored, was only one of the many foci of these reformers. Particularly in England, where massive social and economic problems confronted the new Labour government, mental health reform had a low priority. Further, the English and Swedish policy makers were constrained by their past policy decisions. In the case of mental health, the legacies of past national policy making at the national level in Sweden and England created obstacles to the enactment and promulgation of new mandates. The U.S. was more receptive to innovations precisely because of the paucity of past national initiatives. U.S. change advocates were positioned to advocate policies that could not be contemplated by the English and Swedish reformers.

Assembling a Coalition for U.S. Mental Health Reform

The post-World War II U.S. mental health policy was made possible by the assembly of a sub-government for mental health innovations of the following elements: reform-minded, medical professionals with experience in public medicine; key Senators and Congressmen committed to the expansion of the federal government's role in health and mental health; an effective citizens lobby for mental health; professional associations, pro-mental health and voluntary health organizations; distinguished, university-based bio-medical and social scientists; and, ultimately U.S. Presidents receptive to the reform movement's objectives (Ripley and Franklin, 1980).

The policy precedent for the National Institute for Mental Health (NIMH) was offered by the National Cancer Institute founded in 1937. Prior to World War II, Dr. Lawrence Kolb, PHS Mental Hygiene Division director had called for a comparable mental health institute, but the war mobilization shelved his proposal. However, the NIMH concept was not forgotten. Dr. Robert Felix, who had served under Kolb at the PHS, received his Masters of Public Health degree at Johns Hopkins University. His thesis was a proposal for the organization of a future institute of mental health. In 1945 Felix was asked to activate his proposal by U.S. Surgeon General Thomas Parran. In preparing the plan for a mental health institute, Felix drew not only on his thesis, but also on his experience as assistant chief of the Public Health Services Hospital Division. He consulted with the U.S. Army's wartime Chief of Psychiatry, Dr. William Menninger who was then acting as a consultant to the PHS; Felix also received help from Dr. Francis Braceland, Dean of the Loyola School of Medicine, and Dr. Jack Ewalt, Professor of Psychiatry at the University of Texas.

Thus, the initial planning for a national mental health policy was conducted by the very individuals whose academic training and professional experience favorably predisposed them toward expanding the federal government's role in the treating of the mental disorders. Felix, Menninger, Ewalt, and Braceland were students of the latest bio-medical advances and social scientific understandings of psychiatric disorders. Further, they were convinced of the potentially positive role the national government could play in furthering both basic research, increasing the numbers of trained personnel, and fostering new modes of service delivery. They shared with their fellow professional colleagues the

178

experience of World War II, a war that had demonstrated that national resources--once given a direction--could accomplish great tasks. Given the evidence provided by Selective Service screening test results, the need to eradicate mental disorders was viewed as imperative.

The concept of a national mental health institute was the method adopted by the mental health reformers for involving the federal government in a war on mental illness. Under the U.S. Constitution, the scope for expanding the federal government's role was limited, so a policy innovation had to be carefully constructed. The National Cancer Institute provided the reform advocates with such a policy precedent as well. To succeed, though, the concept of a national institute required the support of the other elements of the mental health reform movement: key members of Congress, the mental health professions, the state mental hospital administrators and staffs, and other potential beneficiaries of this policy development.

Legislatively-based mental health reformers. The 1946 Mental Health Act creating the National Institute of Mental Health passed Congress because the bureaucratic-based reform advocates of the Public Health Service had identified members of Congress favorably disposed to a new national policy initiative. House Bill 2500 and Senate Bill 1160 were enacted into law by the 79th Congress because these bills had gathered an impressive array of sponsors: influential Southerners, Representative Claude Pepper of Florida and Senator Lister Hill of Alabama; impeccable Republicans, Senators Robert Taft of Ohio and George Aiken of Vermont; and, maverick progressive Senator Robert La Follette, Jr., of Wisconsin. Of these supporters of mental health, Senator Lister Hill was to become the mental health reform movement's most powerful and effective supporter. Hill was chairman of the Senate Committee on Labor and Public Welfare until 1968 and had jurisdiction over the future health related bills. Hill spent his career expending the federal role in health research, training, and service delivery (Miles, 1974: 170; Foley, 1975: 1-6).

The reform movement's counterpart in the House of Representatives was Rhode Island Congressman John Fogarty.

Fogarty lacked Hill's family background in health (Hill was the son of a surgeon and his five cousins and two brothers-in-law were doctors), but was considered to be a quick legislative study and soon became a key force in the legislative branch of the reform movements. As Chairman of the House of Representatives Appropriations Subcommittee handling health, education, and labor bills during much of the 1950's and 60's, Fogarty aided the advocates of mental health reform. Thus, the post-war Congress contained members who, by their membership in key committees, furthered the goals of the reformers. These legislators were not only strategically placed, but also inclined to advance the proposals presented by the health experts for enlarging the scope of federal health operations. One key force that shaped the legislative action of Hill, Fogarty, and others was the very bureau that the 1946 legislation created. NIMH, along with the associations for mental hygiene, the professional societies, and the university-based research community now formed a new, powerful mental health reform lobby.

The new bureau's reform mission. In NIMH's founding director Dr. Robert Felix's own words, the 1946 Mental Health Act had three goals:

"...fostering and aiding research relating to the causes, diagnosis, and treatment of neuro-psychiatric disorders; providing for training of personnel through the award of fellowships..., and aid to states, through grants and other assistance, in the formation and establishment of clinics and treatment centers, and the provision of pilot and demonstration programs in the prevention, diagnosis, and treatment of neuro-psychiatric disorders." (Felix, 1967: 47)

The act also established a National Advisory Mental Health Council to review training and research grant applications and to advise the Surgeon General on all mental health aspects of PHS's programs.

By enacting the 1946 legislation Congress began the process of qualitatively altering the structure of U.S. mental health services by mandating a new, activist role for the federal government. Hitherto, the state, county, and city mental hospitals and clinics, departments and bureaus of mental hygiene were not receiving federal support. After 1946, federal funds were available for innovative services, personnel training, and fundamental etiological and epidemiological research. If the states wished to be recipients or beneficiaries of these monies, officials had to comply with federal regulations and guidelines associated with these grants. In this way, Congress created the precedent for the use of federal funds to implement a national policy and to control state and local governments; the ultimate sanction now available to the federal government: the withdrawal of funds for noncompliance with federal guidelines.

A new solo charismatic reformer. At a time when the mental health reform movement was adding new elements, a brash newspaper man, Mike Gorman, came to Washington in the early 1950's and was to play an important role as a lobbyist for the reform movement. As noted, his newspaper articles and book on the neglect of the mentally ill had attracted nationwide attention. In the early 50's, he acted as chief writer and director of the public hearings for the President's Commission on Health Needs of the Nation. In 1953 he was appointed director of the National Committee Against Mental Illness serving as the Committee's one-man staff, lobbyist, and publicist.

Gorman was supported by two philanthropists. Just as Clifford Beers' National Committee for Mental Hygiene was supported by philanthropist Henry Phipps, Gorman's lobbying and education efforts were underwritten by Mary Lasker and Florence Mahoney. Their goal coincided with the expansion of the federal government's role in bio-medical research, the objectives of Felix, Gorman, Hill, Fogarty, and others (Miles, 1974: 174-75; Foley, 1975: 6-7).

The "establishment" reformers exposed. The U.S. National Association for Mental Health (NAMH) was created in 1950 by a merger of three organizations: The National Committee for Mental Hygiene, The National Mental Health Foundation, and The American Psychiatric Foundation.[1] Like their English counterparts, U.S. mental health association members felt their effectiveness would be enhanced by a merger of the often rival and duplicative organizations. However, Gorman (1956) considered the NAMH incapable of mounting an aggressive, reform campaign, specifically a campaign to expand the federal role in mental health (cf. Davis, 1938). In part, Gorman attributed his inability to the organizational weakness of the NAMH that resulted from the lack of formal linkages with state mental health societies. Gorman also attacked the NAMH its antagonism to a federal role in mental health services. Further, in Gorman's view the new National Association for Mental Health was dominated by non-reform-minded "careerists" of National Committee for Mental Hygiene, who failed to appreciate the need for federal funding of mental health research and services:

> "It is really most difficult to portray the negativism of the 'new' National Association for Mental Health. ...At the important Federal level, the Association has constantly refused to face up to its responsibilities." (Gorman: 306)

He blamed the NAMH for not providing all-out assistance in the NIMH appropriations lobbying; he bitterly condemned the NAHM for its 1955 failure to aid in the struggle for the research construction component of the NIMH appropriations bill: "the leaders of the NAMH sat knitting and tatting in their custodial hayloft at 1790 Broadway in New York City while a few of us burned up down in Washington" (Gorman: 293).

Gorman's view of the NAMH seemed to be confirmed by a NAMH policy statement that recalled Franklin Pierce's ideological opposition to federal mental health expenditures; in this document the NAMH executive opposed an expanded federal mental health role. Though the National Committee for Mental Hygiene had backed the 1946 legislation creating NIMH, an anti-federal government dominated the newly formed NAMH; it was not until 1955 that this leadership was over-thrown and a new leadership installed that was willing to assist Gorman, Lasker, and other lobbying allies of NIMH.

182

The Reform Movement at Work: Mapping the Budget

In order to gain an insight into the workings of the various elements of the mental health reform movement one can trace the process by which NIH and NIMH received approval for their budgetary requests.   NIH's goal was expansion of the "obviously inadequate federal medical research base of the early 1950's" (Foley, 1975: 7). Working with Senator Hill and Representative Fogarty, Shannon drew up NIH's appropriation requests, including expert-technical information justifying these increases.   At the next stage in the budgetary process the Congressional-based members gave the NIMH requests for their full support.   Thus, for example,

> "Fogarty castigated the White House, the Bureau of the Budget, and HEW for submitting a budget request for NIH lower than that which NIH had suggested. He elicited from NIH officials, Felix among them, the amount they had initially requested, and corresponding to the one he had before him.   He called for the 'experts.'"
> (Foley, 1975: 7)

Gorman assisted at this stage by providing the experts, such as Dr. Karl Menninger, whose testimony contained justifications for higher budgetary requests than NIMH's original estimates.   In both Houses of Congress this testimony was accompanied by informal contacts and communications all designed to raise NIMH's appropriation.   Shannon responded to Foley's characterization of the process as a conspiracy: "'There was no conspiracy and...generally the Secretary of HEW was as dissatisfied with the BOB [Bureau of the Budget] proposal as was the director of NIH'" (Shannon quoted in Foley, 1975:7; cf. Miles, 1974:173ff).

In this bugetary process, NIMH and other institute requests were forwarded to NIH director Shannon, then passed to the PHS's Surgeon General, and ultimately to the HEW Secretary.   At the Secretarial level requests were adjusted according to Bureau of the Budget (now Office of Management and Budget—OMB) requirements before sending a final bill to Congress.   Once in Congress, Fogarty's House Appropriations

Sub-Committee took control of the process, calling in institute directors and asking them how much their requests were cut. He then obtained expert opinion on what the institutes' budgets ought to look like from assembled health experts of the Citizens Budget Lobby, a branch of the mental health reform movement created by health philanthropist Mary Lasker to further the agenda of the health reformers.[2]

> "At the end of each budget review, Congressman Fogarty never tried to get the rest of his committee to go along with any such increases as the Citizens Budget called for, but was always able to persuade them to make significant increases above the President's budget. (Miles, 1974:176).

Lister Hill followed a similar procedure in the Senate. Together these two legislators helped produce the explosion in federal dollars for health and mental health. Specifically, NIMH was able to increase its budget in a dramatic fashion. Its appropriations rose from $870,000 in 1950 to $18,000,000 in 1956, and finally to $68,000,000 in 1960 (Felix, 1967:56).

Expanding the reform movement's base. Increasing budget allocations meant that NIMH expanded the base of organizational support for ever increasing budgetary allocations. Wildavsky's (1964) conception of the incremental growth in the federal budget does not fully capture the fact that increased expenditures, if carefully allocated, can bring new elements into a reform coalition; an enlarged coalition can apply lobbying pressure more effectively throughout the budgetary process to secure ever bigger allocations for the next fiscal year. NIMH and its reform movement allies provide an example of this strategy.

The 1946 NIMH Act enlarged the potential coalition to lobby for mental health appropriations: universities and research institutes that wished to be recipients of NIMH training and research grants now had an interest in an expanding NIMH budget and thus became a part of a national lobby which could be mobilized at appropriation time to secure further increases in NIMH's funding. Felix's genius as NIMH's director was in defining the scope of fundamental research and training grants in broad terms so as to satisfy all members of this coalition. This broad definition of NIMH's goals meant that universities, colleges, and research institutes were added to the ranks of the mental health lobby, thereby increasing the prestige, power, and credibility of Felix's budgeting requests. Not surprisingly, the NIMH budget grew in a dramatic fashion even before the 1963 Community Mental Health Centers Act was passed.

Reform Movement Turned Interest Groups?

Drew (1967) has used the term "health care syndicate" to label the group that is responsible for the astronomical rise in federal government expenditures. Foley (1975) places NIMH squarely within this noble group of conspirators seeking to increase the federal health budget. In some sense Senator Hill, Congressman Fogarty, Lobbyist Gorman, philanthropist Lasker, administrators Shannon and Felix can be considered a well-meaning special interest group. But these characterizations—syndicate, interest group—are less useful than tha notion of subgovernment developed by Ripley and Franklin (1980).

Subgovernment for mental health. The subgovernments in American politics are "small groups of political actors, both governmental and nongovernmental that specialize in specific issue areas" (Ripley and Franklin: 7). In the area of "distributive policy", where governmental spending promotes private activities that might not otherwise be undertaken (e.g., a private, non-profit mental health clinic in an innercity), subgovernments dominate the policy development and implementation processes. The mental health subgovernment actors were the subcommittees, executive breaus, and small interest groups, like the Hill-Fogarty-Gorman-Lasker-Shannon-Felix group. The relationships among these policy actors were relatively stable for a long period of time, and all the actors gained from the relationships. The visibility of their decision was low; that is, national media attention was more often than not focused on other matters than mental health. The President, his cabinet members, and Congress as a whole was usually not involved in the subgovernments deliberations, while the Congressional subcommittees, the health bureaus, and the elements of the associations, and professional organizations favoring mental health reform were highly involved in these policy deliberations.

The question is, in the cozy world of subgovernmental deliberations (some times called "logrolling"), did NIMH lose its reforming zeal once it had become a part of the federal health bureaucracy? Was NIMH transformed into an agency that came to have interests to defend in addition to reform movement goals to pursue? In other words, were the interests of a reform movement replaced by the interests of a member of the Washington, D.C.-based health subgovernment? In an examination of the reform process in health, Alford (1975) says:

> "Powerful interests benefit from the health care system precisely as it is—with its effective layers of bureaucratic 'planning' and 'administration' and its uncoordinated separate organizational and professional components responding to demands by the sick for care. These interests do not have to exert 'power' to influence particular 'decisions,' except to block proposals for change." (Alford: 6)

While such interest groups may resist proposals for change, the case of mental health subgovernment suggests that at least in the initial phase of establishing a health institute, an agency of the government—in conjunction with its reform and professional associations, Congressional, and other allies—can act to create programs to care for the mentally disordered. NIMH and its allies worked to secure increases in Congressional appropriations, appropriations which benefited the NIMH coalition while at the same time furthering much needed psychiatric research and training and providing funds for demonstration community mental health treatment centers.

The coalescence of reform ideologies. The reform commitment of the mental health subgovernment was enhanced by the convergence of reform ideologies of many of the participants in and out of government. NIMH's director Felix had sketched his views on alternatives to the mental hospital as early as 1942; Gorman's work convinced the muck-raking news reporter that the mental hospital must be replaced; health philanthropist Lasker was supportive of both views and brought Gorman and Felix together with the Congressional leaders who could affect policy changes.[3]

The Crises of Numbers: New Policy-Relevant Intelligence

The newly established NIMH, along with its reform movement allies, did not immediately alter the quality of care provided in the nation's asylums. The funding of fundamental research—bio-medical, psychological, psychiatric, and sociological—was initiated by NIMH and began to further the understanding of the causes, courses, outcomes, and possible treatments of mental diseases. NIMH training grants began to increase the number of psychiatrists and other qualified, therapeutic personnel and encouraged alternative treatment modalities within and without mental hospitals. However, the numbers of patients in overcrowded, understaffed state and county hospitals continued to rise.

The crises of the state mental hospitals. While NIMH began appropriating funds to foster new treatment programs in state and county mental hospitals, the rising numbers of patients in mental hospitals was creating a financial, managerial, and therapeutic crises. Beginning in 1948 NIMH granted each state at least $20,000 (a total of $1.6 million allocated that year); in 1950 this amount was increased to $3.6 million; but, by 1955 appropriations had dropped to $2.3 million. At the same time state mental hospitals were experiencing rising costs associated with the increasing resident populations. The number of annual residents in state and county facilities had risen to 558,922 by 1955, yielding a resident population rate per 100,000 of 344.4. The increase in resident populations ironically was largely a function of the successful public health applications of advances in medical sciences. That is, by developing adequate etiological theories and their concomitant effective therapeutic technologies, a whole host of infectious diseases were eradicated or controlled (Thomas, 1974: 35-42;

Thomas, 1977: 35-46; Knowles, 1977: 57-80). The growth of mental hospital populations is thus traceable to the increase in life expectancies associated with these medical advances. Confirmation of this is provided by Goldhamer and Marshall's (1953) pioneering study that demonstrated that the increase in asylum population to the increase in the percent of the aged in the population is not an absolute increase in the incidence of insanity in society. This relentless rise in mental hospital populations had been viewed as inevitable, something policy makers would always have to cope with. But by the 1950's the state governors, legislators, and hospital administrators began demanding that the federal government assist them with this growing burden.

A solo reformer mobilizes the discontented. As director of the National Committee Against Mental Illness, Mike Gorman had made a career out of advertising the inadequacies of mental health services. Coinciding with this crises of the mental hospital system he sought to mobilize demand at the state level for an expanded, national program to combat mental illness. His contacts with Minnesota's Luther Youngdahl led to the National Governor's Conference sponsoring a comprehensive study of their mental health programs. As a result, Gorman began to build an alliance with Michigan's G. Mennen Williams.

> "I asked the Governor [Williams] if he would be willing to sponsor a resolution at the 1951 National Governors' Conference calling for a specific study of ways in which the states could reverse the rising patient population trend through increased emphasis upon psychiatric research and the training of psychiatric personnel." (Gorman, 1956:167)

The personal lobbying conducted by Gorman with the backing of Williams' staff resulted in the passage of the resolution and a call for a further inquiry. The 1953 report, entitled Training and Research in State Mental Hospitals, was presented to the next Governors' Conference and helped advance Gorman's goals of a national conference devoted exclusively to mental health.

Further, Gorman's lobbying won support for his proposal for a special governors' conference on mental health. At this February 8, 1954 conference, mental health officials, ten state governors, psychiatrists, and other interested parties assembled, discussed the crisis, and issued a ten-point resolution. Following the conference Gorman went on to work among the regional conferences of governors to win acceptance for the implementation of the goals of the national conferences (Gorman, 1956: 175-187).

Enlarging the reform network. Gorman's reform activity enlightened the state officials and brought them in contact with the elements of the reform movement. Robert Felix, Karl Menninger, Kenneth Appel, Jack Ewalt, Henry Brill, and other professionals in psychiatry and public health met with the governors. Policy-relevant information was disseminated that otherwise would not have been directly available to state officials. The governors' mental health education forged new linkages in a growing nation-wide campaign to adopt a national mental health policy. The 1954 governors' resolutions echoed pleas for greater financial support made by NIMH; the governors supported similar demands of Mary Lasker's Citizens Budget for more money for basic health research, personnel training, and preventative treatment. Thus, in an orchestrated campaign, the state governors became another vital element to the post-war reform movement network, a subgovernment dedicated to expanding a sphere of public activity.

Joint Commission on Mental Health: a Formal Reform Network

The 1954 special national governors' conference on mental health call for a national study of the financial and social dimensions of mental illness was seconded by the American Psychiatric Association. The APA's Dr. Kenneth Appel urged the federal government to undertake a study comparable to the 1910 Carnegie Foundation funded Flexner Report on medical education. In 1955 Congress heeded this demand. In February Senators Lister Hill and John F. Kennedy were among the co-sponsors of Senate Resolution 26 urging a federal mental health study act. Felix, of course, participated in the testimonial and lobbying efforts; Dr.

Winfred Overholser, of the national mental hospital, St. Elizabeth's, spoke of the depressing increase in the number of hospital residents and the increasing risk of institutionalization; he argued passionately:

> "'It is not only a question of emptying the hospital or reducing the load, not only restoring the patient to his family, but making him again a productive unit in society.'" (Overholser quoted in Foley, 1975: 16)

Dr. Daniel Blaine, medical director of the American Psychiatric Association, introduced the Congress to the concept of the community mental health center. He cited efforts to establish such centers in England, Holland, and other nations and urged federal funding of such experimental programs. Support for alternatives to the state hospital were presented by the National Association for Mental Health, the American Nurses Association, and the American Psychological Association. The APA president, Dr. Filmore Sanford, secured Congressional support for the participation of behavioral and social scientists in the national policy study. After two months of such testimony all House bills were reduced to H.J. Res. 256. This bill was unanimously passed and sent to the Senate were it was passed without dissent on July 28, 1955 (Foley, 1975: 17ff).

The law required NIMH to establish the commission. Felix appointed the treasurer of the American Psychiatric Association, Jack Ewalt, as Commission head. Ewalt followed Felix's approach of consolidating support for mental health by broadening the Commission's institutional support through appointments to the Commission professional representatives from the AMA, APA, American Academy of Neurology, and governmental and voluntary organizations concerned with mental health. One organization was included that had no history of direct interest in mental health: the American Legion. Here Ewalt's intent in designating the American Legion was to bring a potential adversary and critic into the investigation, review, and reporting process, thereby forestalling criticism of the Commission's recommendations.

NIMH had no way of knowing in 1955 that the strategy of building a broad based mental health coalition would ultimately work; there were no guarantees that the American Legion or other members of the Commission might not resign over substantive or procedural differences, embarassing NIMH and undermining the credibility of the final report. As it turned out, Ewalt was successful in maintaining the confidence of the Commission's disparate membership. Cooptation worked as a tactic in policy-making.

Toward a new U.S. mental health policy mandate. The Joint Commission's final report represented the triumph of the efforts of the mental health reformers to broaden the base of support for a new U.S. mental health policy. Further, the supporters of the Joint Commission's report were to find that their lobbying efforts and coalition building were to pay off even more handsomely than they had hoped. When John F. Kennedy was elected U.S. President the reformers found they had one of their own--a Senatorial supporter of the Joint Commission, an ally of NIMH appropriations fights--occupying the highest office. Beginning in 1960 the reform movement mobilized for the translation of the lofty Commission recommendations into a legislative proposal.

Yet the description, analysis, and recommendations contained in the report, entitled Action for Mental Health, did not immediately become translated into executive or legislative action. Though the Commissioners recommended that community-based treatment programs should become an integral part of a national policy, the characteristics of this program were not specified. Their final report said:

"A national mental health program should recognize that major mental illness is the core problem and unfinished business of the mental health movement, and that the intensive treatment of patients with critical and prolonged mental breakdowns should have first call on fully trained members of the mental health professions." (Joint Commission, 1961:262)

In addition, the Commission called for the expansion of acute-treatment facilities, including community-based alternatives to hospitalization. The Commission did not envision a network of community care clinics, completely separated from existing hospital based care, constructed and staffed with NIMH monies. The recommendation of the report was to develop an integrated system fully utilizing the long-term facilities:

"Community mental health center clinics serving both children and adults, operated as out-patient departments of general or mental hospitals, as part of State or regional systems for mental patient care, or as independent agencies, should be regarded as a main line of defense in reducing the need of many persons with major mental illness for prolonged or repeated hospitalization. Therefore, a national mental health program should set as an objective one fully staffed, full-time mental health clinic available to each 55,000 of population. Greater efforts should be made to induce more psychiatrists in private practice to devote a substantial part of their working hours to community clinic services, both as consultants and therapists." (Joint Commission, 1961:262-263)

Thus, the Commission's intent was not to subvert or abandon the extant network of state and county mental hospitals, but to expand and prolong their usefulness by locating clinics in the institutional legacies of 19th-century mental health reform. This recommendation for community clinics was sufficiently ambiguous to enable later advocates of the community mental health centers to claim that the Joint Commission had explicitly called for separate, federally-funded outpatient treatment centers. This reinterpretation of the Joint Commission's report was to serve an important legitimation function in the lobbying for community mental health centers and in the attacks on the mental hospital.

Unanticipated development: a decline in residential population. As the Joint Commission began its work a reversal of a historical trend began in state and county mental hospitals. As Table I shows, up until 1956 U.S. state and county mental hospitals had increased their residential population. This development had created the pressure from state leaders for a solution to the financial crisis posed by an ever increasing resident population. Beginning in 1956 the U.S. and other nations experienced a decline in the numbers of mental hospital residents and in the rate of institutionalization. The U.S. resident population in state and county asylums reached its peak in 1955 when 558,000 persons were in residence in state and county hospitals; in 1956 this number dropped to 551,400; in 1960 the number had dropped to 535,500. Thus a historical trend had begun to reverse itself, without the intervention of the federal government[4] (Kramer, 1977: 78).

This reduction in resident patient population was due in part to administrative changes and in part to the introduction of psychoactive drugs coupled with the use of experimental treatment modalities developed in England, Holland, and other nations (Mechanic, 1969; Jones, 1973; Swazey, 1974). In fact, this trend, once established, gave impetus to the federal reform process because an initially more hopeful prospect for the treatment of mental disorders was offered by the use of these drugs in combination with new treatment modalities. Only later did the iatrogenic-impact of long-term use of psychotropic drugs become evident, but then the locus of treatment had been changed by policies in this optimistic period from 1956-1963 (See Table I).

The U.S. legislative process in the 1960's. From the mid-1940's on the mental health reform movement steadily increased its strength. With a firm bureaucratic base in the federal government, with allies on Capitol Hill, with a growing legion of supports in the academic and professional communities, and with a reactivated reform association, the stage was set for further policy advances. Thus, though NIMH and the other elements of the reform movement had interests to defend, they also were poised to realize their broad policy objectives.

English Post-War Mental Health Policy Making

The post-war policy environment in England was very different from that of post-war America. First, England was

TABLE 1

Number of resident patients, total admissions, net releases, and deaths, State and county mental hospitals, United States, 1950-1973.

YEAR	NUMBER OF HOSPITALS	RESIDENT PATIENTS AT END OF YEAR	ADMISSIONS	NET RELEASES	DEATHS
1950	322	512,501	152,286	99,659	41,280
1951	322	520,326	152,079	101,802	42,107
1952	329	531,981	162,908	107,647	44,303
1953	332	545,045	170,621	113,959	45,087
1954	352	553,979	171,682	118,775	42,652
1955	275	558,922	178,003	126,498	44,384
1956	278	551,390	185,597	145,313	48,236
1957	277	548,626	194,497	150,413	46,848
1958	278	545,182	209,823	161,884	51,383
1959	279	541,883	222,791	176,411	49,647
1960	280	535,540	234,791	192,818	49,748
1961	285	527,456	252,742	215,595	46,880
1962	285	515,640	269,854	230,158	49,563
1963	284	504,604	283,591	245,745	49,052
1964	289	490,449	299,561	268,616	44,824
1965	290	475,202	316,664	288,397	43,964
1966	298	452,089	328,564	310,370	42,753
1967	307	426,309	345,673	332,549	39,608
1968	312	399,152	367,461	354,996	39,677
1969	314	369,969	374,771	367,992	35,962
1970	315	337,619	384,511	386,937	30,804
1971	321	308,983	402,472	405,681	26,835
1972	327	274,837	390,455	405,348	23,282
1973	334	248,518	377,020	387,107	19,899
1974	323	215,573	374,554	389,179	16,597

Note: For all years net releases were obtained by summing the resident patients at beginning of year and admissions and subtracting from this deaths and resident patients at end of year.

Source: Appendix Table 5, p. 78. In Psychiatric Services and the Changing Institutional Scene, 1950-1985. Morton Kramer. NIMH Series B, No. 12. US HEW PHS, ADAMHA, Rockville, MD.: 1977.

economically exhausted by war. Second, while the U.S. was experiencing relative continuity from the Roosevelt to Truman administrations, England was embarking on a dramatic experiment with democratic socialism under a Labour Government. From the outset of peace, England's Labour government viewed themselves as "the masters now," with a mandate to reconstruct Britain along socialist lines (Howard, 1963).

One of the sectors of British society requiring such a reconstruction was the health care industry. An examination of the social conditions in which this commitment to a massive reorganization of health care is founded will reveal why mental health policy reform took second place in this fundamental reconstruction of an ailing industry. In contrast, no such federal government intervention was deemed desirable, economically necessary, or politically feasible in the United States. Hence the U.S. mental health reformers had a much greater scope for policy initiatives. By exploring the very different English socio-political environment, one can understand why this environment was less favorable for mental health reform.

David Lloyd George's health and welfare legislation did not survive with the twin disasters of the 20th century--the Great Depression and World War II. The war in fact was a catalytic force in the formulation of a new English social policy. At the war's height Winston Churchill's coalition government appointed William Beveridge to develop a national social security policy for a new post-war Britain. The government also commissioned a plan for a national health service (Marshall, 1970: 24ff; Furniss and Tilton, 1977: 104ff; cf Wilensky, 1975: 11).

The 1944 White Paper on health: centralized policy making. The coalition government's plan for health was based on its experience with the Emergency Medical Service (EMS) and the Beveridge report principles. The 1944 White Paper on health called for a comprehensive, government sponsored and funded service that could coordinate the health care provided by the hospitals, general practitioners, and local authorities. The basic principles outlined by Minister of Health Henry Willink were these:

Hospitals. The government was advised to form Joint Health Authorities for hospital administration and planning with the central government taking control of the municipal hospitals. However, all voluntary (i.e., private, philanthropic) hospitals were to remain independent if they so desired. Subsidies would be provided to the voluntary sector as inducement for them to join the public sector.

General practitioners. General practitioners who desired to do so would contract with a central medical board, whose tasks would be to insure equitable GP distribution and to set salary rates and reimbursement schedules for special services rendered. GPs were encouraged to form group practices or to participate in the health center concept.

Specialists. The proper distribution and remuneration for medical specialists attached to the prestigious teaching and voluntary hospitals was to be assured by the hospital authorities, though specific mechanisms were not spelled out in this potentially explosive issue.

Special health services. Planning for home nurses, midwives, clinics, blood transfusion, and other services was to be handled by the joint health authorities, with the administration left to local governments. Dental services required special development, both in financing training and in terms of planning services.

Finance. All services were to be "free" at the time of access. Voluntary doctor participation and patient use was stressed. General tax revenues coupled with local taxes and some payroll insurance deduction would pay for the service (Min. of Health, 1944; cf. Eckstein, 1958:133-140; Lindsey, 1962:23-46).

Like the Beveridge Report on social security, the 1944 Health White Paper on health was widely acclaimed. Parliament's debate heaped praise on Minister Willink and approved the principles he outlined. Yet, the British Medical Association (BMA) was alarmed and began acting as a threatened interest group by lobbying the Tory-dominated coalition cabinet to obtain concessions on a number of issues the BMA felt threatened the profession's independence. The Labour

Party, anticipating a post-war governmental role, announced that it would not be bound by any deals struck by the government and BMA. Thus, confrontation with the professions and other interest groups was set within an environment of popular endorsement of the White Paper's principles.

The 1944 White Paper's proposal for the mental hospitals. The coalition government's 1944 White Paper called for a comprehensive health service envisioned that private and public mental hospital services would be nationalized and integrated into a health service, though mental health service needs presented a problem:

"The inclusion of the mental services also presents some difficulty until a full restatement of the law of lunacy and mental deficiency can be undertaken. Yet, despite the difficulty, the mental health services should be included. The aid is to reduce the distinctions drawn between mental ill-health and physical ill-health and to accept the principle declared by the Royal Commission on Mental Disorder (1924-26)." (Min. of Health, 1944: 9)

The White Paper went on to call for the creation of health services by local governments as necessary additions to hospital and family doctor services. Mental health clinics were envisioned by the report as an essential element in such a network of out-patient, health care services (Min. of Health, 1944:40). Thus, even in the initial stages of national health policy development a new role for mental health care, integrated within a comprehensive service, was viewed as a positive necessary step.

A more advanced statement of future shape of mental health care was embodied in the Future Organization of the Psychiatric Services (June, 1944). This report stressed the need to place psychiatry on an equal basis with other medical specialities, reflecting deliberations between the Royal Medico-Psychological Association, the BMA's Psychological Medicine Section, and the Royal College of Physicians.

Differing the coalitions for health reform. In contrast to the United States, the English coalition for health re-

197

form had reached consensus on the broad outline of a nationalized health service, including psychiatric services, to be provided for by the health authorities of municipal and county governments. In the U.S. no such national connsus existed: the organized structural-interest groups (the American Medical Association, insurance companies, and their allies) had blocked President Harry S. Truman's proposals for national health insurance (cf. Marmor, 1973:7-28).

The post-World War II legislation which did meet with Congressional approval--the 1946 Hill-Burton Hospital Construction Act--was supported by the AMA for precisely the same reasons. That is, the foundations of entrepreneurial medicine were not challenged by the Hill-Burton Act, rather, the federal subsidies for hospital construction maintained and enhanced the special privileges enjoyed by doctors at hospitals. And, the 1946 legislation creating NIMH was not opposed because federal mental health programs were not perceived to be direct threats to vested interests and were popular with the newly emergent mental health professions.

In England the medical professions and hospitals had already experienced de facto nationalization as a result of the war-necessitated mobilization. Many health insurance schemes operating under the 1911 Act were financially exhausted, and popular opinion was mobilized in favor of a comprehensive, equitable solution to the health crisis. The question facing the health professional was not whether health would be nationalized, but what sort of nationalized solution would be finally passed by Parliament.[5] Further, the priorities of health reformers--William Beveridge, the association of socialist doctors in the British Medical Association, the Labour Party activists, the Fabian Society, the mental health and allied health voluntary organizations, and the like--all desired a comprehensive solution. A piecemeal, incremental strategy employed by U.S. health reform advocates was not acceptable.

Comprehensive health reforms. The thorough-going approach of English reform advocates was epitomized by the view of the new Labour government's Minister of Health, Aneurin Bevan:

"'...it (the N.H.S.) takes away a whole segment of private enterprise and transfers it to the field of public administration. A free health service is a triumphant example of the superiority of collective action and public initiative applied to a segment of society where commercial principles are seen at their worst.'" (Bevan quoted in Jenkins, 1963:244)

Mobilized against Bevan's approach were the interest groups that felt they had something to lose: the British Medical Association (BMA), the Royal Colleges for the several medical specialties, London's world-famous teaching hospitals, the insurance schemes (so-called Friendly Societies), the local health authorities, and the financially hard-pressed general practitioners.

Yet, when a settlement between the Labour government and the interest groups was struck after Parliament passed the 1946 Act creating a National Health Service (NHS), some interesting differences among the interest groups emerged. For example, the specialists practicing at the most prestigious London teaching hospitals were ultimately willing to join the NHS after the right contract terms had been presented, terms that preserved their descretion to accept private patients, that maintained income differentials, and that continued their control over their specialties. Bevan was willing to strike such a deal to save the general concept of the NHS.

Further, the case of the BMA-Bevan struggle over NHS also raises questions as to whether all participating groups shared the same structural interests and acted in a coherent fashion to block reform proposals (cf. Alford, 1975). The evidence provided by the numerous studies of the NHS creation process suggests that branches of the medical profession may favor a socialist solution to the health care crisis, and that most doctors, hospitals, and other interest groups can agree upon acceptable compromises that permit their participation in a nationalized health industry. The inevitability of structural-interest group blockage of any and all reform proposals is not confirmed by the English data (Willcocks, 1967).

Psychiatric services within the NHS 1948-1973. From the standpoint of mental hospitals, the compromise creating the NHS benefited the consulting psychiatrist and also put the mental hospital on a sounder financial basis as an integral part of a regional hospital service. Plans for an expanded, post-war psychiatric service had been proposed by a semi-official report jointly sponsored by the Maudsley Neuropsychiatric Institute and Hospital and the Ministry of Health (Blacker, 1946). It called for coordination between mental hospitals and general hospitals in the management of the mentally disordered. The study also recommended a doubling of outpatient psychiatric services; the construction of several small mental hospitals reflecting the latest therapeutic concepts; a set of minimum standards for ratios of psychiatric social workers in mental hospitals (there were only 27 for all 101 mental hospitals in 1946!); and suggested minimum standards of 100 beds per one million persons for all non-psychiatric hospitals and units. The 1946 NHS legislation, by beginning the integration of somatic and psychiatric services, reflected the Blacker recommendations and also those of the 1944 Ministry of Health White Paper. Further, the agenda of English mental health reform, though uncompleted, had been set in 1930 in the Mental Treatment Act: expansion of outpatient care; the innovation of post-hospitalization services, and voluntary admission to treatment. It remained for the NHS to attempt to realize these reform goals. This implementation was hampered by the legislation creating the NHS.

The 1946 Act created not one but several health services. This plurality of services was a product of the compromises necessary to insure doctor participation in a comprehensive health service. The NHS's three basic divisions--hospital, general practitioner (including dental, pharmaceutical and optical), and local authority public health--also reflected an acceptance of the extant divisions in health care as it had evolved under the Poor Laws and public health legislation.

Psychiatric hospital services: organizational discretion permits treatment innovation. All hospitals--teaching, voluntary, poor law, municipal and county, mental institutions, and clinics--were nationalized and placed under the control of the Ministry of Health. The actual administrative responsibility, under the NHS legislation covering 1946-74, resided with fourteen regional hospital boards; each administrative board acted for the ministry as planning, budgetary, and personnel management agencies. The day-to-day management of a hospital was actually conducted by management committees. For psychiatric facilities these management committees played a crucial role. They served as advocates for facilities within a health service that was biased by emphasis on acute somatic care facilities. The members of these committees were appointed by the minister and received no pay for their services. As a result, these committees could act as advocates and liaisons for the needs of mental hospitals that sometimes lacked the necessary attention that a London teaching hospital would more naturally enjoy. Further, the nationalization of the county asylum could begin the process of rehabilitating its institutional reputation now that it was no longer destined to serve as the home for the most chronic of insane persons.[6]

More importantly, the mental hospital potentially could serve as a site of treatment innovations within a health service that aimed at providing comprehensive, life-time health care for an entire nation. Innovators in psychiatric care could experiment at the level of the asylum with alternative modes of delivering psychiatric services. The formal, highly centralized organizational structure of the NHS did not block treatment innovation at the local levels. Reform in psychiatric care could take expression in an organizational structure that permitted a great deal of local and institutional autonomy and discretion in how a broad policy mandate was implemented. Thus, within the NHS a local hospital could design an imaginative solution to the problems of providing community care. Those solutions demonstrated what could be done, though they were not necessarily translated into a national pattern of organized care.

General practitioners and mental health. The 1946 legislation created a second element in the tripartite health service: the nationwide network of 138 councils to administer general practitioner, dental, optical, and pharmaceutical services. These councils were appointed by local governments and acted as record-keeping and salary-dispensing agencies for the NHS. From the standpoint of psychiatric services, the general practitioners were considered to be a key element in a network of patient treatment. GPs were to be the frontline in psychiatric care, identifying patients in need of intensive psychiatric treatment at a mental hospital or psychiatric department of a general hospital, and managing those patients with milder symptoms whose problems-in-living did not require the attention of the already overly-burdened psychiatric services. The GP service was conceived as the primary point of referral for the NHS mental health services. Yet, in implementing this plan, it became clear that there was variation among GPs in their capacity and willingness to perform the initial psychiatric assessment and provide an appropriate referral.[7]

Local authority services. Under the Poor Laws local authority health services provided public and environmental health services. After the 1828 Mental Health Act, the county health authorities were responsible for the construction and operation of public mental hospitals. Under the NHS, local health authorities delivered child welfare services, home health visitors, home nurses, ambulance services. And, a restructuring of services meant local authorities were to create the health centers envisioned by Bevan as comprehensive community-based health service delivery centers.

In the mental health area, the 1946 NHS Act removed the responsibility for psychiatric institutional services from the counties. Control of mental hospitals passed to NHS Regional Boards, while the Ministry of Health's Board of Control continued to have responsibility for the provisions detentions. The original NHS mandate stripped local authorities of their control of hospitals--the chief institutions providing psychiatric care. At the same time, NHS requested that local authorities provide alternatives to hospitalization in a mental institution and provide comprehensive posthospitalization care. Thus, the NHS created a delimma for local health officials. They were mandated to provide psychiatric services but lost control over the resources to provide such services. The chief issue facing post-war mental health reformers was how to create community services in the absence of resources for such services.

The Problems of Implementing Mental Health Reforms in the NHS

The NHS structure created new opportunities for treatment innovation within an organizational structure that appears to be highly centralized and directed by the Ministry of Health. The full, nationwide, implementation of the intent of the 1946 NHS Act and earlier psychiatric legislation was extremely difficult. There were many reasons for the implementation problems dedicated social reformers encountered.

Maintenance of descretion. An important feature of the NHS was the flexibility permitted local health administrators and hospital managers within a system that appears to be overly centralized. For example, up until 1959, local authorities were charged with the responsibility under the Act's section 28 for "prevention, care and after-care" of psychiatric patients, yet this was a "permissive" feature of the act. That is, local authorities may provide such care, but they were not required to do so. This discretion in implementation accounts, in part, for the variation on the experiments with coordinated psychiatric treatment, involving both hospitals and outpatient services. Some of these experiments were highly publicized and many were viewed as successful (Williams and Ozarin, 1968).

Organizational barriers. The corrollary to the flexibility and discretion permitted by the NHS's organization structure was a problem of developing linkages between the general practitioner, hospital, and local authority services. One health area illustrates this liaison problem.

"In Lancashire...there were within the Regional Hospital Board area seventeen county buroughs each operating its own mental health services, and seventeen divisions of the county councils. One local authority might have patients in eight or nine different hospitals. One hospital might have patients from thirteen or fourteen different local authority areas." (Jones, 1972:284)

203

Further, the hospital branch, containing Regional Hospital Boards and Boards of Governors of teaching hospitals, did not correspond to local authority boundaries. One hospital board could contain many local authorities. In London, the reverse was true, one local authority—the London County Council—contained four Regional Hospital Boards, 25 hospital Management Committees, and 26 independent Boards of Governors for teaching hospitals. For mental health local authority services these jurisdictional problems hampered the implementation of community care.

Antiquated admission laws. A third barrier to full implementation of the 1946 policy mandate was the outmoded admission and detention laws. Real advances in therapy and treatment were possible only in institutions where hospital administrators were capable of overcoming barriers presented by legal restrictions on voluntary treatment. English law had to catch up with the new orientations to psychiatric disorders so that greater flexibility in the use of facilities could be fostered and so that admission to treatment could be removed from the judicial system. Reforms had begun in the 1920's, but had not gone far enough.

Demands for changes were made in the 1924-26 Royal Commission Report. The 1930 Mental Treatment Act embodied many of the new psychiatric orientations. The 1930 law enhanced the possibility of voluntary admission; authorized local government to establish out-patient treatment; modernized psychiatric terminology, abolishing terms like pauper, asylum, and the like; and, transformed the hospital inspectorate, the Board of Control, into a full-time salaried body responsible to the Ministry of Health. Unfortunately, the 1946 NHS Act did not go far enough and eliminate the "pauper" lunatic image of public treatment, the isolation of mental hospitals from the main stream of health care, and the discretion by local authorities to provide out-patient care.

The crisis of numbers. Besides these organizational and legal difficulties, the NHS also faced the same crisis of numbers that motivated U.S. state governors to demand a greater federal role in managing the mentally disordered. In 1949 there were 144,700 patients in residence in English mental institutions; by 1954 this number had increased to 151,400 (Board of Control: 1949, 1955). The magnitude of the problem is further reflected in the fact that 42% of all hospital beds of the NHS were being taken up by mental patients. This historical trend was temporarily reversed only by the wartime need for hospital beds.

Thus, some of the same elements favoring reform in the U.S. were present in England. The crisis of numbers, combined with a realization that the past mental health legislation was increasingly a barrier to new treatment modalities, led to calls for reform.

The Royal Commission on Mental Illness

In 1954 Parliament debated a proposal to change mental health laws. In this debate, Kenneth Robinson (who was to serve as Minister of Health in the 1964-70 Labour government) and member of the National Association for Mental Health urged an improvement in mental hospital conditions, especially the relief of overcrowding. With Parliamentary leaders like Robinson, the English mental health reformers created a demand for a formal review of national mental health policy. Though the outmoded 1890 Lunacy Act spoke eloquently for its reform, the Parliamentary deliberations to draw up new legislation did not occur spontaneously. An organized reform movement within and without Parliament was required to bring about a national debate.

In practical terms, the task before Parliament and the Ministry of Health was the completion of the work of the Macmillan Commission, 1924-26. Given the institutional context of psychiatric services provided by the 1946 NHS Act, the long neglected reconstruction of the mental health code required both to bring English psychiatric law in line with the advances since 1890 and to complete the integration of the national somatic and psychiatric services as envisioned in the 1944 White Paper on the Nationalized Health Services. Parliament's Commission on Mental Illness was to be the instrument both for the completion of an unfinished policy agenda and for the realization of the goals of mental health reformers within and without Parliament.

The Percy Commission. Like the United States Congress, Parliament empowered an expert panel to assess the conditions in mental institutions and their staffs, consider the inadequacies in the legislation governing admission, detention, discharge, review detention laws, and consider the significance for public policy of the latest advances in psychotherapy. Lord Eustace Percy, who had served briefly on the Macmillan Commission of 1924-26, chaired the commission. Besides Lord Percy, a number of members of the mental health reform movement also served on the panel. Dr. T. P. Rees, who had developed the "open door" policy at Warlington Park Hospital prior to the introduction of psychoactive drugs, represented a therapeutic innovator able to directly translate his reform agenda goals into practical treatment programs within the NHS organizational constraints. Mrs. Elizabeth Braddock, MP, a tribune for the urban poor, provided understanding of the correlation between mental disorders and poverty. Lady Adrian represented the voluntary associations (e.g., the National Association for Mental Health) that had demonstrated the effectiveness of alternative modes of treatment as well as had lobbyied Parliament for reforms of the mental illness laws.

Thus, the mental health reform movement was able to participate directly in the process of adoption of a national mental health policy. Of course, there were other members of the commission who represented other perspectives on the legislation. Rather than being explicitly associated with the reformers, these persons could be classified as representatives of interest groups: the president of the Confederation of Health Service Employees; a consulting psychiatrist specializing in mental retardation; the neurologist Dr. Russell Brain; and two lawyers qualified to rewrite the complex 1890 law and its amendments.

The Percy Commission's final report. The commission recommendations were published in the 1957 final report reflecting a new approach to the treatment of mental diseases:

"It is not now generally considered to be in the best interests of patients who are fit to live in the general community that they should be in large or remote institutions." (Percy Report, 1957:46-48)

The report also argued for a division of functions between hospitals and the local authorities in which the local authorities should be responsible for preventative and all other forms of community-based care, e.g., day-care, residential treatment centers, job training, pre- and post-hospitalization care, and the like.

The deliberations of the Royal Commission on Mental Illness revealed that the 1890 law was a tangled web of laws and regulations that hampered the effective treatment of mental illnesses. Under the 1890 law the Board of Control scrutinized 4,000 documents per week in the admission, care, and discharge of patients (Watkin, 1975:385). Ultimately, recommendations for new laws governing detention were the chief product of the commission's final report.

"Though the discussions later recorded in the Minutes of Evidence were to range over a wide field, the Commission was...limited to legal and administrative issues, with a clear directive to the effect that they were to consider ways of reducing the existing formalities of admission and discharge, and ways of extending community care" (Jones, 1972:304)

Unlike their U.S. counterparts, English mental health reformers did not obtain a comprehensive reform proposal from their national commission on mental disorders. Given the historical concern of psychiatric reformers with the legal aspects of admission, detention, and release, the Percy Commission was unable to expand the scope of its concerns. The limits on the Percy Commission were re-enforced by the belief that the NHS creation had already "solved" some of the organizational concerns of the reformers (e.g., the isolation of mental hospitals from the mainstream of medical care). Thus, the Percy Commission recommendations were far more modest and technical than the proposals recommended by the U.S. Joint Committee.

There is another reason why the English reform proposals were less sweeping: the lack of a bureaucratic base for mental health reform. The U.S. mental health reformers possessed such a bureaucratic base in NIMH; English mental health reformers lacked such a base. The subsequent analysis will reveal how this difference between England and the U.S. accounts, in part, for differences in the outcome of reform activities.

Swedish Mental Health Services in the Post-War Reform Era

The post-World War II process of health welfare reform in Sweden was calculated and deliberate, in contrast to the often ad hoc policy-making process in the U.S. and England. The political stability and predictability provided by the hegemony of the Social Democratic Party, the administrative control of a tenured, apolitical, professional civil service, and the popular consensus of a small, homogeneous nation all contributed to a non-crisis atmosphere in which public policy alternatives were proposed, debated, agreed upon, and implemented (Anderson, 1972; cf. Wilensky, 1975)[8]. The reforms in the laws pertaining to admission, detention, and discharge of psychiatric patients and the reorganization of somatic and psychiatric services were not exceptions to this deliberate pact of the Swedish policy-making process.

Reform Agenda of the Social Democrats

The post-war world of Swedish psychiatry was confronted with the fact that the laws pertaining to the admission, detention, and discharge of psychiatric patients were woefully outdated. Like England's much criticized 1890 legislation, Sweden's 1929 Mental Health Act was increasingly perceived as a barrier to modern modes of psychiatric care and to the re-integration of ex-mental patients into society. And, as in England, the reform of the 1929 Act was not as high on the post-World War II agenda as other items (e.g., health insurance), and it was not until the 1960's that new legislation was enacted and implemented.[9]

The organizational context of reform. In the post-war reform era Sweden's centrally administered mental hospitals were under the governance of the National Board of Health and Welfare.   This central management of mental health coupled with the historic hospital bias of Swedish health services had meant that the post-war policy impulse was to construct more mental hospitals.   Every fifteen to twenty years, hospital inventories conducted by the Board of Medicine determined the need for more beds.   Given the Swedish incentive structure, such evidence calling for construction of yet another mental hospital resulted in that hospital's construction.   Unlike England, Sweden's robust post-World War II economy generated a taxable surplus that could be appropriated for mental hospital construction.   Sweden did not have to "make do" the way England's Health Ministry has had to do with outdated facilities.

The hospital construction response to the rising numbers of mentally ill persons was not automatically translated into a building program in the post-war years. Surprisingly, a national debate was sparked by a call of a 1950 Board of Medicine Commission report to expand the central government's network of traditional, remote psychiatric hospitals. This report did not conceive of therapeutic or rehabilitative functions newer types of facilities could perform, but rather viewed the hospital's function as a custodial one. Crafoord (1976) notes that

"...voices were raised in protest especially from the medical profession. The doctors pointed out that the system of mental care was in a state of catastrophe [and was] unworthy of a civilized society." (Crafoord, 1976: 2)

A debate ensued among the Board of Health and Welfare's mental health administrators, the psychiatric profession, and concerned citizens over the need to modernize detention laws that usually required compulsory admission procedures and presented restrictions on patients discharged from mental hospitals (cf. Leche, 1970).

This reassessment of the traditional concepts of psychiatric treatment was not directly translated into a new administrative approach to providing mental health services. It was not until the 1960's that new legislation was passed and implemented that altered the detention laws, provided an alternative method of hospital management, and encouraged new modes of treatment. In contrast to the U.S., Swedish mental health reformers, like their English counterparts, did not possess the organizational strength to begin the process of constructing a bureaucratic base for a mental health reform coalition.

In sum, though the concern about the outmodedness of psychiatric detention laws was mounting, an immediate post-war legislative effort to remedy the increasingly anachronistic detention legislation did not take place. Further, a reorganization of mental health services would also have to await reform until higher priority health agenda items received attention (e.g., national health insurance). Thus, in the absence of a national crisis atmosphere, and within the context of an incrementalist approach to initiating policy changes, the Swedish national mental health policy received attention at a later date than it did in either England or the United States.

New approaches to psychiatric treatment. Langfeldt (1961) notes that if the formal process of reform of detention laws and psychiatric services proceeded more slowly in Sweden than some other nations, advances were achieved in the training of psychiatrists. The program of post-World War II Rockefeller Foundation and Fulbright grants for overseas training in the United States resulted in the exposure of Scandinavian psychiatrists to psychodynamic modes of treatment and to non-organic etiological theories of mental disorders. As a result of this knowledge dissemination process, social and other environmental determinants of mental disorder that had previously received less attention in Sweden were included in research conducted in this period.

Psychotropic drugs and psychiatric care. In a country where the organic view of mental disorders remained predominant, despite exposure to alternative orientations, the introduction of psychotropic drugs resulted in their widespread adoption. As in the U.S. and England, Swedish hospital psychiatrists adopted drug therapy because they

210

were not adherents to Freudian and other psychodynamic theories and because they faced a crisis of numbers of patients. Thus, the adoption of psychotropic drugs was facilitated by Sweden's psychiatric profession's training and orientation to mental disorders.

As in England, Swedish psychiatrists interested in reform were experimenting with new modes of treatment that attempted to minimize the deleterious consequences of long-term confinement in a mental hospital. Though Swedish hospital resident bed data do not reflect as dramatic a decline as such data do for the U.S. and England, the Swedish hospital utilization data do reveal that a new pattern of treatment was being initiated and that preceded the detention law reforms and an administrative reorganization of mental health services. In 1950, prior to psychotropic drug revolution the psychiatric bed occupancy rate was 350 per 100,000 persons; this number had risen to 375 per 100,000 in 1960, and had declined to 344 per 100,000 in 1970, following the institution of administrative and legal reforms (Social-styrelsen, 1973). These crude bed-population ratios are not as revealing as the data which suggest that an increase in the utilization of psychiatric services accompanied the adoption of psychotropic drugs and new psychotherapeutic treatment techniques. In Chapter Eight I will explore in greater detail the pattern of utilization of these Swedish psychiatric services by analyzing their mental health service statistics.

Psychotropic Drugs and Public Policy

English and U.S. deliberations over a new national policy for mental health was initiated during the time of the revolution in psychopharmacology. The synthesis and testing of chlorpromazine and other psychotropic drugs had begun in the post-World War II period. By the mid-50's these drugs were having a seemingly dramatic effect on the treatment of mental illnesses. While NIMH's 'experts' were testifying for the necessity of clinical trials, drugs were being used in Europe, Australia, and the U.S. Coincidentally, within one month of the introduction by Senators Hill and Kennedy of their resolution calling for a national study

211

of mental illness and its cures, the U.S. Food and Drug Administration approved Smith, Kline, and French Laboratory's marketing application for the drug CPZ to be called Thorazine (cf. Cole and Gerard, 1959). At the same time that the Percy Commission and the Joint Commission were conducting deliberations, psychiatrists were conducting clinical trials with chlorpromazine (CPZ). Their tests were to have a dramatic impact on treatment of mental patients, facilitating the policy-shifts contemplated in the U.S., England, Sweden, and other nations.

The origins of chlorpromazine. Swazey (1974) traced the history of the development of chlorpromazine as a way of mapping the diffusion of innovation in psychopharmacology.[10] Though CPZ was only one of many psychopharmacological substances, it serves as an example of how a technological breakthrough can have an impact on the public policy sector.

By controlling or suppressing the symptomatology of psychological disorders, the family of psychoactive chemicals made possible the reduction in long-term hospitalization or confinement for many patients in a wide variety of facilities--psychiatric departments of general hospitals, special centers, and clinics. The impact of these drugs was in part dramatically reflected in the decrease in the numbers of inpatients in mental hospitals.[11] In England a similar decline occurred, with inpatients declining from their pre-CPZ high of over 160,000 to a 1972 low of 105,000 (Office of Health Economics, 1975:21).

In the U.S. NIMH had been supporting research on CPZ since 1953. In 1955 Felix appointed an ad hoc committee on psychopharmacology that ultimately resulted in a November, 1955 conference on psychoactive drugs. This conference along with the experiments in state, county, and Veterans Administration hospitals all contributed to a report that asked for a NIMH study of psychopharmacology's impact. Carstairs (1961) says of psychotropic drugs:

"Few would claim that our current 'wonder drugs'
exercise more than a palliative influence on

psychiatric disorders. The big change has been
rather one of public opinion." (Carstairs,
1961: 56)

Introduction of psychotropic substances did not inaugurate a
new orientation in psychiatry. The adoption of community-
care proposals and the development of the "open door" policy
pre-date the widespread use of these drugs. Dr. T. P. Rees
at Warlington Hospital had experimented with the innovation
of unlocking the wards prior to CPZ's widespread use. As
noted, Kenneth Robinson, Labour MP, chairman of the Mental
Health Committee of the Western Regional Hospital Board, and
mental health reformer, had introduced a bill in the 1953-54
Parliamentary session calling for a review of the laws
governing detention, admission, care, and discharge in mental hospitals before the full implications of the synthesis
of CPZ and other drugs had been realized.

True, as in the U.S., the psychopharmacological revolution gave support to the English mental health reformers'
demands for new national policies. Yet, the undesirable
consequences of long-term psychotropic drug use were not
fully known, and drugs were only gradually perceived to be
even more powerful and effective forms of social and psychological control. However, in the 1950's and early 1960's,
the psychotropic drug revolution served as an important
legitimation function for the demands of psychiatric reformers for dramatic new national policies and programs, e.g.,
the work of Gorman in the U.S. (cf. Gorman, 1956:89-134).

In sum, CPZ obviously did not act alone, but in combination with other factors to push national and local governments to deepen their involvement in the treatment of mental
illnesses. To borrow a pharmacological term, CPZ acted as a
potentiator in public policy-making, furthering the reform
process. Both the U.S. Joint Commission and the English
Royal Commission pointed to the advances made in psychopharmacology that could facilitate policy innovations. Only
recently have the deleterious consequences of the widespread, long-term use of psycho-active drugs been widely
noted. Only recently have the policies partially predicated
on drugs been criticized.

Conclusions

The post–World War II policy environment was conducive to reform. The specific pattern and timing of the reforms adopted varied in England, Sweden and the United States. The U.S. mental health reformers were more successful in advancing their cause than their English and Swedish counterparts because the subgovernment for mental health had branches in the bureaucracy as well as in the legislature and had well-developed connections with the associations, professional societies, and research and training communities. English and Swedish mental health reformers were less successful in realizing their policy agendas because they lacked the bureaucratically-based elements of a reform movement that could effecitvely mobilize change-advocates and follow-up on policy initiatives.

Chapter Eight trace the policy-making developments in the 1960's and considers the new issues of the 1970's to explain how U.S. mental health policy reformers have been successful in fully realizing their goals and to determine if English and Swedish reformers were able to overcome the handicap of not possessing a bureaucratic-base on which to anchor their campaigns to adopt and implement community-care alternatives to the classic mental hospital.

In the early 1900's the National Committee for Mental Hygiene (NCMH) had worked closely with the federal government in gathering data on mental hospitals. Though an accurate and thorough census of hospitals and their patients awaited the establishment of NIMH, the initial, rudimentary NCMH data-gathering operation necessitated cooperation between the federal civil service and the voluntary associations. These cooperative relationships grew as a result of World War I.

However, by World War II the NCMH had experienced a loss of reform zeal. This decline can be attributed, in part, to the factors identified by Davis (1938). Davis located a middle-class bias in the mental hygiene movement. Their bourgeois conception of positive mental well-being flowed from a psychologistic theory of the determinants of mental disorders and synonymous with middle class morality. Further, in an analysis of the backgrounds of 51 members of the mental hygiene movement, Davis found that they were mostly upper-middle class professionals with white Anglo-Saxon Protestant backgrounds who had risen to prominence through their own initiative.

> "It follows from their background and is exemplified in their writings, that they believe in empirical science and have taken the American humanitarian religion seriously enough to apply scientific results zealously to the welfare of society." (Davis: 58)

Gursslin, et al. (1959-60), in their late 1950's content analysis of the publications of the New York State Department of Mental Health and the National Mental Health Association, supports Davis' earlier study (cf. Ginsberg, 1955 and Stanton, 1970).

2. Up until 1973 NIMH was not the only institute of the National Institute of Health (NIH) that was benefitting from the generosity of Congress. Miles (1974) identifies the NIH grant system, that generated increasing, aggregate appropriations: first, bio-medical research would thrive best where the most talented researchers work--universities, teaching hospitals, non-profit institutes--and second, the allocation of grants to such talented teams should be made by advisory teams of scientists, not the bureaucracy itself.

> "The combination of decisions resulted in a national research dominated by thousands of small projects generated by scientists themselves wherever they were institutionally based." (Miles: 177-78)

The result was that NIH appropriations have risen from $464,000 in 1938 to $2,015,196,000 in 1973; from 1948 to 1968, the years roughly of Hill-Fogarty dominance, the appropriations rose from $26,573,000 to $1,178,924,000.

3. Solo-charismatic reformer Gorman viewed the mental hospital in these polimical terms:

> "...the typical state mental hospital of today is an anachronism, a vestigial appendix of earlier superstitions which pictured the mentally ill as incurably possessed of evil thoughts and demons and therefore to be consigned to asylums far removed from the eye and conscience of 'civilized' society." (Gorman, 1956:10)

Adopting this stance, Gorman self-consciously placed himself in the tradition of Dorothea Dix and William Lloyd Garrison; he viewed himself as the tireless ally of the mentally ill in their struggle for humane treatment.

Miles (1974) says bureaucratically-based reformer Felix partially shared Gorman's orientation:

216

"[As NIMH's]...director, Robert Felix was dedicated to the proposition that most state
mental hospitals built in the late nineteenth
and early twentieth century were a blot on
the national conscience, that they were custodial institutions where progressive therepy
and hope were rarely found, and that they be
simultaneously upgraded in quality and replaced as rapidly as possible by community
mental health centers and other similar forms
of treatment." (Miles:204)

This example of convergence demonstrates the ideological linkages between the bureaucratic-based reformers
and a solo lobbyist of the mental health reform movement; such agreement permitted the coolaboration between
these very different groups and ultimately furthered the
cause and made possible policy advances in the 1950's
and 60's.

4. This development also occurred in other countries. Wing
    and Hailey (1972) examined hospital bed occupation rates
    in England and noted that from 1900 until 1954 the num-
    bers of persons in residence at year end always in-
    creased, "but then quite unexpectedly the number of beds
    occupied began to decline." (Wing and Hailey: 88) From
    the 1954 high point of 344 mental patient beds per
    100,000 persons, the numbers have steadily declined to
    231 per 100,000 in 1970. A similar drop can be noted
    for Scotland, from a 1954 high of 410 per 100,000 to 339
    per 100,000 in 1970. Though Sweden's data do not show
    such a dramatic decline, the numbers have stopped
    growing: in 1950 the psychiatric bed rate per 100,000
    was 350; it rose to 375 per 100,000 in 1960 and has
    since leveled off at 344 per 100,000 in 1970
    (Socialstyrelsen, 1973: Table A4).

5. The BMA's curious role in the public as well as in the
    private debate over NHS negotiations is not the central
    focus of this study, but we need to make passing refer-
    ence to the struggle. Eckstein (1958:122-131; 43-163)

217

recounts the BMA's policy changes in the struggle over the form of nationalization (cf. Anderson, 1972).

6. A major complaint made by mental hospital administrators voiced in my 1975-76 interviews was the loss of the special direct relationship with the Regional Board and the Ministry of Health under the newly reorganized version of the NHS. But to discuss reorganization at this point in the analysis can only confuse the reader, so I only provide a description of NHS as it functioned from 1948-73. Eckstein notes the delegation of actual administrative duties by the Regional Boards and Management Committee to their subcommittee and even more directly, to the NHS administrative salaried personnel (Eckstein, 1958: 186-192).

7. The general practitioner service is a feature of the NHS which is not understood by the AMA and other critics of socialized medicine. At a time when a call is being made in the U.S. for a reevaluation of primary care (cf. Rogers, 1977; Enthoven, 1978) and the number of general practitioners has fallen to its lowest levels ever, it is interesting to note that the proportion of British MDs who engage in general practice has held fairly constant since nationalization. In Sweden, the county hospital-based medical services also suffer from the fact of this lack of a coordinating focal point for patient care (cf. Anderson, 1972).

8. The adoption of national health insurance differed from this process because the interests of doctors and the county council were threatened by the nationalization scheme proposed by the Board of Medicine head Dr. Axel Höjer. The political conflict which followed the Höjer's presentation of his proposals was a deviation from the bureaucratically-dominated process of policy adoption and implementation (cf. Anderson, 1972: 77-79).

9. The 1929 legislation (and subsequent amendments) enabled persons to be confined to a mental hospital against their will on the basis of petition from a relative and a certificate provided by a medical doctor (doctors other than psychiatrists could certify persons in need of confinement). Self-admission was possible, but under this procedure discharge was possible only with the approval of the chief of psychiatry. Though a central appeals board was available to hear and review the petitions of patients desiring discharge, its composition was weighted in favor of the medical and legal professions, not the patient. A chief inspector of the Board of Health was responsible for assessing the quality of patient care in all state asylums but the protests over the inhumane treatment and prolonged confinements testified to the ineffectiveness of this officer (Leche, 1970).

10. Swazey's (1974) work on CPZ is a case study in innovation and diffusion. CPZ alone did not create the drug revolution. A second major class of tranquilizers, the rauwolfa alkaloids, also entered Western psychiatry in the early 1950's, though they had been used extensively in India for over 1,000 years to treat psychosis.

Once CPZ was in use, other substances entered psychiatry rapidly; by 1956, 26 tranquilizing agents were listed in the literature. A new class of drugs, the antidepressants, entered the field in 1956. Swazey's tracing of their history demonstrates a pattern similar to CPZ's.

This pattern of dissemination is also a means whereby one can map the international character of psychiatry and the treatment of the mentally ill. The case of CPZ not only is a latter-day example of this international dissemination, but also reveals a new dimension to innovation diffusion--the increasing speed with which innovations spread in a much denser, tightly interconnected world of the 1950's. For example, Rhone-Poulenc distributed samples of CPZ in France in April, 1951 for the first clinical trials. Within one year the U.S. firm of Smith, Kline, and French had acquired marketing rights. By the fall of 1953 the first psychiatric symposium on CPZ was held in Basel, Switzerland, and selected U.S. state mental hospitals had begun to administer CPZ. Further, the publication in February, 1954 of the first North American report of clinical trials conducted by Lehmann in Canada was followed swiftly by the first British publication in April, 1954. Finally, by May, 1954 CPZ, under the SK&F marketing name Thorazine, was approved by the FDA for U.S. distribution. Thus, within three years, CPZ made its way into psychiatry, from France throughout Europe and on to North America (Swazey, 1974: 266-67).

11. Drs. Henry Brill of New York and Martin Fleishmen in California were two participants in early 1953 trials with CPZ. Brill said:

> "'I was searching for a treatment that was simple to administer and so safe it could be administered to large numbers of patients without any special, elaborate techniques that were slow and burdensome. I always believed that such a treatment would be forthcoming; in the early literature I read about chlorpromazine encouraged by belief. Once I had seen a small handful of cases that confirmed what had been said, I had no more doubts. The most memorable experience I remember was walking into the dayroom and seeing this small group of patients dressed, quiet, cooperative, and in surprisingly good contact--with their psychiatric symptoms wiped away. That was perhaps the most spectacular demonstration anyone can ask.'" (Brill in Swazey, 1974: 201)

Fleishmen also reported a decrease in hallucinations and delusions, the increase in the predictability and intelligibility of patients as a result of the administration of psychotropic substances. Brill and Fleishmen accounts show how CPZ sold itself to overworked administrators of mental hospitals. These psychiatrists had rarely been able to practice psychotherapy under the appalling conditions of most state mental institutions. They were looking for a cure, one which was more effective on a wider range of patients than electro-convulsive therapy.

One of CPZ's main selling points was the cost-savings realized by the administration of CPZ. But the test's initial results were discouraging; for example, the California experiments revealed a higher readmission rate for former mental patients, thus undermining the initial cost-savings associated with CPZ. A. Alan Post, State Legislative Analyst, was critical of CPZ because of the high relapse rate and dubious about its benefits. SK&F's Task Force investigators were naturally disturbed by these reports from such a key state mental hospital system. And their investigation found that the problem lay with the low after-care dosages prescribed by family physicians unfamiliar with CPZ and wary of possible side effects of this "wonder" drug.

By 1961, the advances in methodology coupled with the progress in the VA studies convinced NIMH's director of Psychopharmacology Service Center, Jonathan Cole, of the feasibility of an NIMH collaborative study. Rigorous in design and execution, the study analyzed the results of tests to demonstrate the differences between phenothiazines and placebos.

> "The findings of this study lend strong support to the rising optimism about and confidence in the effectiveness of treatment of acute schizophrenic psychoses. Even among the placebo-treated group, almost half the patients were rated as having improved to some extent. Almost 95 percent of the patients treated with one of the three phenothiazines improved. More significantly, the effects of phenothiazine therapy are not only quantitative, in that a large percentage of patients improved; but they are also qualitative, in that a wide range of schizophrenic symptoms and behavior are favorably altered." (Swazey, 1974:255)

CHAPTER VIII

VARIATION IN THE ADOPTION AND
IMPLEMENTATION OF COMMUNITY CARE:
THE SECOND CYCLE OF POST-WAR REFORM

In the 1960's England, Sweden, and the United States all
converged in their adoption of further mental health reforms
of their national mental health policies; however, the
specific form these policies took varied considerably from
nation to nation. This chapter focuses on the role the
different mental health reformers played in each nation in
shaping the community-care policies and programs by exploring different national policy-making processes and their
outcomes.

This chapter presents evidence from the three nations
under study that support the theory of mental health reform.
Specifically, the data will show that variation in the success of national elites in implementing community-based care
for the mentally disordered is a function of the variation
in the development of the organizational base of mental
health reformers. A nation whose mental health reform movements acquired and developed bureaucratic bases for the
operation of mental health reformers was more successful
than nations that had not constructed such a foundation for
reform work.

Toward Community Mental Health Centers in the United States

The creation of the National Institute for Mental Health
in 1946 and the formation of the U.S. Congressional Joint
Commission on Mental Illness and Health in 1955 set the
stage for policy innovations in the 1960s. The turbulent
decade of the sixties saw the U.S. mental health reform
movement succeed in developing policies and programs that
would outstrip policy advances in England and Sweden. Though
in all three nations therapeutic innovations continued and
advances in psychiatric research and training proceeded, and
even accelerated in the decade, the U.S. out-distanced

England and Sweden in the creation of community-care alternatives to the classic mental hospital. The following analysis offers an explanation of this divergence of national policies and programs.

The inauguration of John F. Kennedy's fabled thousand-day administration also marked the beginning of the zenith of the bureaucratically-based reformers of NIMH and their legislative, professional, and associational allies. Because of his family's involvement in mental retardation reform, Kennedy was a member of the legislatively-based mental health reform movement. As a Senator, he co-sponsored the Joint Congressional Resolution calling for an investigation of the causes and cures of mental diseases. Though less influential than NIMH's ally Senator Lister Hill, Kennedy nonetheless could be counted on to aid in the passage of NIMH appropriation requests and in other ways to further the cause of mental health reform. As a Presidential candidate, he had read the final report of the Joint Commission; as President, Kennedy moved in several directions to effect mental health reforms. One of his first acts was to appoint the Presidential Panel on Mental Retardation, with sister-in-law Eunice Shriver as its head. On the mental illness front, Kennedy acted in November, 1961 by appointing Department of Health, Education and Welfare Secretary Abraham Ribicoff, and later his successor Anthony Celebrezze, to head up an inter-departmental task force to develop proposals to implement the Joint Commission's recommendations.

Bureaucratically-based reform policy making process set in motion. The Kennedy created inter-departmental task force provided NIMH with an opportunity to fully realize its ambition of adding a direct-service component to their research and personnel training functions. The task force was chaired by HEW's Boisfeuillet Jones and consisted of Bureau of the Budget's Robert H. Atwell, Under Secretary of Labor Daniel Patrick Moynihan, representatives from the Council of Economic Advisors and Veterans Administration, and NIMH's Doctors Robert Felix and Stanley Yolles.

Felix instructed his staff that assisting the task force was their number one priority; he placed Yolles specifically in charge of developing NIMH's own legislative proposal based on the Joint Commission's report. Yolles had already been working with Atwell on such a response, so that it was logical for him to continue the coordination task at this crucial stage in the policy process.[1]

In developing a community mental health policy proposal for Kennedy, the interagency task force departed in their legislative recommendation from the Joint Commission's proposals. While the Joint Commission's recommendations envisioned the state mental hospitals as one of many sites for community mental health services, the interagency task force recommendations called for community mental health care to be placed outside of the mental hospital and to be under the direct authority of NIMH. This marked a fundamental shift in the mission of an Institute of Health: federal health institutes were to fund and conduct research (both pure and applied), assist in personnel training, and only indirectly assist in service delivery through demonstration projects.

NIMH's direct-service operations were limited in the numbers of persons served, of clinics funded, and of dollars expended for community care projects (e.g., NIMH Prince George's County laboratory). The inter-agency plan envisioned that NIMH would directly fund services to provide a nation-wide network of illness treatment centers. Kennedy was presented with a legislative proposal that reflected NIMH and its allies' desire to expand the scope of NIMH operations and alter the intent of the Joint Commission report.

The consequences of a public health service training. In a task force dominated by NIMH, the concerns and goals of NIMH gained a hegemony; these goals and concerns reflected the training of the NIMH leadership.

"The two most important factors in the development of a proposal by the NIMH task force were its members' public health training and access to the findings of the Community Services Branch of NIMH. (There were more staff members holding Masters of Public Health degrees in the NIMH in 1959 than in

any other division of the Public Health Service.)
Not only did the members of the NIMH task force
possess a public health philosophy, they had also
been traumatized by their work experience in the
state mental hospitals." (Foley, 1975:35-36)

Felix, foremost among the bureaucratically-based reformers,
was not favorably disposed towards the state mental hospital
system. In 1963 testimony that called for community-care
centers before Senator Lister Hill's committee Felix said:

"'I wish to God I could live and be active for 25
more years because I believe if I could, I would
see the day when the state mental hospitals as we
know them today would no longer exist.'" (Felix
quoted in Connery, 1968: 51)

As NIMH director, Felix ultimately assumed responsibility
for research conducted on the mental hospital. Studies by
Stanton and Schwartz (1954), Belknap (1956), and Goffman
(1961) had provided significant insights into the socially
and psychologically corrosive processes of institutionalization (cf. Clausen, 1970). These research findings rein-
forced the training and professional experience that had
favorably predisposed them towards a public health service
model of service delivery. Thus, professional training,
combined with extensive understanding of the workings of
mental hospitals, meant that most of NIMH's policy innovators shared, along with other elements of the reform movement (e.g., Gorman's National Committee Against Mental
Illness) an antipathy towards the state and county mental
hospital. The community mental health center concept cor-
responded with many of the reformers' objections to the
hospital while it simultaneously advanced the relative
status of NIMH among the other institutes of health.

The lobby for the reform legislation. Gorman and his
allies also had been mobilizing support for the coming
certain legislative confrontation with the opponents of an
expanded federal health care role. Along with NIMH, he had
prepared a resolution for the November, 1961 National Governors' Conference that endorsed community psychiatric services. Additional meetings were held in early 1962 with

state and territorial mental health authorities to brief
them on interagency policy deliberations and to obtain their
support of federal funding of community services.   HEW's
Jones also met members of the AMA Council on Mental Health
to persuade them that federal staffing grants for community
services would not lead to socialized medicine: grants
could support private as well as public community mental
health centers.

Thus, NIMH's Felix and Yolles, along with interagency-
committee head Jones and lobbyist Gorman, had assembled most
of the coalition to support the legislative proposal President Kennedy would make to Congress in his State of the
Union address.   The development and adoption of the Community Mental Health Centers Acts thus illustrates the importance of assembling a broad-based reform coalition that
combined effective lobbying with connections to key legislators and linkages to other supportive associations and
organizations (cf. Felicetti, 1975:28-30; 45-56 ff.).

NIMH's reform goals vs. state hospitals' interests.
While it was natural that the task force should draw on the
resources of the professional staff of NIMH, the consequence
of this decision was to give greater weight to the particular reform interests that Felix, Yolles, and the entire
consultative team that developed the legislative proposal
represented.   The specific proposal of the interagency task
force was that NIMH direct and finance the new, community-
based treatment centers.   However, the agreement over the
need to provide such services did not mean that all task
force members were committed to this alternative to the
mental hospital.[2]

The state mental hospital system was the main governmental effort to promote mental health and treat mental
diseases.   Atwell and Fein argued that the states could not
be expected to raise additional monies to construct and
staff a whole new network of facilities: the state mental
hospitals would continue to function, but only as "dumping
grounds."   Further, Atwell and Fein predicted that the
entrenched mental health interest groups (e.g., hospital
workers, administrators, and state mental health departments) would be obstacles in implementing any new mode of

treatment. More importantly, the "crisis of numbers" was being resolved by the introduction of psycho-active drugs, leaving state mental hospitals with a reduced number of patients for whom to care. Hence, the interests of state hospitals would not necessarily be served by the establishment of a competing system of patient care. The decline in resident populations, combined with the opening of federally-funded, community care centers, would leave hospitals and their staffs vulnerable to closings imposed by fiscally-conservative state governments.

Kennedy resolves the policy dilemma. The task force report was given to President Kennedy for his approval, but in giving approval Kennedy also had to resolve a conflict between different reform advocates.[3]

The task force had agreed that NIMH would fund the construction and operation of up to 2,000 community-based mental health centers. These centers would serve as the major ambulatory treatment facilities for the nation. This nationwide network would mean that at least one center would be placed in every Congressional district, insuring the continuing interest of a Congressman's constituents in the long-term funding of such centers. Thus, the reform movement strategy sought to build into this program a continuing demand for the funding of these treatment facilities.

Kennedy was determined to see the NIMH program go forward, but he had to deal with the conflicting advice of his staff. The new HEW Secretary, Anthony Celebrezze, had differed with the interagency task force recommendations over the issue of federal support for new staffing grants, and had informed Kennedy that he felt the states should pay for staffing. The Bureau of the Budget also had objections and told the President that the recommendations to expand training funds for community psychiatry would rob acute, somatic-care services of needed new personnel.[4] Kennedy used his prerogative to ignore these objections and accepted the NIMH proposal as his legislative proposal.

Mental Retardation Takes Precedence in the Policy Adoption
Process

Though agreement had been forged on a legislative proposal, Kennedy held up the announcement of his administration's mental health package until the Report of the Panel
on Mental Retardation was issued. Gorman said of the delay:

> "'We had to hold off on mental health legisla-
> tion because Jack Kennedy and Eunice Shriver,
> through Mike Feldman, said there would be no
> Presidential initiative until the panel on
> mental retardation reported in 1962.'"
> (Gorman quoted in Foley, 1975: 53)

When Kennedy's panel on retardation issued its report on
December 11, 1962, the President launched the mental health
centers legislation, using the network of mental health reformers within and without Congress. The substantive legislative proposals were introduced as HR 3688 by Representative John Fogarty and referred to his House Committee on
Interstate and Foreign Commerce and in the Upper Chamber as
SB 755, introduced by NIMH's chief legislative ally,
Alabama's Lister Hill.

The mental retardation linkage and incrementalism. The
bills considered by Congressional committees again linked
the reform agenda of the mental illness and retardation
lobbies. This linkage in part reflected Kennedy's affinity
for the mental retardation legislation and in part because
the mental retardation component of the bill was thought to
be less objectionable to potential opponents, e.g., conservative Republicans and Democrats and the bulk of the American Medical Association's membership. Hence, community
mental health centers were tied with the construction and
staffing proposals for the mentally retarded to assist in
the passage of these more controversial mental illness
proposals.

Kennedy, along with NIMH and the mental health reform
lobby, also tried to buy "legislative insurance" by mini-
mizing the amount of legislation which would have to obtain
Congressional approval.[5] In this way the reformers hoped

to neutralize the opposition to health legislative proposals (cf. Marmor, 1970). Ultimately, Kennedy and NIMH would have to compromise and settle for a more minimal program than they had originally envisioned, hoping that the limited legislative victory would establish the precedent of federal funding of services to the mentally disordered.

Anti-mental hospital intent? In the Congressional testimony on HR 3688 the anti-mental-hospital interpretation of this policy was revealed. HEW's Jones said:

> "'So what we are really advocating, Mr. Chairman, is, in a sense, removing the care of the mentally ill from complete, almost complete, responsibility of the state through tax funds and direct operations in these isolated large state mental institutions, and putting this care back in the community to be financed and supported and operated through the traditional patterns of medical care to which we have become accustomed in this country. This means providing for the mentally ill in precisely the same pattern that we provide for physically ill.'" (Jones quoted in Foley, 1975:63)

HEW thus advocated two concepts: the placing of mental health services on an equal footing with somatic health services and the supplanting of the institutional legacy of 19th century era reform, the asylum.[6]

In addition to HEW's testimony favoring community-care facilities independent of the mental hospitals, the mental health reform lobby coordinated testimony from a wide range of groups with health and mental health interests. The National Association for Mental Health, the National Association for Retarded Children, the American Psychiatric Association, the American Hospital Association, the American Public Health Association, the AFL-CIO, the American Psychological Association, the National Association of State Mental Health Programs and the pharmaceutical industry supported the House and Senate bills. Gorman's National Committee Against Mental Illness lobbied for the bill's passage. The legislative allies of NIMH, Veterans groups and the VA supported the bill (cf. Felicetti, 1975:57-60).

But the AMA House of Delegates balked at endorsing its own Mental Health Council's positive recommendation. Staffing grants were equated with salaried service, and hence socialized medicine. The AMA's House of Delegates directed its lobbyist to oppose the bill's sections on the staffing of centers, even though the AMA's own Committee on Mental Health had advocated AMA's endorsement of the bills and testified for the bills (Felicetti, 1975:76-80).

Are all doctors' interests the same? As revealed above, there was a split within the AMA's ranks over the CMHC Act, P.L. 88-164. This division suggests that Alford's (1975) medical-structural-interest group concept requires revision. The AMA internal conflict shows that medical specializations can differentially evaluate the same piece of legislation. Thus, the political interests of the medical community are not necessarily homogeneous, and the political behavior of medical professionals associations can be divergent. It can be concluded that Alford's concept of structural interests does not capture the subtle, yet very real conflicts between two AMA factions that Foley (1975) and Felicetti (1975) reveal.

The range of variation in the AMA's attitudes reflects the fact of the division of labor in medicine creating different structural conditions which will shape perceptions and understandings (cf. Larson, 1977:19-39). More specifically, Alford's use of the structural-interest group concept ignores the variation in medical training and careers, variation which is a function of the increasing specialization due to the transformation of the scientific-technological foundations of medical practice. Psychiatry has emerged as a branch of medicine, though its roots lie in the asylum. The present-day American Psychiatric Association (APA) was originally founded in 1844 as the Association of Medical Superintendents of American Institutions for the Insane (Overholser, 1944). In contrast to the AMA, the APA is linked to a specific institutional mode of treatment, a mode that has been largely governmentally supported. Thus, the members of the APA were less threatened by the growth in federal health programs and expenditures because their practice had originally been funded by state and local governments. Further, the 1946 creation of NIMH had enhanced psychiatry's stature among the branches of medicine, and the entry, via the community mental health legislation, of NIMH into the subsidy of direct services would further increase the scope of psychiatric practice.[7]

In contrast to the APA, the AMA continued to speak in 1963 with several policy voices. The AMA's Council on Mental Health argued for the staffing grants because of the need for "seed-money" for these innovative programs. The bulk of the AMA officialdom favored only a limited Hill-Burton style involvement; that is, a mental health program that used federal monies only to construct community health centers. The split in the AMA widened when the AMA House of Delegates voted to direct their lobbyists to oppose the staffing grant concept. Battling any program that provided a policy opening for socialized medicine, AMA conservatives were able to mobilize the association's resources in opposition to the Council on Mental Health's position. The AMA, in alliance with GOP and conservative Democrats, was successful in deleting the staffing grants from the legislation.

The AMA prevails in round one. In October, 1963, Kennedy signed the Mental Retardation and Community Mental Health Centers Act, Public Law 88-164, but the law was incomplete from the mental health lobby's perspective; the AMA had been able to delete from the act the provisions relating to staffing. While Lister Hill had obtained Senate approval of the staffing grants, the House of Representatives had been persuaded by the AMA to delete these grants. The conference committee that formed to reconcile these two versions of the act dealt the "staffing" advocates a defeat. The compromise bill as reported did not contain provisions for staffing, acknowledging that the AMA had the power to kill the original bill.

"The conferees could not agree that the bill would pass the House with an 'initial staffing' provision in it (an extra $169 million). Virtually all conferees acknowledged the value of the staffing

money to the states, but the majority of the House
conferees were reluctant to jeopardize the bill by
restoring the staffing position." (Foley, 1975:
75)

The 1963 funds authorized by P.L. 88-164 were $329 million:
$179 million for construction of mental retardation centers
and $150 million for construction of mental health centers.
The mental health lobby promised itself and others that the
staffing funds would be added in the next session of Congress. The mental health lobbyists felt that the facts
created by the act's construction provision—the bricks and
mortar—would speak eloquently for the staffing grants in
future Congressional deliberations.

And, the mental health reformers were correct. The
AMA's defeat of the staffing grant provisions was only a
temporary set-back for the mental health lobby, as was
Kennedy's death. With Presidential backing for mental
health reform continued, mental health reformers' defeat on
staffing created a policy precedent for future federal funding of P.L. 88-164. The AMA's opposition to staffing CMHC
staffs weakened because the AMA was battling a far more
threatening piece of legislation: Medicare and Medicaid.
Also, in 1963 the AMA lobby was effective because it called
every member of Congress, usually using Congress members'
personal physicians to lobby for a "no" vote on mental
health community center staffing. This tactic was far less
successful after the 1964 election that swept many members
of the GOP and conservative Democrat block from Congress and
gave President Lyndon B. Johnson an overwhelming endorsement
to complete the martyred Kennedy's unfinished legislative
agenda (Chu and Trotter, 1975).

Incrementalism in Policy Adoption

Though CMHC's staffing grants were defeated in 1963, the
mental health lobbying branch of the reform movement had
established a policy beachhead. Policy analysts have developed several concepts to capture this phenomenon. In
Wilensky's terms, mental health reformers had opened the
policy "back door":

"When ideology and practice are far apart, the chief mechanism for reconciling them and getting on with the business of solving real problems is back-door entry. The principle of back-door entry is evident in Medicare and veterans' programs in the United States and in family allowances everywhere." (Wilensky, 1975:41)

Wilensky's conceptualization converges two other policy analysts. Bardach (1977) says that an incrementalist strategy --what he calls "piling on"--is a risky way to gain a policy's adoption; attempting to pile onto an adopted policy new programs will not necessarily lead to the desired result, and may lead to future administrative problems. Marmor (1973) calls this process the politics of incrementalism. In the struggle over Medicare its proponents were able to use the aged as a "shield" to deflect the opposition. The AMA attacks thereby enact a piece of legislation that while only partially realizing the goal of national health insurance, created the precedence for such insurance and incremental additions to it (Marmor:14-20 ff.).

Whatever concept one uses one can see that all three policy analysts have converged in their attempts to describe and explain the process whereby a policy can grow gradually as the political climate permits, once an initial, and even quite limited mandate has been agreed to. In the case of the Community Mental Health Centers Acts (1963, 1965, 1973), the staffing grant setback suffered by the reform movement forces could be relatively quickly reversed given the 1963 precedent. When CMHC amendments were placed on the agenda of unfinished business by the new Johnson administration, they were quickly passed by an activist, liberal Congress intent on solving social problems.

Implementation of the community care concept. Once Kennedy signed the CMHC Act (1963) into law, the task for the reformers was implementing the law. Felix and his NIMH staff assumed that they would write the administrative guidelines, handle the disbursement of funds, approve service plans, and the like, but competition for control of the construction of health facilities emerged quite quickly, and NIMH had to fight to control the programs it had designed.[8]

In the implementation phase, the CMHC legislation was up for grabs among the various HEW agencies. CMHC's legislative mandate did not insure that NIMH would control the construction funds. The Hill-Burton agency of HEW's Bureau of Medical Services (BMS) viewed P.L. 88-164 as a "bricks and mortar" law because Congress had stipulated in the act that states and localities use the 1946 Hill-Burton pattern of funding, including a state plan requirement. NIMH, in contrast, felt that as the creator of the CMHC concept, it should implement it. Thus, ambiguity in the policy mandate created competition between the Bureau of Medical Service and NIMH over control of the implementation process, not an unusual development in implementation (cf. Pressman and Wildavsky, 1979; Bardach, 1977).

This struggle over a program illustrates how a poor program definition can result in inter-agency struggles to control a program. NIMH was able to thwart the plans of the Bureau of Medical Services because NIMH enlisted its powerful allies to assure NIMH's control. If in 1963-64 NIMH had lost control of construction grants it would have had greater difficulty in pressing for legislation authorizing funds for staffing; in other words, the policy "back-door" would have been shut. In maintaining control of CMHC construction programs, NIMH called on powerful and strategically-placed allies like Senator Lister Hill and Congressman John Fogarty and other elements of the mental health reform movement, the sub-government for community care.

The Operationalization of the Community-Care Concept

P.L. 88-164 also created other ambiguities. Congress did not give NIMH's regulation writers—Felix and his staff —an operational definition of community. NIMH had the discretion to create this definition constrained only by the act's intent. An examination of P.L. 88-164 shows how almost any operationalization of community could be developed.[9] Title II of P.L. 88-164 defines community as:

"...an area or that portion of an area served or
to be served by a program providing at least the
essential elements of comprehensive mental
health services." (U.S., CMHC Act, 1963:5951)

Hence, the law creates an interesting tautology: a community mental health center offers services to persons
residing in a community; a community is defined as the
locality in which such services are provided. As such,
community-care centers may serve something no more clearly
defined than a catchment area for facilities providing services, if a catchment area is defined as a community. And
the catchment areas may be an inner-city district of a
municipality, with ethnic homogeniety, or the whole of a
sparsely-populated state (cf. Titmuss, 1961).[10]

Once CMHC was enacted, the NIMH staff had to implement
the concept of community; or more exactly, the staff had to
find some social, scientific, psychiatric, or statistical
justification for regions to be served by up to 2,000 CMHC
centers. The NIMH staff charged with the task took Felix's
ratio of 1 center per 100,000 as their point of departure
and began a review of the social science literature (circa
1960's) on community in order to derive an operational definition. The difficulty of synthesizing this literature on
community meant that:

"'We came down to simply numbers of people because
the other approaches--political, geographic, ethnic, or socio-economic boundaries--did not work.
'Quantities of population' was the last resort.'"
(Cain and Felix in Foley, 1975:92)

The final formula agreed upon was that a community center
should serve not less than 75,000 and not more than 200,000
people [Regulation 54,203(b) (2)], with a clause included
which granted discretion to the Surgeon General to grant
exceptions and make modifications. The centers were to be
"accessible" to the population, within the geographical and
political boundaries.

This translation of the act's intent raises a serious
question: do CMHC centers reflect the original vision of an

235

accessible, alternative care system? The CMHC Act had
raised popular expectations that such a system would be
created. As will be shown, the law also created the opportunity for widespread misinterpretation and disillusionment
by not fulfilling its promise. Like other Great Society's
policies and programs, the CMHC programs were to fall short
of the policy's promise (Moynihan, 1969; cf. Levitan and
Taggart, 1976).

Winning the Staffing Grant Appropriations: Another Great Society Program

The 1964 $35 million appropriation for construction of
mental health centers was not being expended at anywhere the
rate anticipated. The states and localities were reluctant
to match federal dollars to build centers when the staffing
monies were not authorized. The death of Kennedy removed a
key element of the reform movement, and the commitment of
President Johnson was unclear. Though President Johnson
intended to complete Kennedy's unfinished domestic agenda,
the mental health lobby did not take Johnson for granted.
In 1964 the lobby went to work. Members including Atwell,
Gorman, and Yolles, along with Dr. Philip Sirotkin, met with
and received a commitment from then HEW Assistant Secretary
Wilbur Cohen that the Johnson administration would introduce
the staffing legislation. President Johnson personally
followed up on this meeting with his own 1964 election eve
statement endorsing staffing grants:

> "'We must step up the fight on mental health and
> mental retardation. I intend to ask for in-
> creased funds for research centers, for special
> teachers training, and for helping coordinate
> state and local programs.'" (Johnson, quoted in
> Foley; 1975:105)

With his electoral mandate, Johnson could deliver on his
commitment to mental health. For this second legislative
struggle, NIMH again prepared a legislative package. As in
the early 60's, NIMH was strategically-based; reformers are
at an advantage to realize policy goals when they possess an
agency itself in control of the policy design process. Gor-

man and his allies collaborated with NIMH and its Congressional allies in drafting legislation completing the 1963 program goals for CMHC thwarted by the AMA-GOP alliance.

The Medicare diversion. The AMA was not able to block CMHC staffing grants because the campaign to defeat national health insurance for the aged and poor had diverted their lobbying resources (Marmor, 1970: 19). The formidable AMA lobbying effort did not place opposition to CMHC-staffing grants as high on its list of priorities as it had in 1963. But AMA opposition to staffing grants persisted as evidence by the AMA President's statement to the February, 1965 conference of the American Psychiatric Association:

> "'The AMA is firmly committed to the proposition
> that the local community is most responsive to
> the health needs of its citizens and that it
> should assume the basic responsibility for their
> needs.'" (Ward quoted in Foley, 1975:109)

State and federal support should be forthcoming only if local governments' commitments proved inadequate. But the Medicare battle was more crucial, and in any event, the huge liberal Democratic majorities meant the AMA could not lobby against Medicare as successfully as it had in 1961-63.

In 1854 President Pierce perceived Dorothea Dix's proposal for land grants for the mentally ill as supplanting the state's rightful role in mental health administration and finance, and so he vetoed it (Deutsch, 1949; cf. Piven and Cloward, 1971). In 1963 and 1965 Pierce's successors had reversed this precedent-setting veto, and so threatened state hospital systems.

P.L. 88-164 called for state plans for new mental health services, but the states were slow to initiate the planning process. The failure of states to develop plans that would obligate capital-spending funds meant that the goal of comprehensive mental health planning was being imperfectly realized. Further, besides not planning for services, many states were reluctant to match the construction grants without certain knowledge that the federal government was going to provide the staffing funds. Thus, the 1963 construction

237

grants were not being expended at the rate NIMH anticipated. Yolles' 1965 testimony revealed the gap between CMHC promise and performance and identified the failure to enact staffing grants in 1963 and the requirement to prepare state plans as its cause:

> "No center facilities were under construction in March, 1965 because the money became available in November, 1964 and the state plans, mandatory by law, had not come in yet. No application could be approved until the state plan was approved. Certain communities would not submit plans until they were assured of operating costs." (Foley, 1975: 110)

Further, federal appropriations do not necessarily equal state and local expenditure. In the case of P.L. 88-164, the policy door was ajar, but it was not permitting much traffic to pass through. The 1965 CMHC amendments were necessary to enable often ideologically-reluctant, cash-starved states to commit themselves to construct treatment centers. If a certain seven year federal commitment to maintain these facilities was evidenced by a new federal mandate, Felix's dream could be realized. Also, the state had "sunk-costs" in the form of their investments in their mental hospital systems, though some had developed community treatment programs (e.g., California's Short-Doyle Program).

The lobby for staffing grants was also well orchestrated for the battle to fulfill the intent of the 1963 legislation. As in 1963, Gorman coordinated the testimony, including that of retired NIMH Director Robert Felix, and this time the mental health reform interests were triumphant. In May, 1965, the unanimous positive report of the House Interate and Foreign Commerce Committee was followed by a 390-0 vote of the House for CMHC staffing.

In the Senate, Hill's Committee on Labor and Public Welfare met in executive session with NIMH's Yolles on June 24, 1965; on the same day the committee unanimously reported the bill out to the Senate. The Senate bill, which increased the House appropriation by $57 million, was passed on a voice vote on June 28, 1965. A House-Senate Conference was needed to reconcile the two bills, and the agreed upon compromise set initial staffing grants of $224,174,000 for seven years. President Johnson signed P.L. 89-105, Community Mental Health Centers Act Amendments of 1965 into law on August 4, 1965, thus culminating a twenty-year campaign to expand the federal government's direct role in the provision of mental health care (Felicetti, 1975: 31 ff.).

CMHC Legislation Assessed

P.L. 89-105 is an intriguing piece of legislation for several reasons. First, as a legislative mandate, it commits the federal government to a policy of by-passing the state mental hospitals. As noted, initially state mental hospital directors supported CMHC 1963, in the belief that it followed logically from the Joint Commission's recommendations. But later the National Association of State Mental Health Program Directors opposed NIMH's move into direct-service delivery:

> "[Yolles said that] 'state hospital directors thought community mental health centers would be located mostly in state hospitals. When they realized they would not get funds, they started screaming bloody murder.'" (Yolles quoted in Chu and Trotter, 1974)

The federal "seed-money" concept, with its requirements for state and local matching funds, was predicated on the assumption that localities were willing to assume an ever increasing financial burden for operating programs originating with the federal government. Mental health reformers discovered that simply obtaining a positive federal mandate did not eliminate state and local barriers to full program implementation. The commitment of localities and states to these new policy initiatives is always highly problematic, especially so in a country with fifty states, and layers of regional, county, municipal, and special service district governments (Wilensky, 1975: 52-54; cf. Myrdal, 1960).

The success of the CMHC concept. The goal of the CMHC Acts (1963, 1965) was the construction and staffing of 2,000 centers, but by 1967, 286 centers had been funded. Implementation was more problematic than anyone had thought, but the 1970's data show a dramatic increase in the number of psychiatric episodes, i.e., the sum of the patients under care in any facility and the over-all admissions to these facilities as well as a dramatic shift and a change in the loci of those treatment episodes from 1955 to 1973 (where an episode is defined as the sum of all resident patients plus all admissions to an institution). When psychiatric episodes increased 350% from 1955 to 1973, from 1.7 million patient episodes of 5.2 million. The pattern of utilization changed. In 1955 no CMHC facilities existed, but in 1973 such centers were the site of 23% of the episodes; outpatient psychiatric services increased their share of these services from 23% to 49%, a 113% increase from 1955 to 1973. In contrast, the state and county mental hospital experienced a 75% decline in their share of these patient treatment episodes, from 49% in 1955 to 12% in 1973 and smaller decreases were experienced from VA hospitals, private mental hospitals, and general hospitals' inpatient psychiatric units. In 1973 the number of patient episodes occuring at CMHC facilities was 1,747,498, more than twice the 651,857 episodes occuring at state and county hospitals, once the dominant locus of psychiatric care (Kramer, 1977: 4-5). Thus, the $1,014 million spent from 1965 to 1974 to develop the CMHC facilities had dramatically altered the character of U.S. psychiatric treatment (see Table 2).

These dramatic changes in the loci of care were not achieved without considerable continuing political activity on the part of mental health reformers located within the federal bureaus, in Congress, and in the professional practitioner associations. The continuing and expanding role of federally-funded, community-care centers was sustained despite the concerted efforts of the Nixon and Ford Administrations to transfer CMHC-type programs to state and localities, to decrease the budgets of NIMH, and to empound expenditures authorized by Congress for mental health services. The analysis of this struggle between the mental health reformers and the Nixon and Ford administrations will occur after an assessment of the reform of mental health services in England and Sweden. Only after an international evaluation of the politics of mental health reform in two other

240

TABLE 2

Numbers and Percentage Distributions of Inpatient and Outpatient Care Episodesa in Mental Health Facilities, by Type of Facility in the United States, 1955 and 1973.

Type of	1955		1973	
Institution	Number	Percent	Number	Percent
INPATIENT SERVICES				
State and County Mental Hospitals	818,832	48.9	651,857	12.4
Veterans Administration Hospitals	88,355	5.3	208,416	4.0
Private Mental Hospitals	123,231	7.3	122,831	2.3
General Hospitalb Psychiatric Units	265,934	15.9	475,448	9.1
OUTPATIENT SERVICES				
Outpatient Psychiatric Servicesc	379,000	22.6	2,586,672	49.3
Community Mental Health Centersd	NA	NA	1,174,498	22.3
TOTALS	1,675,352	100.0%	5,249,722	100.0%

a. Patient care episodes are defined as the sum of the number of patients under care of a specific type of facility as of the beginning of the year and all the admissions actions to these facilities during the following 12 months.

b. According to national reporting system of NIMH general hospital inpatient psychiatric units include both separate psychiatric units and general inpatient psychiatric services not provided in separate units.

c. These are separate facilities whose primary purpose is to provide nonresidential mental health services.

d. Comprehensive sommunity mental health centers are those facilities operating under PL 88-164 and PL 88-165 and providing inpatient, outpatient and day treatment care; emergency services; and community consultation and education.

Source: Appendix Table 3: "Number and Distribution of inpatient and outpatient care episodes and rate per 100,000 by type of psychiatric facility: United States, 1946, 1955, 1963, and 1973," p. 75. In Psychiatric Services and the Changing Institutional Scene, 1950-1986. Morton Kramer. NIMH Series B, No. 12. US, HEW, PHS, ADAMHA, NIMH. Rockville, MD., 1977.

advanced societies it will be possible to place U.S. policy developments of the 70's in perspective.

English Mental Health Policy Adoption and Implementation

The policy dilemmas posed by community care proposals are not unique to the United States. English mental health reformers also faced the task of how to realize their goal of establishing local or community-based alternatives to the mental hospital. The English reformers encountered difficulties in translating the recommendations of the Royal Commission on Mental Illness (the Percy Commission) into workable, fundable programs that could be implemented by local health authorities, authorities not directly controlled by the centrally administered National Health Service. In exploring the policy implementation difficulties it is necessary to analyze how the Percy Commission proposals were translated into legislation and what consequences that enactment process had for community-care concepts advocated by refomers within and without the government.

The fate of the Percy Commission report. The Royal Commission on the Law Relating to Mental Illness and Mental Deficiency, 1954-57 (cmnd. 169) presented its report to Parliament in May, 1957. As with the U.S. Congressional Joint Commission report, the Royal Commission's final report had been influenced by a number of innovations in the management of mental disorders. The Percy Commission members attempted to reflect these influences, while at the same time remaining within the Parliamentary mandate that limited them to a consideration of detention laws. In contrast to the U.S. case, the charge to Lord Percy and his fellow Commissioners was much more delimited than that of the U.S. Congressional Joint Commission. The Percy Commission was asked to determine how laws could be revised so that mental patients could be treated voluntarily; to review the detention procedures and treatment given persons under the NHS; and to propose ways of expanding community care. These specifications were reflected in the Commission's final product: a complex series of 146 clauses designed to strip away the 19th-century legalistic approach to admission and detention (cf. Jones, 1972:306-320).

242

Legislative passage of the reform Act. The recommendations of the Percy Commission were almost completely accepted by the Conservative Government of Harold MacMillan. The Minister of Health, Derek Walker-Smith, presided over the translation of the Percy Commission recommendations into the government's bill. But in this policy mandate design process the government made two departures from the principles adopted by the Royal Commission on Mental Disorders. First, a new category of patient--subnormal (e.g., mentally retarded in U.S. parlance)--was added to the forms of mental disorder recommended as legal categories: mentally ill, psychopathic, and severely subnormal. From policy-analytic perspectives this addition was necessary, but not crucial; it merely insured that the category was wide enough to cover the range of subnormal patients requiring specialized care. However, the second of the Tory government's modifications of the Royal Commission recommendations was more crucial for policy implementation. The government decided to permit local health authorities discretion in constructing and staffing community-based treatment facilities.

Originally, the Royal Commission had recommended that categorical grants be made by the Ministry of Health to local authorities for the specific purpose of constructing community care facilities. The Percy Commission was aware of the failure of the NHS to realize the concept of health centers due to the lack of funding (Marshall, 1970:124-5). True, the local authorities had increased their expenditures for psychiatric services from 2.5 million pounds in 1954-55 to over 4 million pounds in 1958-59. This real increase (discounting inflation) was cited as evidence for the case that the central government need not mandate spending, because local authorities were already demonstrating a willingness to expand their community mental health efforts. Still, the discretion inherent in the legislation could enable fiscally conservative local authorities to avoid expanding their psychiatric facilities and services.

Discretion and policy implementation. By proposing that local mental health expenditures not be required, Health Minister Walker-Smith was seeking to preserve local authorities' organizational discretion. An ambitious local authority could fulfill the spirit of the law by constructing and staffing a community-based preventative and treatment service, but all local authorities were not legally required to do so. Further, the Ministry of Health lacked the power to withdraw health funds from local authorities who failed to comply with the spirit of the community care mandate.

Watkin (1975) believes that this Conservative government's proposal the local discretionary funding of services for hostels, after-care facilities, diagnostic centers, and the like stemmed from the Conservative government's commitment to the block grants concept. This concept, in turn, was based on the belief that the local county and municipal governments should retain the control to set their own expenditure priorities.

The Conservative Party's defense of local government's discretion reflects Tory hostility to centralized government, especially to the Labour government-created welfare state. The Conservative government sought to maintain what discretion local authorities possessed, in part because Tories have tried to champion the rights of local governments vis-a-vis the encroachments of the central government. Further, English Conservatives, like U.S. Republicans and Southern Democrats, are much more likely to be hostile to increases in expenditures required to comply with the central needs of social selfare services. Finally, Tories were much more responsive to the complaints voiced by local authority residents over the possibility that community-based treatment centers might be located in their district, town, or village. In England, as well as the U.S., the distrust of the mentally ill can be a cause of neighborhood opposition to the location of a treatment facility in a community.

The passage of the 1959 Act. The English mental health reformers that sought to require local authority spending on community-care alternatives were not without supporters in both Houses of Parliament. For example, the English Mental Health Association was in part represented by Conservative Christopher Mayhew and Labourite Kenneth Robinson in the House of Commons; Lord Feversham, head of the National Association for Mental Health and Lady Wotton, the social scientist, both sat in the House of Lords. Though these mental health reform movement representatives were able to present the views of the NAMH on the necessity for requiring the local authorities to expend funds for psychiatric services, they were not successful of attaching such an amendment to the legislation. The Conservative government's commitment to granting local authorities discretion in implementation was sufficient to insure that the intent of the Percy Commission was not fully realized.[11]

The legislation was readily adopted by Parliament without requirements for community care. The debates and amendments resulted in the July, 1959 reconciliation of the House's and Lord's versions of the bill; and it received Royal assent on July 29, 1959. It is important to recall that unlike the CMHC Act that explicitly funded services, the 1959 Mental Health Act in England was primarily intended to revise the complex tangle of laws pertaining to admission, detention, and patient discharge.[12] Thus, the English reform coalition that was effective in obtaining passage of laws regarding definition and treatment of mental patients, enhancing patients' civil liberties in the process, was not able to launch a separate mental health services. The goal of community care was still not specifically mandated. Only a reallocation of existing NHS resources, coupled with local efforts, could achieve the broad policy objectives. Predictably, the lack of explicit mandates and funding requirements has retarded the full-scale development of local psychiatric services.

The Implementation of the Community Care

Under the English constitution officials who implement a legislative act are often the same persons who designed the bill. Government ministers further have discretion in how they will administer the bureaus they manage. In 1961 the members of the English National Association for Mental Health were among the first to learn from the Minister of Health of the hospital plan for England and Wales, and hence the plan for how the 1959 Mental Health Act would be implemented. The annual NAMH meetings had become a national forum for review of psychiatric advances, health service administrative issues, and criticisms of the treatment of the mentally ill under the NHS. The British political, social, and medical establishment was represented at meetings that also drew academics, practitioners, former mental patients, and representatives of other associations concerned with mental disorders. The Minister of Health was always invited to give the keynote address, since he was ultimately responsible under the NHS legislation for the treatment patients received in every hospital and clinic in the coutry.

The Powell proposal for dismantling the asylum. In 1961 the English NAMH heard an address from the newly appointed Conservative government's Minister of Health J. Enoch Powell. The interest in his speech stemmed from the knowledge that the government was preparing a comprehensive, ten-year plan for somatic and psychiatric services that in part would provide clues as to how the NHS would realize the 1959 Act's goals. What the members of the organized reform movement were not prepared for was Powell's position regarding the asylum. The new minister announced the NHS's intention to eliminate 75,000 mental hospital beds. He condemned the legacy of Victorian and Edwardian institution building as out-moded and meriting destruction:

> "'There they [asylums] stand, isolated, majestic, impervious, brooded over by the gigantic water-tower and chimney combined, rising unmistakable and daunting out of the countryside--the asylums which our forefathers built with such immense solidity.'" (Powell in NAMH, 1961: 6)

Powell cautioned his audience that the planned phase-out of mental hospital beds would not be easy; the institutions which had survived this long would resist destruction. Yet, he predicted that the asylum was a doomed institution and said he was lighting the mental hospitals' "funeral pyre" (Powell in NAMH, 1961).

The statistical justification for Powell's policy. Powell's rhetoric was grounded in a statistical study conducted by the Ministry of Health and the Registrar General's office that projected a decline in the hospital resident population (Tooth and Brooke, 1961). As in the United

States, the introduction of psychotropic drugs, new therapeutic modalities, the expansion of out-patient treatment,
and local innovations in community-based care had produced a
decline of 8,000 resident patients between 1954 and 1959.
This trend would continue, according to the NHS commissioned
study, rendering useless the asylum. Though the data were
published in The Lancet after Powell's speech, as Minister
of Health Powell had prepublication access to the data which
enabled him to spring these projections and their policy
implications on the assembled delegates.[13]

Interestingly, the same NAMH that had often called for a
new departure in national mental health policy greeted
Powell's proposal with skepticism and even hostility. In
part, the NAMH audience was at a disadvantage, not having
had access to the Ministry of Health data, and hence resented being surprised by both the data and the government's
proposals; in part, the audience was deeply distrustful of
the motives of the well-known, ultra-conservative critic of
the English welfare state turned manager of one of its cen-
terpieces, the NHS. For example, Elizabeth Braddock, MP and
member of the Royal Commission, believed the destruction of
the mental hospital was a retrograde step; she urged the
NAMH to adopt as its policy the Royal Commission's recommendation for a ten-year grant for new and expanded local
authority mental health services, to be linked and integrated with hospital services; Dr. H. B. Kidd of Towers
Hospital, Leicester wondered how the chronic mentally ill,
young and old would be accomodated under a phasing out of
patient beds, given that hospitals for acute somatic cases
and new psychiatric units in general hospitals were not
intended for long-term care. Probably most telling of all
was the criticism leveled by sociologist Richard Titmuss.
He said:

> "'I have tried and failed to discover in any pre-
> cise form the social origins of the term commu-
> nity. Institutional policies, both before and
> since the Mental Health Act of 1959 have assumed
> that someone knows what it is.'" (Titmuss in
> NAMH, 1961:66-67)

Given the difficulties in defining community and given the paucity of examples of community care services (the York and the Worthing cases were experimental, and possibly not generalizable models of care), Titmuss thought it strange that the Ministry of Health should embark on a campaign to dismantle the hospitals. Further, Titmuss pointed out the lack of real growth in local authority expenditures for the mentally ill: when adjusted for inflation, the increase from 1.3 million pounds in 1949-50 to 3.5 million pounds in 1959-60, was actually a decline to 1.25 million pounds. In addition, given the increase in the numbers of persons being treated, the English were spending less per capita on community care than in 1951. Powell's policy proposal would mean abandoning of the asylum without a commensurate real build-up in local services:

> "To scatter the mentally ill in the community before we have made adequate provision for them is not a solution; in the long run not even for H.M. Treasury. Considered only in financial terms, any savings from fewer hospital inpatients might well be offset several times against more expenditure on the police forces, on prisons, and probation officers; more unemployment benefits measured as sickness benefits; more expenditure on drugs; more research to find out why crime is increasing." (Titmuss, 1961: 68)

The Jones' critique of Powell's policy. The debate over Powell's policy proposals continued in the years following the NAMH conference. The chief critic of the Health Minister's approach was a student of social policy and administration, Kathleen Jones. She noted in speeches and papers a number of flaws in the Powell approach to providing community care (Jones, 1964.). In fact, Powell's projections of the reduction in mental hospital beds from 3.4 per 1,000 in 1959 to 1.8 per 1,000 in 1975 could be in error because of economic changes, variation in the propensity of people to use mental health services, the adoption of new treatment techniques requiring longer residency, or the reductions in the effectiveness of long therapy. Fundamentally, Jones contended that Powell's ideological commitment to scaling down the NHS was conveniently reenforced by the Tooth   and

Brooke (1961) data projections. That is, given that the NHS represented a major achievement of the socialist-trade union movement, and that the policy of nationalization was anathema to an unreconstructed 19th-century liberal, it was natural that Powell was committed to scaling down the major public-sector institution. The Tooth-Brooke data only lent legitimacy to Powell's policy intentions, a point Powell denied when confronted by Jones with the charge that his policy's intent was to reduce NHS operations (Jones, 1975: personal communication).

Reform movements' relative impotence. Despite Titmuss, Jones, and others' objections, the debate over the intent of Powell's policy exposed relative impotence of the English reform movement in the face of attack on the mental health services. The Conservative Government had first deviated from the Percy Commission's recommendation for ten-year central government grants to local authorities to explicitly expand coordinated, community-based psychiatric services. Now, backed by the Tooth-Brooke "official" statistical evidence, Powell recommended dismantling the only other facilities that could serve the mentally disordered in the absence of a rapid expansion of alternative care facilities. Interestingly, the NAMH, and its Parliamentary allies, could not actively enlist elements of the government to do battle with Powell and the other opponents of the NAMH policy wishes. The English NAMH did not possess (as did the U.S. reformers) an autonomous, bureaucratic-based branch of the reform movement that had money to expend in service of mental health reform.

The fusion of psychiatric and somatic hospitals under the NHS administration, while not inhibiting therapeutic innovations, had resulted in a loss of autonomy and discretion at the ministerial level of health governance for the proponents of mental health reform. Coupled with the tradition of civil service administration of the day-to-day affairs of a ministry by well-rounded amatures, the British system of health care under NHS militated against the capturing or creation of a governmental bureau dedicated to mental health reform. Further, the organizations and procedures of the English legislative process were not founded on the committee system dominant in the U.S. Congress. As was noted, U.S. mental health reformers had been successful in cultivating and maintaining alliances with committee chairmen who could further the reform goals of both bureaucratic and associational members of the reform movement, thereby forging a mental health sub-government.

The Decline of the Asylum

Despite the objections of Powell's critics, the general outlines of his policy for English mental hospitals was partially realized. The data on hospitals utilized in England and Wales tell a story similar to admission and resident population statistics in the United States. In both nations, the numbers of persons in permanent residence in the classic, remote institution declined, though interestingly enough, the data show that the asylum endures despite efforts to abolish it legislatively and administratively.

Trends in mental hospital usage. By 1970 the English residential population in mental hospitals nearly reached the rate of 1.8 per 1,000 projected by Tooth and Brooke (1961): the 1954 rate per 1,000 was 3.44; the 1959 rate was 3.15 per 1,000; and the 1970 rate was 2.31 per 1,000. There is now evidence to suggest that maybe less than 1.0 per 1,000 may be sufficient (Brothwood, 1973; cf. Wing, et al., 1972).

These declines are a product of the decrease in the total numbers of patients in residence from the all-time high of 151,400 in 1954 to 133,200 in 1959, and finally to 103,300 in 1970 (Jones, 1972:359). These data suggest that though Tooth and Brooke may have made errors in calculating the rate of reduction, their projection of the trend was fairly accurate. The question is: to what is this decline due? There are a number of factors which explain this reduction: the liberalized 1959 admission laws; the continued use of psychotropic drug therapy; new ways of classifying hospital beds for census purposes; and, the introduction of local authority services. The following analysis reveals that other variables may account for the decline in hospital residency (see Table 3).

The rise in out-patient treatment. There has been a marked, real increase in the use of out-patient treatment to manage the mentally ills' symptomatology, helping reduce the need for prolonged hospitalization. The total number of new out-patients receiving such treatment increased 32 percent from 160,800 in 1959 to 212,600 in 1973. Total out-patient attendances at all treatment facilities increased 40 percent: from 1,158,400 in 1959 to 1,624,100 in 1973. As in the U.S., the changing locus of psychiatric care in England is, in part, a product of the introduction of psychotropic drugs, but it can also be seen as a result of an increased willingness to treat mental disorders without resorting to hospitalization. The 1959 Act, with its provisions for voluntary admission to treatment, facilitated the use of out-patient services for initial treatment and subsequent episodes of patient care.

The increase in utilization of day hospitals. The numbers of new, day patients at mental hospitals increased 94 percent from 16,300 in 1966 to 31,700 in 1973, total day attendances increased more dramatically from 1,082,400 in 1966 to 2,407,300 in 1973. The day-hospital concept is one that has been implemented with vigor. These numbers demonstrate that old facilities--even the remote, factory-like 19th-century mental hospital--can be converted to new uses, especially in a crowded, geographically compact country like England. In many cases day hospitals are a wing of the aging asylum that is converted to a day treatment center permitting patients to reside at home and yet receive daytime hospital treatment. Again, a combination of stabilizing psychotropic drugs, public policy changes, and therapeutic treatment innovations have created a new locus of psychiatric care.

The increased utilization of psychiatric departments in general hospitals. There has been a 53 percent increase in the use of psychiatric departments of general, district hospitals as the primary site of admissions for observation, diagnosis, and treatment. In 1964 only 15 percent of all psychiatric admissions for treatment were being handled by these relatively new psychiatric departments. Unfortunately, these data are not broken down by first admissions; 32 percent of the admissions were to mental hospitals and 3 per-

251

cent were admitted to geriatric hospitals. By 1973, the distribution of the site of all admissions had changed: mental hospitals admissions had declined to 74 percent, while the psychiatric departments experienced an increase to a 23 percent share of all admissions; geriatric hospitals' proportion remained the same at 3 percent (see Table 4).

While the locus of psychiatric care has not shifted as dramatically in England as in the U.S., these data on psychiatric departments in general hospitals do provide another bit of evidence that the 1959 legislation has changed the character of English psychiatric care within the NHS.

In sum, the data suggest that the decline in the residential population and the shift to new sites of care has been due to a number of factors, interacting with one another, to produce a change in the locus of psychiatric treatment. The hegemony of the 19th-century mental institution has been reduced by the introduction of the day-hospital, the use of out-patient clinics, and the development of psychiatric departments in general hospitals. Further, the utilization data reveal that the mental hospital has not been eliminated to date; that is, Powell's prediction of the demise of the asylum is not borne out by these trend data; and Jones and others' critique of the Powell policy and its impact has not been entirely verified. Both views of the future role of the mental hospital in British hospital-based psychiatric care did not foresee the adaptability of the hospital and did not realize the number of other factors that insured the future of the mental hospital in English psychiatric services.

The "new" long-stay patients. Tooth and Brooke (1961) assumed a linear reduction in the decline in mental hospital residential population. Wing and Hailey (1972) point to the phenomenon of the "new long-stay" patient in their detailed analysis of the utilization of psychiatric services in Camberwell, South London. Their analysis of the patient trend data show that a steady decline of long-stay patients will not result in the death of the asylum. The data show a growth in the number of patients requiring long-term psychiatric care, a growth that Tooth and Brooke did not foresee. That is, when the actual rate of reduction is plotted,

TABLE 3

Numbers and Rates (per 100,000) of Resident Patients in Mental Hospitals and Other Institutions in England and Wales for Selected Years from 1904 to 1970.

Year	Number	Rate
1904a	117,200	349
1909	128,200	366
1914b	138,100	377
1919	116,700	309
1924	130,300	339
1929	141,100	356
1934	150,300	371
1939	ND	ND
1944	ND	ND
1949	144,700	334
1954	151,400	344
1959c	133,200	290
1964	127,600	270
1969	105,600	220
1970	103,300	210

ND: No Data Reported

a. Data for 1904 and 1909 based on the Reports of the Lunacy Commissioners to determine the numbers of persons of "unsound mind," both "lunatics" and "idiots" whether in public asylums, private hospitals, nursing homes or other forms of care.

b. Data for 1914-1954 are numbers of patients in state institutions, mental nursing homes, general hospitals, and mental hospitals as reported in the Annual Reports of the Board of Control.

c. Resident patients in all mental institutions and psychiatric hospitals of the National Health Service, December 31st each year.

Source: Appendix tables 1, 3, and 4, pp. 356-358. In Kathleen Jones, A History of the Mental Health Services. London: Routledge and Kegan Paul, 1972.

TABLE 4

Total Admissions and Percentage Distribution of Admissions to England and Wales' Mental Hospital, General Hospital Psychiatric Departments, Geriatric Units, and Children's Units, 1964 and 1970-1973.

YEAR	TOTAL ADMISSIONS				PERCENTAGE DISTRIBUTION			
	Mental Hospitals	Psychiatric Units	Geriatric Units	Child Units	Mental Hospitals	Psychiatric Units	Geriatric Units	Child Units
1964	127,873	23,151	3,904	374	82%	15%	3%	< 1%
1970	172,931	32,665	4,275	532	78%	19%	2%	< 1%
1971	131,806	35,000	5,809	615	76%	20%	3%	< 1%
1972	129,683	38,984	5,849	636	74%	22%	3%	< 1%
1973	128,588	39,678	5,248	657	74%	23%	3%	< 1%

Source: Table A-3, p. 17. In DHSS Psychiatric Hospitals: In-Patient Statistics From the Mental Health Enquiry Year 1973, Statistical and Research Report No. 12. London, HMSO, 1974.

it reveals a curvilinear pattern; there is a buildup of "new," long-stay patients, suffering from senile dementia, schizophrenia, or requiring more extensive treatment than had been anticipated. These new, long-stay patients will not replace the losses due to the death and discharge of old long-stay patients. Thus, the Camberwell data suggest that the chronicity of these new, long-stay residents (mainly young schizophrenics) will require long-term care facilities but not at pre-1955 levels. Wing and Hailey (1972) note that:

> "The rate of recruitment to the long-stay group showed a definite fall off over the years [1964-70] for patients with dementia, though not for other patients." (Wing and Hailey: 168)

Therefore, the hospital will continue to be a feature of psychiatric services because it has proven to be adaptable to new therapeutic demands (day-hospital care, out-patient treatment), but also because its inpatient role will not be eliminated by the natural wastage of its resident patients. In a word, the asylum has not and will not wither away. Yet, does the NHS hospital remain important not just for all the above factors, but precisely because the mental health reform movement has not been successful in their efforts to require local authorities to construct alternatives to hospitalization? Recall that in the early 1970's nearly half of all U.S. psychiatric treatment episodes were occuring in out-patient departments of hospitals and that nearly another quarter were occuring in the NIMH's community mental health centers; in contrast, in England the mental hospital was still the site of nearly three quarters of all admissions.

Local authority psychiatric services. In contrast to U.S. CMHC-funded services, the English local authority psychiatric services have not been as lavishly funded, nor have they grown as dramatically as a locus of care. In economic conditions that have often times restricted the initiation of new services, local authorities have made efforts to increase their expenditures as well as to provide a greater range of services. The aggregate data show that local authority expenditures have increased 834 percent from fiscal year 1958-59 to fiscal year 1970-71, from 3,687 thousand

TABLE 5

Total Admissions and First Admissions to Mental Hospitals in England and Wales, 1964 to 1973.

YEAR	TOTAL ADMISSIONS	FIRST ADMISSIONS
1964	155,302a	75,411a
1965	155,554b	81,369b
1966	160,523b	83,699b
1967	165,095b	87,308b
1968	170,527b	90,699b
1969	171,714a	90,076a
1970	172,931a	63,480a
1971	173,230a	61,904a
1972	175,152a	60,118a
1973	174,171c	58,450c
1974	170,827c	56,140c
1975	175,111c	57,376c

a. From Table A-3, p. 17, DHSS Statistical and Research Report No. 12, London: HMSA, 1973.

b. From Table 6, p. 360. In K. Jones. A History of the Mental Health Services. London: Routledge and Kegan Paul.

c. Data since 1973 are for England alone, and is thus not strictly comparable with previous time-series including Wales. From Table 9.4, 9.5, pp. 152-153, DHSS Health and Personal Social Statistics for England, 1977. London: HMSO.

pounds to 34,448 thousand pounds. The percentage of local authority expenditures in relation to NHS mental hospital expenditures rose over the same period from 14.6 percent to 20.5 percent, a 40 percent increase. In percentage terms, the growth of local authority mental illness expenditures has grown less rapidly than the absolute increases; this is because NHS mental hospital expenditures were also increasing. Further, the local authorities mental illness expenditures in the NHS mental illness budget is remarkably close to the share for all local authority expenditures: from 1958-59 to 1970-71, all local authority mental health care expenditures rose from 18.5 percent to 21.8 percent of all NHS expenditures; thus, mental illness expenditures have narrowed a 3.9 percent gap in 1958-59 to 1.8 percent in 1970-71.

Therefore, in the absence of explicit requirements that local authorities expend money for community-based psychiatric services, such services did not grow as rapidly as envisioned by the advocates of mental health reform. The English case suggests that if a policy of community-based psychiatric care is going to at least partially meet its goals, such a policy needs the full backing of central governmental authorities. Fiscally-conservative localities have other spending priorities, and localities have been noticeably hostile to the placement in their community of psychiatric patients. Thus, ironically, though the social scientific evidence suggests community care is more desireable for most psychiatric patients, such treatment must be imposed by central governments on many reluctant localities. In the absence of a strong central government commitment to constructing and staffing local psychiatric services, the English mental health reformers have been consistently frustrated in their efforts to obtain implementation of community care.

Swedish Psychiatric Reform in the 1960's

Like their English counterparts, the Swedish psychiatric services have undergone administrative integration into somatic services while the laws pertaining to patient admission, detention, and release have been liberalized. The question for a comparative analysis of English, Swedish, and U.S. national mental health policy-making is this: did this organizational and legal reform further the goal of commu-nity psychiatric care?

Rationalization of Somatic and Psychiatric Services

Prior to 1967 reforms, Sweden had a dual system of health care: the central government administered the mental hospitals and the county councils (<u>landsting</u>) operated the hospital services. In 1967 the National Board of Health and Welfare (<u>Socialstyrelsen</u>) departed from this century old division of functions and implemented 1962 legislation that authorized the transfer of all 25 psychiatric hospitals to the 25 <u>landsting</u>.[14] The policy goals of this restructur-ing were several. As in England, the Sweden health admini-strators hoped to end the isolation of psychiatry by inte-grating the management of these hitherto separate branches of the health services. Health officials hoped the goal of altering the locus of psychiatric care from 19th-century-style asylums to psychiatric departments of general hospi-tals would be more effectively achieved if the administra-tion of these two services was consolidated. Further, the policy goal of creating a community-based, out-patient psy-chiatric treatment might be more fully implemented if the <u>landsting</u> assumed full responsibility for all aspects of psychiatric treatment (Rexed, 1971). Until the 1967 trans-fer the Board of Health and Welfare has retained its overall supervisorial functions: <u>Socialstyrelsen's</u> psychiatric-care department still sets broad policy with the <u>landsting</u>, moni-tors trends in patient care, gathers national statistics, inspects complaints about patient care, and interprets the laws and regulations. In this way, the devolution of autho-rity to the <u>landsting</u> had been accompanied by continued direction from the national board, retaining the Swedish tradition of national board policy guidance, albeit in an altered form.[15] Formally, the mid-60's mental hospital administration reorganization has rendered Sweden's psychia-tric services much more comparable, organizationally, to U.S. services: localities now have a greater direct say in the operation of mental health services.

From a policy analytic perspective, the question is: has this transfer of responsibilities to county authorities and functional re-alignment achieved the stated reform policy goals? This question can be answered only after the reform of psychiatric admission and detention laws also has been considered. The reorganization of psychiatric services alone could not alter the patterns of patient treatment; the legal barriers to modern, out-patient treatment had to be removed to effect the utilization of these services.

Modernization of the Swedish detention laws. In part, the slower, more deliberate pace of Swedish social reform explains why Sweden has lagged behind England and the U.S., in adopting legislation that facilitates voluntary, out-patient treatment for mental disorders. Though the 1929 Laws governing detention of the mentally disordered had been revised, no major modernization revisions occured until the 1960's. New legislation was finally enacted in 1966 (SFS 1966: 293) that incorporated the new orientations to psychiatric care (Crafoord, 1976). The updated legislation sought to restrict the conditions under which one could be involuntarily admitted for psychiatric treatment and to encourage voluntary admissions to out-patient care. In this way law makers and mental health professionals hoped that transfer of control of psychiatric hospitals to counties would result in an increased use of new modes of psychiatric treatment. Yet only an analysis of Swedish hospital utilization data can tell us if these changes in the detention legislation and administrative reforms have had the desired effects.

Changing loci of care in Sweden. Hospital and clinic utilization statistics reveal that these administrative changes, combined with new treatment modalities, have begun to alter the character of Swedish psychiatric care. For example, the number of psychiatric hospital beds had been growing up until 1960 when there were 26,153 hospital beds available in the classic mental hospital. In 1973, this number had dropped to 19,984. As in England the numbers of beds available in psychiatric departments in general hospitals had increased from 1,334 in 1960 to 8,389 in 1972 (Socialstyrelsen, 1974: tables 3: 1 and 4). Admissions to treatment also reveal the "revolving door" phenomenon experienced in England, the U.S., and all European nations for which we have data (May, 1976: 34-44). The numbers of all admissions to psychiatric treatment stood at 37,603 in 1960; in 1970, shortly after the reforms of psychiatric detention legislation and the transfer of mental hospitals to the landsting, the total number of annual admissions rose to 96,739; by 1973 this number was 110,449 (Socialstyrelsen, 1973: table A4).

These developments all suggest that the previously mental hospital dominated psychiatric services can be altered by the revisions of the psychiatric detention laws as well as by the changes in the organization of mental health services. What these Swedish developments also suggest is that the dramatic changes in the site of psychiatric care, as experienced in the U.S., can only take place when reform mandates specifically authorize the construction and staffing of non-hospital, community-based psychiatric care. For example, in Sweden, 70 percent of all psychiatric beds are still located in the classic mental hospitals. And though there were 9,671 places available in mental nursing homes in 1973, this constituted only 26 percent of all psychiatric care beds. Therefore, the hegemony of the classic mental hospital persists in a health care delivery system that is itself hospital dominated. Among European nations Sweden ranks second only to Ireland in 1972 in the number of mental health facility beds per 1,000 population: Ireland ranked number one with 5.8, in comparison with Sweden's 4.9; Norway's 4.8, Finland's 4.7, and England's ratio of 3.8 (May, 1976: figure 4). Thus, while Sweden has been altering the character of its psychiatric services, the dramatic shifts to community care experienced in the United States have not occurred.16 The explanation for the underdevelopment of Swedish community-care alternatives to the classic mental hospital is similar to our explanation for the lagging local authority psychiatric services in England: the absence of a powerful, bureaucratically-based, dedicated cadre of mental health reformers.

The underdeveloped mental health reform movement. Up until the 1960's most of Sweden's mentally ill were treated by psychiatrists in mental hospitals run by the central government and administered by the tenured health bureau-

TABLE 6

Numbers of Mental Hospital, Mental Nursing Home, and Psychiatric Departments of
General Hospitals in Sweden from 1950 to 1972.

Year	All Mental Hospital Bedsa	Mental Hospitalsa	Mental Nursing Homesa	Psych. Dept. in General Hospitalsb
1950	28,300	23,016	5,284	NA
1960	32,940	26,153	6,787	1,334
1970	30,288	21,753	8,535	5,774
1971	28,835	20,097	8,738	7,131
1972	28,935	19,984	8,951	7,389

NA: Not Available

a. Data for these facilities comes from Table 3.1, "Hospital beds, official number
    at end of year," In Abstracts from Public Health in Sweden, 1972. Stockholm:
    Socialstyrelsen, 1974.

b. Data for these facilities comes from Table 4, "Bed-Strength development of
    departments in general hospitals, official number of beds," In Abstracts from
    Public Health in Sweden, 1972. Stockholm: Socialstyrelsen, 1974.

crats of the National Board of Medicine (later the omnibus Board of Health and Welfare). These administrators are not comparable to the reform advocates who founded NIMH and instituted new community-based mental health services, (Felix, et al.), nor to individual hospital psychiatrists who initiated "open door" policies (e.g., T. P. Rees), nor to mental health activist-politicians who assisted the framing of new mental patient detention laws (e.g., Kenneth Robinson). Rather, revision of Sweden's 1929 lunacy law and reorganization of mental hospital service proceeded in typical, non-controversial Swedish fashion as the product of official, national board policy deliberations. True, in the shift in responsibility for mental hospitals or in proposals for new mental health laws, the psychiatric profession, the voluntary mental health association, the legal community, and others were consulted and their suggestions solicited. But at the end of these policy decisions, the very same professionals, who were in control of Sweden's hospital dominated mental health services before "reforms," preside over "new" psychiatric services that retain their hospital bias in the delivery of mental health care.

In short, Sweden has not witnessed the creation of a bureaucratically-based, reform-dedicated mental health activists, convinced of the necessity of transforming the character of psychiatric care. Sweden has instead experienced a number of shifts and adjustments that have modernized the hospital-based mode of psychiatric treatment (e.g., new laws that foster voluntary admissions) and created the opportunity for new modes of hospital-based psychiatric care (Furman, 1965; cf. Vail, 1968: 68-115).

Conclusions

The goal of this chapter was to demonstrate the impact that variation mental health reform movements can have on these three nations' psychiatric services. By comparing the modifications of national mental health policy in three nations, this chapter illuminated the crucial role played by mental health reformers in creating and implementing these policies. Specifically, the cases of the United States, England, and Sweden demonstrate that the community care

TABLE 7

Numbers and Rates (per 100,000) of Resident Patients in Mental Hospitals and Other Mental Health Facilities in Sweden for Various Years from 1930 to 1973.

	MENTAL HOSPITALSa		MENTAL NURSING HOMES	
Year	Number	Rate	Number	Rate
1930	15,743	256	NA	NA
1940	22,272	349	2,401	38
1950	24,720	350	4,206	60
1960	28,054	375	6,354	84
1970	28,253	350	8,785	108
1971	27,874	344	9,100	112
1972	28,052	345	9,382	115
1973	28,021	344	9,671	119

NOTES: Due to inexplicable reasons the hospital bed totals reported in this Socialstyrelsen Publication do not correspond to hospital bed data reported in <u>Abstracts from Public Health in Sweden, 1974.</u>   Tables 3.1 and 4.

NA: Not Available.

a.   The data are for the numbers of mental hospital beds available at the end of the year, December 31st.

Source: Table A4, in <u>Förhandredovisning av vissa tabeller</u>, i AHS 1973, (Stockholm: Socialstyrelsen, 1973).

TABLE 8

Total Admissions and Admission Rates (per 100,000) to Psychiatric Facilities in Sweden for Selected Years from 1930 to 1973.

	MENTAL HOSPITALS		MENTAL NURSING HOMES	
Year	Total Admissions	Rate of Admissions	Total Admissions	Rate of Admissions
1930	7,154	116	NA	NA
1940	8,416	132	955	15
1950	19,756	281	1,320	19
1960	37,603	502	3,983	53
1970	96,739	1,197	6,018	75
1971	102,060	1,258	6,360	78
1972	107,528	1,323	5,973	73

NA: Not Available

Source: Table A4 In <u>Förhandsredovisning av vissa tabeller</u>, i AHS 1973. Stockholm: Socialstyrelsen; 1973.

policy will be most likely to succeed when such a policy can be imposed upon often-times unwilling localities by a powerful, central government-based advocate of reform. Thus, ironically the successful implementation of a community care policy will be enhanced when a nationally-based mental health authority can apply the pressure necessary to obtain local authority compliance with a central government's objectives. The U.S. case gives a clear example of the success of this strategy of policy design and implementation.

The case of England illustrates how a well-intentioned reform movement, with numerous allies in Parliament, could not fully realize their policy objectives in the absence of a firm bureaucratic-base for reform activities. In addition, the local authority discretion in implementing a new national mental health policy frustrated national reform objectives. This organizational discretion in policy implementation, coupled with continuing economic constraints, has thwarted the National Health Service in its efforts to meet national policy objectives. Thus, ironically, in a nation much more formally centralized than the U.S., the persistence of local governmental implementation discretion, combined with the under-development of the bureaucratic-base of a reform movement, has contributed to under-development of mental health community care.

The Swedish case illustrates how the continuing hegemony of professional doctor-administrators in a psychiatric service that is both hospital-based and is infused with an organic view of mental disorders will minimize efforts to establish non-hospital-based alternative modes of treatment. This case, like the English example, also reveals the necessary connection between a dynamic bureaucratically-based reform movement and the achievement of reform objectives. A bureau--in alliance with professional and associational allies of mental health reform--is the most effective force for securing specialized community services for the mentally disordered. In sum, the different cases of England and Sweden reveal the importance of the bureaucratic-based, yet dedicated, reformers in a campaign to adopt a new national psychiatric policy and alter the nature of psychiatric treatment.

1. For Yolles the preferred service model was NIMH's own demonstration project in Maryland's Prince George's County. Since 1946 this project had been operated by NIMH to provide state and local governments with an example of how a community-based treatment program could operate. Given that NIMH was designated by the inter-agency task force as the agency to provide Americans with a new mental disease management, it used the Prince George's facility as its policy template. NIMH would later have to fight to retain this designation, but in the initial stages of policy adoption, the reformers entrenched within the bureaucracy were able to insure that their preferred policy proposal was adopted, casting the die for its ultimate adoption in the national implementation phase of the community mental health care's life cycle (Foley, 1975: 35-36).

2. While Felix wanted the mental hospital qualitatively altered, he did not believe it was politically wise to by-pass the states entirely; he was supported in this view by Moynihan and Jones (Foley, 1975: 39). The state mental hospitals would remain major centers for treatment until the massive federal network was con-structed, and hence, required continued encouragement and support to implement the latest treatment modali-ties; elimination of the state institutions was not feasible, given the constitutional realities of the federal-state division of responsibilities.

3. The specific programmatic aspects of the agreement forwarded to Kennedy were these:

    i)   categorical programs in which federal grants-in-aid assisted in the construction of comprehensive mental health centers;

    ii) operating, staffing grants;

    iii) comprehensive, state planning grants in which

states and localities developed an inventory of extant resources and planned for future needs;

iv) federal support to improve the quality of service in state and county hospitals;

v) encouragement of private insurance carriers to include psychiatric treatment in their coverage offerings;

vi) professional training grants to colleges and universities to expand the pool of qualified personnel;

vii) federal support for mental health research.

4. Foley's (1975) interviews with Felix and Fein discovered that Kennedy explicitly rejected Celebrezze's recommendation and ignored the Bureau of the Budget's objections and told the HEW Secretary to put the staffing costs into the legislative proposal. The NIMH proposals thus won Presidential approval, over his HEW Secretary's objections and BoB's disapproval (Foley: 44).

5. The New Frontier's legislative proposals had been blocked by the Congressional conservative coalition of Southern Democrats and Republicans, the fourth political party (cf. Burns, 1963: 204ff). In order to minimize the opposition to this legislative proposal, the legislation was designed so that the bulk of the interagency recommendations could be implemented through increased NIMH appropriation requests; only the construction and staffing of centers required new authorizations. The bill's construction titles were modeled on a mode of financing health care with which Congress was familiar and which the American Medical Association would not find objectionable: the 1946 Hill-Burton formula for support of hospital construction. Under the mental health centers act the federal contribution would range from 45% minimum to a 75% maximum for support of facility construction; the staffing grants were to range 75% federal support in the first fifteen months, declining to 65% in year two, then 45% and 30% in the third and fourth years.

6. The Joint Commission's director Jack Ewalt strengthened the arguments for community health centers by reinterpreting the meaning of the Joint Commission's recommendation so as to include the Kennedy concept.

> "Ewalt's testimony was crucial, since it created the political myth that the Joint Commission suggested a bill designed to direct the major federal effort into the community and not into the state mental hospital system." (Foley, 1975: 65)

7. Earlier, in the mid-50's debate over the Congressional resolutions calling for the Joint Commission studies, the split between the AMA and the APA was also evident. APA spokesman Dr. Daniel Blain said:

> "...when we speak of a national program, I do not think we have in mind a detailed blue-print for everyone to follow in exact detail, but rather to focus on the major problems and all the possible ways of approaching solutions." (Blain in the U.S. Senate Hearings, 1955)

Blain's comments can be interpreted as attempting to allay the anxieties of the more conservative AMA that viewed the Joint Commission's recommendations as a prelude to an expanded federal health care service.

Thus, the AMA spokesman took a narrower view of the government's role in health care. Dr. Leo Bartemeir spoke for the AMA in 1955 testimony:

> "We emphasize, however, that our support is limited to temporary Federal programs in this area, since it is our sincere conviction that the entire question of defining local and Federal responsibilities in the public health field should be carefully analyzed by Congress." (Bartemeir in testimony before U.S. Senate, 1955)

8. NIMH's 1963-64 struggle to keep CMHC programs was pre-dated by a late 1950's early 1960's battle to divest NIMH of some of its functions (cf. Foley, 1975). Having won mental health centers construction grants meant that the policy "back-door" was open, and the mental health reform sub-government could work to realize the goal of community care.

9. The concept of community is often used and abused in politics with consequences that are usually never anti-cipated by those invoking the concept. I think that what the framers of U.S. mental health legislation and programs meant by the term community is the locality and network of family, friends, work, and leisure which make up the "everyday life" of those persons residing in the locality. The question is, can this be a community which provides "care" for the "mentally ill"? That is, what are the assumptions underlying the belief that the locality of catchment area coincide the with supportive network assumed to be more likely than the remote mental hospital to improve the condition of the patient (cf. Mutso, 1975)? Even in England, a more ethnically homo-geneous society than the U.S., with strong traditions and identifications with village, town, county, and region, the definition of community when applied to mental health care is not clear. The 1960 conference of the National Association for Mental Health Minister of Health Enoch Powell unveiled a new policy for mental hospitals. Powell's plan for the elimination of the Victorian and Edwardian-era mental hospitals sparked a debate on what would constitute the community care alternative to the old facilities. Though many agreed with the need to find alternatives, many felt Powell was only seeking to save money and was not confronting the issue of the costs of providing new modes of care delivery. Others, Richard Titmuss among them, felt Powell's proposals were begging the questions: would the facilities and programs provided by the local authorities constitute community care? In other words, what would community care mean for what kinds of patients?

Thus, this confusion over just what the term community means is trans-Atlantic phenomenon. The Chief of the New York State Mental Health Research Unit, in a paper read at the Syracuse Psychiatric Hospital in 1963 said:

> "'I do not know what community psychiatry is. Community psychiatry is the name that will be applied to what we will do in the next ten years... we can expect the words community psychiatry to cover a multitude of different programs.'" (Quoted in Connery, 1967:475)

These examples illustrate the vagueness of the concept of psychiatric community care. Vagueness has, I believe, unanticipated, yet highly significant consequences for the implementation of the current community mental health legislation, and other similar great society programs (Moynihan, 1969; cf. Estes, 1979).

10. While testifying Felix had suggested that the nation ought to construct and staff 2,000 centers; he arrived at this number by simply dividing the nation's approximate population at the time by 100,000 (Foley, 1975: 92). This number of 2,000 centers was not based on an assessment that the center to population ratio was the correct one; Felix had not conducted research to demonstrate that 1 center per 100,000 population was going to increase access to treatment, improve the quality of mental health care, or prevent unnecessary hospitalization. Rather, this 1 per 100,000 population ratio was a promise of Felix's that had to be justified in some way after the legislation was adopted.

11. The forces for mental health reform in England have still not grasped the significance of this preservation of local authorities' discretion in fully complying with the 1959 law's intent. The critics of Britain's NHS point to the failure to live up to this and previous legislation yet do not seem to understand why NIMH was successful with CMHC. That is, English reformers do not

understand how the U.S. mental health reformers presided over the design, adoption, and implementation of a major capital expenditure program, and why NIMH succeeded in this way and they did not. Before NHS, the network of county hospitals and clinics for the treatment of the insane, while admittedly antiquated, was under local control. NHS transferred the control of these county hospitals to hospital boards under the terms of nationalization. Thus, the physical plant which could have been employed for new purposes was not available to local authorities. Local authorities were left with a mandate to provide community care without any facilities. The construction of totally new facilities was required of local authorities if they were to meet the law's intent. The English mental health policy formulation provides us with yet another example of the process whereby governments commit themselves to broad policy goals and then undermine those goals by failing to assemble adequate machinery for the implementation of these goals. In a word, England's community mental health policy was "ill-fated:"

> "The term 'ill-fated' implies a judgment, and that is precisely what I offer: to wit, that the program is carried out in such a way as to produce a minimum of social change its sponsors desired, and bring about a maximum increase in the opposition to such change, of the kind they feared." (Moynihan, 1969: lv)

12. The 1959 Mental Health Act did represent an important breakthrough in the treatment of the mentally ill. Some of the law's chief accomplishments were:

    i.   modern definitions of mental illness and subnormality were entered into the statute books;
    ii. a hospital was defined so as to include any specialized facility and accommodation of local authorities;
    iii. the Board of Control, heir to Lord Ashley's hospital inspection commission was abolished and new Mental Health Review Tribunals took over their

function of reviewing cases of illegal detention and patient discharge requests;

iv. informal admission to any NHS facility was not sanctioned, so as to encourage patients to come for treatment; the separate designation of mental illness beds and all others was abolished;

v. safeguards against illegal detention, patient abuse, leave of absence, discharge, and guardianship were updated, reflecting a new humanism in psychiatric treatment.

13. Powell's projections of mental health hospital bed requirements were based on a study prepared by Dr. G. C. Tooth and Eilene Brooke for the Ministry of Health and Registrar General's Office. This report was published in The Lancet in April, 1961 and was reflected in the Ministry of Health circular MH (61) 25, a policy position paper to guide health administrators. Tooth and Brooke used data on hospital residency from 1954 to 1959 for projecting trends in bed-occupancy, and hence the need or lack thereof for new facilities in the 1970's. The decline in residents from a high of 3.4 per 1,000 in 1954 to 2.9 per 1,000 (151,400 to 133,200) represented a real change, one which if projected into the 1970's would yield a rate of 1.8 per 1,000 in 1975. In a 1962 adress to the Royal Medico-Psychological Association, Jones attacked the Tooth and Brooke projections. She noted that residential patient trends needed to be examined with the following caveats in mind:

i. difficulty in making long-term projections from a limited data base;

ii. limitations in the reduction in mental patient populations by the wide-spread application of drug therapy;

iii. administrative policy changes, not any advances in therapy techniques, accounts for much of the reduction;

iv. statistical reclassification of beds accounts for part of the drop in patient populations. (see Jones, 1962)

271

These issues sparked a pilot study in the Leeds Area Hospital Authority that was designed to evaluate the future need of hospital beds. The results reported in The Lancet (August 29, 1964) showed that the Ministry of Health's Hospital Plan for England and Wales (1962) projected the numbers of hospital beds would be reduced to 5,840 by 1975 due to natural attrition. Jones and her colleagues found that at least for the Leeds Region the range of need of beds needed to accomodate the aged, chronic schizophrenics, untreatable psychotics, and others, would be between 8,645 and 9,455. A gap in services would have to be made up some how. The record of local authority construction and staffing of alternatives to hospitals suggested that the families of mental patients would most likely be the ones to fill the gap (Gore, et al., 1964; cf. Jones, 1964).

14. On January 1, 1967 the 1962 law (SFS: 1962: 242) that changed the ownership of psychiatric hospitals was implemented. This five year gap between enactment and implementation is yet another example of the deliberate, unhurried pattern of Swedish social policy making (Anderson, 1972: 74-75).

15. The 25 landsting have formed an association and act as an interest group, lobbying the Riksdag and the relevant national boards to insure that their concerns are being addressed. The landstings' Association of Swedish County Communes (Svenska Landstings for bundet) also provides its members with legal, administrative, and budgetary advice, represent the landsting in salary negotiations with the employees public workers trade unions, publish journals and engage in other educational activities, operate central puchasing services, and the like. "In general, they have through long practice come to act as pressure groups representing the interests of local governments vis-a-vis the state" (Board, 1970: 223).

16. These data were reported to the European office of the World Health Organization in a 1972 survey of the 27 national mental health services. Mental health facility beds include all beds in mental hospitals, psychiatric departments in general hospitals, and mental nursing home beds; facilities for the mentally retarded are excluded in this comparison. Interestingly, Ireland consistently ranks the highest on many bed/population ratios because the successful Irish Sweepstakes continually generates money for the expansion of the Republic of Ireland's hospital facilities. Also, it is not accidental that Sweden's ratios are so close to those of Finland and Norway: both of these nations were at various times governed by Sweden and the pattern of convergence persists today, even in hospital bed/population ratios (May, 1976).

CHAPTER IX

THE FUTURE PROSPECTS OF MENTAL HEALTH REFORM
IN AN ERA OF SCARCE RESOURCES:
THE CASES OF THE UNITED STATES AND ENGLAND

Up until 1970, the mental health reform movements in the United States, England, and Sweden all had succeeded in accomplishing the main reform agenda goals. However, the decade of the 1970's marked a beginning of challenges to the programs won by mental health reformers in United States and England. The assumptions that had guided the elements of the coalition for reform were questioned in these two nations. The desireability of continuing and expanding governmental financial support for mental health services was evaluated. Political allies of mental health reform were often no longer present to defend the previous decades policy victories. Economic conditions created increasing competition among governmental services for scarce resources. Further, the very policy successes of reformers in the 1960's made it more difficult to duplicate such policy victories in the 1970's. The goals for many American and English mental health reformers was merely retaining policy advances won in the previous decade.

The Conservative Challenge to U.S. Mental Health Reforms and Reformers

In 1969 the mental health reformers faced their most serious challenge to date when the Republican Administration of President Richard M. Nixon proposed to dismantle service programs of NIMH. Nixon's policy, the "New Federalism", was presented as a renewed partnership between the national and state governments. The policy's centerpiece was the allocation of block grants, under the label of Federal Revenue Sharing, to state and local governments. The grants were to not only to give local authorities greater discretion in setting their own spending priorities, but also to enable the Nixon administration to attempt to disassemble the direct-service programs enacted during the Kennedy-Johnson years (cf. Estes, 1979).[1]

The mental health centers were identified for elimination from the federal budget and for transfer to the states and localities. Local governments desiring to continue funding the community mental health centers would not require it of them. The federal government would grant states discretion in their use of revenue sharing monies, and many would probably choose equipment over services. The Nixon assault on the centers, and hence on NIMH itself, began in earnest with HEW Secretary Casper Weinberger leading the attack. 513 centers had been constructed, and 75 more were operating without federal funds (New York Times, March 22, 1971). Weinberger argued that the federal government had fulfilled its obligation to initiate a new mode of managing the mentally disordered. Now the states and localities ought to assume their funding burden.

> "Federal support for developing community mental health centers should be seen both for what it is and for what it was originally intended to be--a demonstration project that helped set in motion a major new trend. It was nevet intended to be a categorical permanent aid program, and it whould not be transformed into one simply because it already exists." (Weinberger in San Francisco Chronicle, October 5, 1973)

Thus, the Nixon Administration's overt position was that the CMHC ought not to be a continuing federal categorical grant program. Along with all the War on Poverty and related social programs, CMHC's ought to be supported by those governments that believe in these programs.

However, the covert policy of the Nixon Administration was somewhat different than the call for a "New Federalism." By turning the funding responsibility over to the states and localities, the Republicans hoped to kill off programs they found ideologically objectionable. Nixon and his advisers trusted in the inherent fiscal conservatism of local governments, hoping that the social reforms of the 60's would die at the hands of tight-fisted local officials.

CMHC's could not only be eliminated from the federal budget, but also would fare poorly at the hands of local politicians reluctant to burden taxpayers with a continuing obligation to support expensive psychiatric services, especially when states and localities were already paying for their own network of mental hospitals and local clinics.

The mental health reform lobby re-mobilized. The U.S. mental health reform movement's powerful Washington, D.C. lobby was again mobilized to defeat Nixon's proposed destruction of the CMHC center concept. The character of the late-60's lobby had altered due to a number of personnel changes: Dr. Stanley Yolles had retired as NIMH director, succeeded by Dr. Bertram S. Brown; Senator Lister Hill had retired, leaving a void in the U.S. Senate Committee on Labor and Public Welfare; Congressman Fogarty's untimely death in 1968 had removed NIMH's staunch House of Representatives ally. But the lobby, though missing Felix, Hill, and the rest, was still a potent political force as Nixon, Weinberger, et al. soon discovered, mainly because of an addition to its ranks, CMHC centers themselves.

Like state asylum directors of the 19th century, the directors of CMHC facilities had formed an organization, the National Council of Community Mental Health Centers (NCCMHC). It was to be a new, vital element in the mental health reform coalition, which included the already bureaucratically-based reformers of NIMH, the State and Territorial Mental Health Program Directors, the National Association for Mental Health, the American Psychological Association, the American Psychiatric Association, NIMH training grant recipient universities and colleges, and others. The NCCMHC was fostered by Yolles during his tenure as NIMH director and formed a new element in the interlocking mental health reform network. Benefiting directly from an ever increasing NIMH budget, the NCCMHC has a vested interest in the outcome of HEW appropriation votes. With Hill and Fogarty gone, this new addition to the reform movement coalition played a key role in the Congressional lobbying campaigns, educating new members of Congress about mental diseases and the role CMHC played in combatting them (Foley, 1975: 126-127; cf. Felicetti, 1975: 35-43; 52-67).

The crucial test for the enlarged mental health lobby was this Nixon-Weinberger "de-funding" effort. The mobilized lobby secured on March 27, 1973 Senate passage of NIMH appropriations using the testimony of American Psychological Association President Dr. B. E. Moore and American Psychiatric Association head Dr. A. M. Freedman. These experts provided the Senate with arguments to continue CMHC funding; "de-funding" would result in a decrease in the number of psychiatrists, as well as a dramatic reduction in the availability of psychiatric services for the poor (in 1972, 53% or 846,336 of CMHC clients earned less than $5,000). The campaign was effective. The House of Representatives was overwhelmingly in favor of continuing CMHC funding, and on March 23, 1973 it voted 372-1 for CMHC.

In May, 1973, 350 mental health professionals arrived in Washington, D.C. to lobby for the CMHC concept. They were drawn from the National Association for Mental Health, the National Council of Community Mental Health Centers, the American Psychiatric Association, the National Association of Social Workers, and the National Committee Against Mental Illness; these persons met with over 305 Congressmen and Senators. In addition, their organizations launched a mail campaign to follow-up on their personal lobbying. Accepting defeat on June 19, 1973 the Nixon Administration agreed to a one-year appropriation extension, hoping to defeat the lobby the next year (Fellicetti, 1975: 67).

The creation of a new, independent bureau. As part of the Republican proposed functional realignment of bureaus and agencies, certain Public Health Service bureaus were restructured. NIMH was placed in a new federal agency with two new institutes, the National Institute on Alcohol Abuse and Alcoholism and the National Institute on Drug Abuse. This new branch of the PHS was named the Alcohol, Drug Abuse, and Mental Health Administration (ADAMHA). Though the new agency's creation supposedly reflected the Nixon Administration's commitment to wage war on drug abuse, budgetary cut-backs plagued the new agency. In 1974, when the ADAMHA budget was $399.4 million, the new fiscal year appropriation was reduced to $367.5 million. This budget was also eroded by inflation; further, the usual three-year funding commitment was not forthcoming from HEW Secretary

Casper Weinberger (New York Times, February 23, 1974). Thus, the mental health movement was threatened not only with the loss of CMHC programs, but also had to contend with the Nixon Administration's efforts to reorganize--and intentionally underfund--the bureaucratic base of the reform movement. Not suprisingly, these cut-backs in NIMH appropriations, coupled with reorganization moves, left many convinced that the Nixon Administration had adopted a multipronged attack on the mental health movement and its past legislative victories.

Subgovernment for mental health triumphs. As the events of the so-called Watergate scandle unfolded and consumed Nixon and his staff, NIMH and ADAMHA were freed briefly from direct White House pressure, though inflation continued to erode the NIMH budgets. Once President Gerald R. Ford assumed office, the battle against the CMHC Act resumed. A fiscal conservative, Ford was also convinced that NIMH ought to withdraw from the psychiatric service business. The Democratic-dominated Congress, responsive to the bureaucratically-based reformers and their allies, disagreed; and the House and Senate overrode the objections of HEW Secretary Weinberger. The House voted 359 to 12 on August 12, 1974 to continue CMHC funding and added detailed administrative requirements to the appropriations bill. The Congressional specifications of administrative requirements were felt to be necessary to prevent the impounding of funds. The Nixon administration had been impounding HEW appropriations until U.S. District Judge Gerhard Gesell of the District of Columbia had directed the President's Office of Management and Budget to spend legally authorized monies. Now the Congress wanted to insure its will was carried out by a recalcitrant Administration, and so detailed specifications were added to the bills.

Despite the executive branch's objections, both Houses of Congress followed the recommendations of the mental health within and without Congress. Happily, the anti-Nixon interests of a Democratic Congress, of NIMH, the National Council of Community Mental Health Centers, the National Association of State Mental Health Program Directors, the National Mental Health Association, and others coincided. Congress was eager to assert itself as a co-equal branch of government after the abuses of executive power by the Nixon Administration, and the mental health reform movement sought to maintain control over its service programs. Every bill opposed by the executive branch thus became a symbol of the Congressional determination and ability to act as a counter-balance to the Presidency. The White House opposition to the extension of CMHC was thus transformed into one of many struggles for dominance between two branches of government. Fortunately, interests of the mobilized lobby of the mental health reform movement and Congress coincided, with the result the CMHC appropriations requests passed with "veto-proof" margins. Thus, the Senate Committee on Labor and Public Welfare followed the House's overwhelming vote by reporting a bill to continue health service delivery programs and health revenue sharing. Senator Edward M. Kennedy, who introduced this bill (SB 3280), was both a literal and spiritual heir to the leadership role of the mental health reform movement. As a member of Lister Hill's Committee on Labor Public Welfare, Kennedy carried on the family tradition of supporting the expansion of the federal government's health sector. In the case of SB 3280, the combined forces of the mental health reform lobby support, Senator Kennedy, other liberals, and general Congressional hostility towards the Nixon Administration would insure Senate passage of the CMHC Act extension. The House and Senate compromise was reached in November, 1974. The Senate agreed to the compromise by a voice vote on December 9; the House approved it by a 372-14 margin on December 9, 1974. On December 25, 1974, President Ford vetoed the Health Revenue Sharing and Health Service Act of 1974, including its Title II, Community Mental Health Centers. In 1975 Ford's veto of CMHC funding was overturned because the coalition of community mental health center directors, state mental health program officials, the mental health associations, and NIMH was successful in mobilizing the sub-government for mental health. In sum, the alliance between these community-care advocates and key legislators insured that the Nixon and Ford Administration's attack on CMHC Acts funded.

Mental Health Reform Gains in the Carter Years

With the election of President Jimmy Carter, mental health reformers were able to again attempt to expand the policy gains won under the Kennedy and Johnson Administrations. Carter was committed to forming a President's Commission on Mental Health to review the latest psychiatric research findings, to evaluate CMHC and other mental health, drug abuse, alcohol control, and related programs, and finally to suggest new directions for future federal programs. Mental health reformers within and without the government thus once again had in the White House an ally in its campaign to increase the level of research and training grants and to expand the scope of CMHC's service (Koran, 1978; cf. President's Commission on Mental Health, 1978).

The reporting of the President's Commission on Mental Health: recurring concerns. Mental health reformers found the newly elected Democratic President Jimmy Carter a politician committed to furthering the goals identified by the subgovernment for community care. Executive order No. 11973 issued on February 17, 1977 established a Presidential Commission that placed the President's wife, Rosalynn Carter, at the head of research committees charged with evaluating the advances in knowledge and practice and updating the 1960 Joint Commission report.

The President's Commission report is of interest precisely because it has very little if anything new to say. The issues in 1978 are the same as they were in 1955 when the Joint Commission undertook its study:

   i. develop and maintain a network of comprehensive community care centers;

  ii. secure adequate public and private financial support for mental health;

 iii. provide properly trained personnel for all those requiring treatment;

  iv. address the special needs of the elderly, children, adolescents, and other populations;

280

v. improve coordination between somatic and psychiatric services, both hospital and community-based;

vi. increase support for basic research; and,

vii. enhance preventative services.

The only really new emphasis added to the list of goals was a concern with the protection of the human rights of mental patients (President's Commission, vol. I, 1978: viii) Thus, this latest federal policy statement illustrates the persistence of the problems of the mentally disordered. The well-intended solutions of one generation of policy-makers are discovered by a new generation of reforms to have been incompletely realized. And, in this process, new problems become salient, requiring new solutions. In the case of the Carter Presidency, the re-identification of mental illness as an issue resulted in a renewed commitment to solve the persistent social ill that has eluded a policy solution.

The Carter Presidential Commission exmplified this renewal of a policy commitment. At the top of the Commission's list of proposals was the expansion of the CMHC system:

> "Over the past 15 years the Community Mental Health Centers Program has been the major Federal vehicle for providing comprehensive mental health services in local communities. Since 1963, over 1.5 billion Federal dollars have been invested directly in this program. By October of 1978, there will be 647 centers in operation throughout the country; another 57 centers will be funded but not operational; and an estimated 14 centers are now approved but unfunded." (President's Commission, 1978: 17)

The Commission noted that though approximately 25 percent of patient care episodes are being handled by the CMHC facilities, these facilities consumed far less than 5 percent of the national budget for treating the mentally ill. Given the cost-effectiveness of the centers and their demonstrated record in reducing reliance on the mental hospital mode of care, the Commission recommended the expansion of the centers program, with an emphasis on the targeting of new specialized services for the poor, elderly, children, adolescents, underserved areas, minorities, and the chronically mentally ill. The Commission went on to call for a $75 million appropriation in fiscal year 1978-79 to realize their goal (cf. President's Commission on Mental Health, 1978).

The Mental Health Systems Act, 1980

The Carter Commission sparked a campaign to provide a comprehensive solution to the problems of providing mental health care to the diverse populations requiring psychiatric treatment. The mental health reform movement seized the policy momentum generated by the Commission's report. The National Mental Health Association formed a coalition with the National Association of State Mental Health Program Directors and the National Council of Community Mental Health Centers designed to develop a program that could realize the goals outlined by the Presidential Commission. Besides expanding the community mental health center, the coalition envisioned a comprehensive, federally-supported mental health centers serving the specific mental health needs of the elderly, children, adolescents, and minorities (including native Americans, Blacks, Chicanos, Asian-Americans, and others). Further, the coalition identified the chronically mentally ill as requiring special programs to insure that the diverse group of long-term, psychiatrically-impaired were aided by mental health services.

The Congressional passage of reform legislation. In 1979, the Carter Administration developed a legislative proposal that embodied many of the recommendations of the Presidential Commission. The Mental Health Systems Act (H.R. 4156; S. 1177) reflected the efforts of Secretary of Health, Education and Welfare, Joseph Califano, the NIMH staff, and the White House staff to broaden the CMHC concept and address the specific recommendations for new services called for by the Presidential Commission Report.

The omnibus legislation provided for a continuation of funding for the Community Mental Health Centers, but also called increasing state funded alternatives to hospitalization. Further, legislative proposal would permit states to be designated as the sole provider of mental health services (Section 602 of S. 1177). This proposal would permit the designation of a single agency of the state to assume responsibility for administration of the plans and the other aspects of a state's mental health services program. Further, the legislative proposal called for services to be targeted to meet the needs of the chronically mentally ill, racial or ethnic minorities, the poor, rural residents, and any other group with special needs. The legislation also specified the need for preventative services and called for federal funds to assist state governments and local mental health providers in educational and promotional activities designed to bring mental disorders to early treatment.

The Kennedy-Carter rivalry. The Carter Administration's Mental Health Systems Act did not lack for Congressional sponsors. Senate Majority Leader Robert Byrd introduced the bill into the Senate for debate. The most intense examination and discussion of the bill took place in the Subcommittee on Health and Scientific Research of the Senate Committee on Labor and Human Resources, chaired by Senator Edward M. Kennedy. As the last of the Kennedy brothers, he was heir to their political concerns, including reform of programs promoting mental health. In 1976, he was an alternative to President Carter for disgruntled Democrats and the vehicle for a return to power of the Kennedy clan and its allies; as such, he was a natural rival of President Carter. Thus, the Mental Health Systems Act served as not only a method of implementing a Presidential Commission, but also a means to further the political ambitions of Kennedy who sought to lay claim to a landmark piece of legislation.

The Kennedy-Carter rivalry was evidenced in the reception given the Honorary Chairperson of the President's Commission on Mental Health, Mrs. Rosalyn Carter, the First Lady. In her statement on February 7, 1979, Mrs. Carter outlined to Senator Kennedy's Subcommittee on Health and Scientific Research the findings of the Carter Presidential Commission. Not to be outdone, Senator Kennedy's statement pointed to his family's contributions to mental health legislation. While the exchange was formal and friendly, the emphasis Kennedy made on his family's role in mental health policy making was designed to note the clear Kennedy perception that the legislation flowing from the Presidential Commission would bear the Kennedy imprimatur. In testimony on the legislation itself, Kennedy joked about the increasing intense contest between Carter and himself. Thanking HEW Secretary Califano for his testimony, Kennedy said: "See how nicely we get along with the administration these days? [laughter]" (U.S. Senate, May 24, 1979).

The rivalry continued to characterize the legislative struggle to enact the Mental Health Systems Act. And, the outbreak of political warfare between Carter and Kennedy in the Fall of 1979 was a factor, along with many others, that delayed the enactment of the legislation: Kennedy's campaign took him away from his Senate duties, thereby delaying the deliberations; Carter's preoccupation with Kennedy and with international crises (especially the Iranian hostage affair) diverted Presidential energies from the legislative process. The firing of HEW Secretary Califano, in part because he was viewed as too independent and too tied to Kennedy, was yet another factor prolonging the legislative history of the Mental Health Systems Act. And, there were other factors that lengthened the enactment process: the reassertion of states' rights; the fragmentation of the reform coalition; the concern over chronically mentally ill; and, the debate over a balanced federal budget.

Schweiker's concern for the chronic mentally ill. Senator Lowell Schweiker of Pennsylvania focused the attention of the Subcommittee on Health and Scientific Research on the plight of the chronically mentally ill person. In February, 1979, he read into Congressional hearing testimony the entire, Philadelphia Inquirer series on "chronic" mental patients and their mistreatment. The Inquirer's Lacy McCrary and Bruce Keiden conducted research in 1978 in New York, Chicago, Los Angeles, San Diego, Denver, Birmingham, and Philadelphia to document the gaps in the treatment services, and the neglect and exploitation of the chronically mentally disordered. Schweiker used the Inquirer stories as evidence of the gaps in federal and state mental health ser-

284

vices. His remarks exemplify the growing concern that the reforms of the 1950's and 60's were incompletely realized:

> "Nowhere are the failures of our current mental health system more glaring, the needs more acute, as the problems more complex and intractable than in the area of care for the chronically mentally ill. Congress, with its best intentions, encouraged the phasing-out of mental institutions and required community mental health centers to provide aftercare and transitional living arrangements for chronic patients. The sad fact is that in too many cases, the care has simply not been provided. We must work to see that our good intentions are implemented and certain minimum standards of care are provided, while allowing some flexibility." (Schweiker, 1979: 53)

In calling for the elimination of "psychiatric ghettos," Schweiker was not alone. The representatives of the mental health reform movement—the National Mental Health Association and the National Council of Community Mental Health Centers, among others—pointed to the needs of this underserved segment of the population. Secretary Califano—speaking for NIMH—also acknowledged the need to target services to the chronic patient and ex-patient groups. Hence, the subgovernmental elements converged in their assessments of this problem.

States rights and the exclusive agent designation. Title III of the Mental Health Systems Act provided for states to apply for designation as the exclusive agent for mental health services. In the formulation of the bill, the advocates of the CMHC concept felt that any imposition of a state mental health authority between local CMHC facilities and NIMH would lessen the effectiveness of the CMHC's.

In contrast, the states-rights advocates of the exclusive-designation concept believed that the states had been by-passed by the 1963 CMHC Act and subsequent legislation. NIMH's program approval and funding powers had originally been designed to insure that community-based treatment alternatives to the state mental hospital would be constructed and operated, outside the sphere of control of state officials. The intent of the 1963, 1965 and subsequent acts was to by-pass the state asylum--a discredited institutional vestige of a previous reform era. In a policy reversal, the 1980 Mental Health Systems Act provided that new discretionary powers could be granted to the states to permit them to coordinate and cooperate in the creation of local mental health services.

The Title III clause allowing the agent designation was not in the original administration bills, H.R. 4156 and S. 1177. This concept was added by legislators who felt that a power imbalance had developed between the federal and state governments: too often the national government, via legislation, regulations, and court decisions, was directly operating local and state governmentsl services. The CMHC refunding proposals tied to the Mental Health Systems Act bills became a vehicle for proponents of increasing state and local authority and power and for scaling back the directly-funded federal activities at the community level.

A "Bill of Rights" for mental patients. The final version of the 1980 Mental Health Systems Act also contained a title not provided for in the original Carter Administration bills: a statement of the rights of mental patients. This amendment was introduced by the National Mental Health Association and other mental patient advocate organizations. The intent of the amendment was to set national standards for the treatment of the mentally ill as well as for the protection of mental patients' civil rights. Thus, this amendment would attack the variability in the enforcement of the civil rights, forcing states and localities to adhere to a set of minimum standards for the treatment of the mentally ill, as in the case of 1960's civil rights legislation designed to protect black Americans.

Court cases had already begun to redefine the state confinement laws and regulations. In O'Connor v. Donaldson, 433 U.S. 563 (1975), the U.S. Supreme Court found that when a person did not pose a threat to himself or society, his confinement in a mental institution was a violation of the person's freedoms under the U.S. Constitution. If a person was able to function in society, in spite of being diagnosed mentally ill, the _parens patria_ doctrine could not be applied. In an earlier landmark Alabama case, Wyatt v. Stickney, 344 F. Supp. 373 and 387 (M.D. Ala. 1972), several patients were found to have been abused by state commitment procedures. The plantiffs were functionally mentally retarded because of the gross abuse and mistreatment in a non-therapeutic, custodial state mental institution. In another civil rights case a 1978 suit brought the release of a Spanish-speaking woman confined for 30 years in Washington, D.C.'s St. Elizabeth's Mental Hospital. Her original reason for admission: typhoid fever (cf. Clarke, 1979:461-479). A national patient' bill of rights was viewed as a first step to build a uniform safeguard of patient's civil rights and avoid such law suits in the future.

The "bill of rights" amendment attempted to codify the new liberal attitudes towards patient confinement and treatment. Yet, this amendment became something its proponents did not intend: a symbol federal-governmental encroachment into the affairs of state and local governments. The advocates of mental patient rights lost the Congressional battle to impose a standard "bill of rights" on the states. The implementation of Title V remains discretionary, though the legislation urges the states to amend their detention and treatment laws.

The maintenance of local discretion insures variation in the implementation of Title V's frames. As such, this title's enactment was a blow to the mental health reform movement and a victory for the foes of federal regulation of state and local affairs. Like the exclusive-agent designation governmental, the discretionary "bill of rights" title will mean that opponents of future federal health initiatives have limited federal hegemony in state affairs. Both Title V and Title III prefigure the Reagan Administration's call for a devolution of control of health and welfare programs to the states and for a dismantling of federal regulation of local health services. In light of the broad policy intentions of the Reagan Administration, Titles III and V may signify the demise of the original CMHC concept of federal government funding and direction of a categorical-spending program.

The Coming Battle to Implement P.L. 96-398

   Though an embattled President Carter signed the Mental
Health Systems Act (P.L. 96-398) into law on October 7, 1980
and vowed to see this landmark legislation implemented, the
election of Ronald Reagan as President on November 4, 1980
almost insures that the full implementation of the complex
bill will not occur. The mental health reform movement--the
sub-government of officials, agencies, associations, research communities, and training institutions--faces the
most severe and sustained challenge to its cherished policies and programs.

   The policy context in which P.L. 96-398 will be implemented is qualitatively different from the mid-70's period
of challenge posed by the New Federalism of Richard Nixon
and by the budget vetos of Gerald Ford. First, in the 1980
elections, the Democrats lost control of the U.S. Senate.
Thus, the 97th Congress marks the first time in generations
the Republicans control the most exclusive policy framing
and implementing body in the nation. The loss of the Senate
was most painful for the Democrats because it came as the
result of the electoral defeats of many of the well-placed
advocates of domestic social policy reforms. Defeated Senators Frank Church, George McGovern, Gaylord Nelson, among
others, were the tribunes for the poor, disabled, hungry,
ill, aged, and mentally disordered. The forced retirement
from formal governmental policy-making post has created a
void in the reform movement and in the subgovernments of
health, mental health, and other special welfare interests.
The remaining legislatively-based reformers in the U.S.
House of Representatives and Senate will face the difficult
recruitment of new members to the cause of mental health
reform and related reform issues.

   Second, the mental health reform movement's defeats in
the amendment process of the Mental Health Systems Act suggests that a much more conservative Senate and House of
Representatives will be much less sympathetic to the funding
requests of the National Mental Health Association, the
National Council of Community Mental Health Centers, and the
National Association of State Mental Health Program Directors. Third, P.L. 96-398 provided for transitional funding

of the extant CMHC centers, but due to the highly charged national election campaign and the intense international crises of the closing months of the Carter Administration, formal funding authorizations for CMHC's was not enacted by the 96th Congress. Federally-funded CMHC centers had to operate until June, 1981 under a "continuing funding resolution." This funding resolution must be formally renewed or CMHC's cease to exist. Thus, a much more conservative Congress must explicitly refund CMHC's in order to sustain a key organizational feature of the comprehensive mental illness treatment system envisioned by the Mental Health Systems Act. The form and level of such funding can not be predicted because the Reagan Administration plans for federal spending and for block grants have not been implemented.

The 1981 fiscal crisis of the federal government. President Reagan took office in 1981 pledging to cut federal spending and taxes in order to curb the twin ailments of inflation and recession. Since the enactment of federal legislation, such as the 1935 Social Security Act and the turn-of-the-century unemployment insurance bills, an even larger number of U.S. citizens are entitled to transfer payments and in-kind benefits (cf. Levitan and Targgat, 1978; Schulz, 1980; Aaron, 1973; Wilensky, 1975). The Reagan Administration, like its predecessors, faces the problem of how to balance the federal budget when transfer payments are inflation-insured by being linked to a consumer price index, and when inflation-induced recessions push more workers onto unemployment insurance rolls and into in-kind benefit programs like food stamps. In an attempt to quickly gain control of federal spending, the Reagan Administration's budget manager, Director of the Office of Management and Budget, David Stockman, has initially proposed retaining the central features of the New Deal-New Frontier-Great Society income Security programs (Social Security Act transfer payments, food stamps, Medicare, among others), while cutting many of the categorical spending, direct-service programs and subsidies of the Department of Education, Housing and Urban Development, Health and Human Services (HEW), Transportation, Energy, and Agriculture.

The Reagan OMB proposal for mental health marks an even more dramatic departure from the concepts of the Mental Health Systems Act. Reagan proposes to consolidate what monies will be allocated for NIMH's direct-service activities (community mental health centers, et al.) into block social and health service grants to states. States can then determine their spending proprieties and choose to supplement federal funds to realize the objectives of the Mental Health Systems Act and and other recent pieces of social welfare legislation. The questions are: how successful will the Reagan-Stockman approach be? Will Congress approve this radical devolution of administrative responsibility and fiscal control to states and localities? How successful will the mental health reform movement, lacking many past Congressional supporters, be in convincing Congress to fulfill the intent of P.L. 96-398 and similar federal acts (e.g., the Older Americans Act)? Only the political struggles of the coming months will provide the answers to these questions.

Mental Health Services in a Reformed National Health Service

While the gains of the U.S. mental health reform movement were and are threatened by fiscal conservatives, governmental reorganization, and competition from other lobbyists for related health and welfare programs, England's mental health reformers have been similarly attacked. Principle among the foes of English mental health reforms in the 1970's is the continuing financial crisis that has strained English national budgets and the attempts to restructure the administrative system of the social and health services.

England's health service organizational structure was a product of political compromise between the competing political forces seeking to maximize their political goals of to defend their vested interests. In 1945 Labour Minister of Health Aneurin Bevan desired an integrated, comprehensive health service, but the political compromises required by British political realities (and the complexities of the health industry) forced him to adopt essentially a multidimensional health service: a regional hospital service, with a special role for the elite teaching hospitals; a separate general practitioner service, with special provisions for dentists, pharmacies, and optical services; and, a plethora of local authority health responsibilities. The administrative problem is how to operate a non-profit, therapeutically-oriented service, and how to coordinate the NHS branches in delivering medical services to patients. Ironically, since 1948, the reorganization of the NHS has been continuously addressed by both Labour and Conservative Governments. Under the Conservatives, the 1953 Guilleband Report on NHS costs contained the dissenting opinion of Sir John Maud that the tripartite structure created an imbalance which resulted in acute somatic hospital care dominating general practitioners and social medicine's needs. The 1959 Mental Health Act called for greater coordination between hospital and local health services. Enoch Powell's 1962 Hospital Plan for England and Wales of Conservative Ministry of Health offered the district hospital concept. The Bonham-Carter Report and other subsequent reports elaborated on Powell's plan calling for the joint planning of community health and district hospital services.

The first formal proposals for reorganization were made in 1967 by Labour Minister of Health Kenneth Robinson. He called for the unification of the 15 Regional Hospital Boards, 36 Boards of Governors, 336 Hospital Management Committees, the 134 Executive Committees administering general practitioner service, and 175 local health authorities (Leavitt, 1976:19-21). Naturally, in a health service where somatic and psychiatric services are integrated and nationalized, reorganization proposals would have an impact on mental health services, even though the focus such proposed was on somatic health.

Rationalization of governmental services. Under Harold Wilson's second Labour Government a policy of functional reorganization and realignment of many government departments and ministries was implemented: the Ministry of Health was abolished; its health functions were combined with responsibility for pensions into a new Department of Health and Social Security (DHSS), with Richard Crossman as its first head. As DHSS head, Crossman continued to follow Robinson's lead in the furthering proposals for rationalizing of health services to achieve greater efficiency and improve the delivery of services.

Also, various Labour governments royal commissions studied and reported on social welfare services and the structure of local government. Among these were the report of the Committee on Local and Allied Personal Social Services chaired by Frederick Seebohm and the Royal Commission on Local Government in England, chaired by Lord Redcliffe-Maud. The Seebohm proposals called for local authority services, including all health services to be combined into personal social service departments. Redcliffe-Maud envisioned a major functional realignment of local governments, with the new unitary local authorities taking full responsibility for health. The implementation of these recommendations would require NHS restructuring to take into account the social service reorganization and the redefinition of local authority boundaries and responsibilities. Since NHS reform proposals were already being formulated by DHSS under Crossman's direction, it made sense to link these with the Seebohm and Redcliffe-Maud proposals. Thus, Crossman published a second position paper on NHS reform that flowed from and integrated parts of the Redcliffe-Maud and Seebohm reports. The Crossman Report principles were:

> "...that the new health authorities would be independent of local government and directly responsible to the central government; that the public health and personal social services would continue to be the responsibility of local government; that the boundaries of the new health authorities would march those of local government." (Leavitt, 1976:23)

Sir Keith Joseph presides over NHS reorganization. Labour Government's June, 1970 general election loss meant that the Conservative Party's DHSS Secretary Sir Keith Joseph would preside over the development of the NHS reorganization plan. Understandably, the Crossman proposals were modified, reflecting Joseph's belief in the need for a modern, strong-management model of administration of the doctor-dominated NHS (cf. Alaszewski, et al., 1981). The August, 1972 White Paper was followed shortly by the reorganization legislation. By July 5, 1973 the NHS reorganization bill had received Royal assent, and the functionally realigned and managerially more "efficient" NHS emerged.

The NHS created by reorganization differed substantially from the health services of 1946–73.

Most importantly, the tripartite divisions were abolished. Under the 1973 Act, the DHSS Secretary administers a NHS divided into Regional Health Authorities (RHAs), whose functions are planning and supervision for hospitals, general practitioners and related health services. Under the RHA's new Area Health Authorities (AHAs) assume the day-to-day administrative responsibility for somatic hospitals, both teaching and non-teaching, mental hospitals, GP services, related out-patient and auxiliary services. Coordination between the NHS and local governments is achieved because the ninety AHAs correspond to the new local authorities created by the Redcliffe-Maud local governmental reorganization scheme. Finally, the AHAs are divided into districts, each with District Management Teams (DMTs), who assume the administrative activities formerly performed by the Hospital Management Committees, local health departments, and Boards of Governors of teaching hospitals (Manning, 1974).

In sum, the NHS reorganization ended the formal allocational and functional responsibilities for the various aspects of health services among the several structures of the NHS. Now, all functions are administered by regional, area, and district management teams composed of representatives of the various branches within the NHS. In this way coordination is supposed to be fostered and linkages forged in the delivery of services. The question is: how have mental health services fared after such a massive restructuring?

The restructuring of mental health services within the new NHS. From the perspective of the history of mental health reform, the NHS reorganization marks the full reintegration of mental illness management institutions into the health delivery system. The English mental health reform movement had attempted to separate out the mentally ill from other patients and to provide them with specialized treatment. This goal was accomplished in the 19th-century asylum construction campaign, campaigns for mental illness legislation, and the monitoring of hospital treatment of the

mentally ill. In the 20th century a reintegration of psychiatric into somatic services became a goal because of the
separation of psychiatric care had relegated it to second-
class status in health care. Proponents of psychiatry's
reintegration argued that a more efficient use of all
psychiatric beds, whether in asylums, district hospital
psychiatric departments, or day hospitals, would occur,
insuring that acute cases received prompt treatment and that
chronic patients were not isolated from the mainstream of
health care. Reorganization and integration was meant to
enhance greater cooperation between functionally-aligned
local authority social welfare services and the AHA's and to
facilitate coordination between community treatment and
hospital care.

   An assessment of the English implementation process.
The 1973 pre-reorganization symposium on a comprehensive
district psychiatric service reviewed the problems and their
possible solution within the current administrative framework (Cawley and McLachlan, 1973). At this conference that
focused on the medical (i.e., hospital-based) aspects of
delivering psychiatric services then Secretary of DHSS spoke
of the need to address local authority alternative services
to hospitalization:

   "It must be stressed that I well understand that
   it is no good whatsoever trying to improve the
   hospital-based services for mental illness unless at the same time equal--no, probably more--
   emphasis is put on improving and expanding the
   community services. I realize there is a widespread anxiety about the lack of community services and a widespread desire to see both the
   quality and the quantity increased sharply."
   (Joseph, 1973:4-5).

   In 1975 the Labour Government's White Paper Better Services for the Mentally Ill (Cmnd 6233) again admitted the
failure of the DHSS strategy to effect a transformation in
psychiatric care. The government noted statistics showing a
decline in the mental hospital's residential population.
These statistics are impressive. While the resident populations in NHS mental hospitals have declined from the all-

time high of 151,400 in 1954 to 103,300 in 1970 (Jones, 1972:359), the numbers of persons receiving out-patient treatment for the first time increased from 160,800 in 1959 to 212,600 in 1973, a 32 percent increase,and the use of psychiatric departments in general hospitals experienced an even greater increase, up 53 percent (Department of Health and Social Security, 1974).

The local authorities were spending more than ever on psychiatric services (6.5 million pounds); nearly half of local authorities personal social service budget was being spent on day and residential facilities. Still, as of 1975, 31 local authorities had no mentally ill residential housing, and 63 had no day facilities. Psychiatric staffing ratios were still undesirably low, with a continuing problem of the uneven distribution of those personnel, and inadequacies persisted in facilities of the 100 or so hospitals bequeathed to Britain by the philanthropic Victorians. The reports of the Hospital Advisory Service, heirs to 19th-century mental hospital inspection commissions, revealed gaps in services and point to the need for improvements. The Department of Health and Social Security, author of the position paper, acknowledged the problem:

> "What we have to do is get to grips with shifting the emphasis to community care. The problems are many. Social services facilities--hostels, day centers, group homes--have to be built up from their present minimal levels. Staff to run them have to be recruited and trained, and the implications for trained and experienced social work staff have to be recognized and provided for. Psychiatric services have to be developed locally, in general and community hospitals and health centers. The balance of resources between health and personal social services has to be shifted." (DHSS, 1975: ii-iii)

Thus, whether Conservative or Labour, official government's analyses point to the same facts: namely, the implementation discretion granted to local authorities in 1959, coupled with financial constraints that all sectors of English society operate under, has resulted in mental health services losing out in the keen competition for funds to expand local authority services and to transform the 19th-century hospital. Thus, England's pioneering therapeutic work (cf. Williams and Ozarin, 1968) has been accomplished in spite of the NHS' organizational barriers, local authority's discretion, and fiscal constraints. The 1973 NHS reorganization may have removed some of the barriers, but in the "shake-down" phase of reorganization it has been difficult to evaluate how mental health will ultimately fare in an integrated service.

The Irrelevance of the English Mental Health Reform Movement

Recall that in the early 1960's the English mental health reformers faced, on the one hand, a Parliamentary victory that substantially modernized the laws on admission and detention, greatly expanding the scope for voluntary admissions to treatment. On the other hand, the movement had to resist the concerted effort of Conservative Health Minister Enoch Powell to dismantle the nation's mental hospital network. The National Association for Mental Health, students of Britain's welfare state, patient organizations and hospital workers—all could agree with Powell's 1961 critique of the 19th-century mental hospital. But these members of the reform movement sharply diverged on how the alternatives to hospital care were to be implemented. Clearly, the inadequately funded and highly variable local authority mental health services were not meeting the need for community care. The reform movement still had to determine how incentives could be created to induce local authorities to live up to the 1959 Act's intent.

Unlike their American counterparts, English reformers lacked a reform-committed bureau within the Ministry of Health from which they could encourage and monitor expenditure of community-care funds. This meant that English reformers were without the political power and discretion enjoyed by their American counterparts. What English mental health reformers have had is a Parliamentary All-Party Conference on Mental Health that has been a complement to and has formed linkages with the National Association for Mental Health. The All-Party Conference members have been critical

of the Ministry of Health and Secretaries of the Department
of Health and Social Security, noting the failure of all
governments to fulfill the intent of the 1959 Mental Health
Act. While such criticism was useful, it was not a substitute for an alliance between legislative committee chairmen
capable of increasing a mental health budget and a mental
health bureau capable of expanding funds that would construct the facilities and hire the staff for community
psychiatric services.

The reason the mental health budgets of the NHS have not
increased as a percentage of all NHS spending is due to the
dominance of the NHS decision-making by the doctors and
administrators of the acute-care sector. The 1973 reorganization was intended to solve the problems created by the
unique organizational solution hit upon by NHS creator Bevan
in his efforts to win doctor approval. Administratively,
the NHS decision-making was dominated by the acute-care
hospitals and their physicians:

"Between 1948 and 1962 the Service [NHS] had vir-
tually been allowed by the central department to
drift. There was little central guidance and the
general direction of development was the sum of
local decisions. Since key local service providers (consultants in the prestigious acute
specialisms) dominated the local decision-making
process, incremental decision-making resulted in
a policy drift towards high technology medicine
and a neglect of long-stay and the community
services. The results of this policy drift were
escalating costs and a series of scandals in
long-stay institutions and the neglect of facilities in some part of the country." (Alaszewski, et al., 1981:8-9)

This dominance and policy drift continued through the
1970's.

Thus, whether or not a member of the National Association for Mental Health was Minister of Health, the continuing hegemony by the acute-care sector starved the mental
health and other chronic-illness-treatment services for the

funds needed to fulfill the mandates of the 1959 Act. This fact, coupled with the local authority discretion in implementing community treatment alternatives, has continually frustrated the English mental health reformers within and without Parliament.

Reconstruction of mental health reform. The official advocate of reform, the English National Association for Mental Health has acknowledged its shortcomings by a massive attempt to reconstruct and reorient the NAMH. This reform of the reformers was prompted by the limited successes of the post-war era and also by the manifest success of newly formed reform organizations. In the late 1950's, the emergence of new, activist reform groups, with evocative names and well-defined media images, spurred the rather establishment mental health association to contemplate an image change, one which would enhance the marketability of the association's reform proposals. Examples of these new advocate groups are provided by Shelter and the Child Poverty Action Group (CPAG).[2]

Like its U.S. counterpart, the English mental health association had hitherto been a feature of the "establishment." The association had been intimately linked with the government which operated the mental health services over the years both as the recipient of governmental operating subsidies to manage demonstration hostels and halfway houses as well as to fund the national office. Further, NAMH was consulted in the development of governmental mental health policy, participating in the formulation of the latest Royal Commission report and having a review and comment role in the formulation of many of the subsequent implementation strategies. The intimate link between NAMH and the NHS administration was symbolized by the Minister of Health opening the annual conventions with a keynote address.

In a word, in the late 1960's NAMH's leaders felt the reformers were too closely identified with the mental health services administration the NAMH was supposed to be monitoring and evaluating. The CPAG and Shelter, among other new activitist reform organizations, provided NAMH with a model for updating the image of an aging social reform organization, that is, for repackaging the mental health movement, tailoring it to a new climate in which the media image of an association was as important as the message the organization was attempting to convey.

The transformation of NAMH took the following form in 1970. NAMH changed its name to MIND, to enhance its market ability, though the ties with the English governing elite were retained. Vice-presidents (Anna Freud, Dr. Morris Carstairs, England's chief rabbi, the Archbishop of Canterry, the former Minister of Health under Labour, and the former Minister of Education under the Conservatives) symbolized the linkages between the reform society and other social institutions. Further changes occured with the retirement of Mary Applebey, NAMH director for 25 years. She was replaced by the relatively young, pro-civil libertarian, patient-rights advocate, Tony Smythe. The 1973-74 NAMH annual report sums up these changes:

> "MIND has been on the move. When Mary Applebey resigned at the end of last year after 22 years at its head, her selfless intent was to leave MIND free to move in a new direction and under new leadership. Her successor, Tony Smythe, took up office on January 1st. His task is not an enviable task. Fresh to the field, not only has he taken over the Directorship, to which Mary Applebey brought wisdom and years of experience, but also the role which David Ennals so effectively initiated as Director of the three year MIND campaign. Tony Smythe's experience in the field of human rights stands him in excellent stead." (MIND, 1975)

Thus, the English National Mental Health Association's new direction had been marked by a three year campaign to inaugurate the new name and renew the association's reform mission. Whether the new name MIND will evoke greater media recognition and result in greater success in reform actions remains to be seen. The persistence of its ties to the government (by means of operating subsidies) belies the radical departure suggested by the new name.

A new, critical role for MIND. One product of this new image and approach was MIND-sponsored systematic re-evaluation of the 1959 Mental Health Act, with a view towards criticizing the features of the act which still violate the civil rights of mental patients (cf., Gostin, 1975). A second example of the new MIND was the November, 1975 national conference to criticize the Labour government's White Paper and demand a reallocation of national health priorities. The candid White Paper Better Services for the Mentally Ill (Cmnd 6233) had pointed to the lack of residential accomodation in 31 local authorities and of day facilities in 63 local authorities, the shortages of staff (there were in 1975, 835 full-time consulting psychiatrists to cope with 250,000 adult in-patients, 1.5 million out-patient visits, and over 2 million day patient visits), and the lack of funds for community care services (in 1973-74, 300 million pounds were spent on hospital psychiatric services and only 15 million pounds were spent on local authority services for the mentally ill).

At the late-1975 conference, the assembled critics of NHS psychiatric services pointed to these failings, but could not provide a formula for realizing their reform objectives. The diverse conference participants asked governments at all levels simply to fulfill the intent of the 1959 Act: make the community-care dream possible. But this call was in vain as long as the combination of factors- -NHS organizational features, budget constraints, and local authority discretion in implementation--worked unwittingly to thwart the goals for everyone, including the NHS and local authority administrators. The dilemma facing the reform movement advocates of the mentally ill was that though they have obtained government agreements (from both Labour and Conservative) on the nature of the problem (as evidenced by Cmnd 6233), such agreements have not and will not lead to the creation of local psychiatric services unless there are dramatic changes in the allocation of the English mental health budget.

Another new effort by mental health reformers was the May, 1977 suit filed by MIND against the Home Office and the Department of Health and Social Security for the violation of patients' rights. The distinctive aspect of this suit is

300

that it was filed with the European Commission of Human Rights in Strasbourg (The Observer, May 8, 1977). This suit raises a question: will civil suits, along with reevaluations of the 1959 Act, and alterations of the NAMH-MIND media image affect the transfer of governmental resources to the mental health sector of the NHS and local authorities' budgets? The answer is probably not. So long as the structural and organizational barriers remain, enhancing the quality of mental patient life and initiating comprehensive community care will not take place.

Re-Organizing the NHS and the New Conservatism

1979 marked the triumph of the Conservative Party under the leadership of Margaret Thatcher, an avowed foe of the English welfare state. The new government called for spending cuts in health and social services, explicitly trimming the NHS expenditures and "reorganizing" a health service that had suffered from a bad case of "manageralism." The reforms of the NHS had become the scapegoat for many complaints about the NHS: the new management structures involved a new nomenclature, required new patterns of behavior, altered comfortable ties. A new Royal Commission was appointed in 1976 by the Labour government to study proposals for reforming the reform. In its 1979 report, entitled Patients Come First, the Royal Commissioners argued for a new, more local, patient-centered NHS. For example, the locus of decision-making is to be shifted to the district health level:

> "The focus of the district will be the District General Hospital and the associated range of community services. Coterminosity with associated local authority services (personal social services and education) is no longer a key determinant of boundaries." (Alaszewski, et al., 1981:4)

The Royal Commission called for a shift from acute-care services to community services dealing with the mentally ill, chronic somatically ill, and elderly patients. Further, the Commission considered local discretion in policy implementation as a way to more appropriately adapt national policy proposals: the strong centralized, management model of the Joseph plan was rejected.

What are the chances of success of this further restructuring of the NHS? Specifically, what will be the fate of mental health services under this latest plan? Given the stated intentions of the Thatcher government to cut spending, the competition for increasingly scarce national resources will intensify. The losers of yesterday's budget battles—mental health services—are probably going to be the losers of tomorrow's priority-setting processes. Secondly, the new 1979 reorganization proposals really consist of yet another rational-technical solution to the NHS crises of public management. Such proposals do not really offer the possible creative, innovative, locally-generated solutions to the NHS' problems a chance to be heard. Third, as long as mental health is fused administratively with somatic health, as long as mental health reformers lack an independent national base of operations, and as long as localities have discretion in implementing community care, the English version of comprehensive community mental health centers remains a dream. Thus, one can predict that NHS services for the chronically ill, including mental patients, will suffer at the hands of budget slashers and administrative reorganizers. And, MIND and allied associations will be able to do little more than protest and criticize from the policy-making sidelines.

A Final Comment

This comparison of the adoption and implementation of U.S. community mental health policy, coupled with an assessment of English policy developments, suggests that the success of U.S. mental health reform movement is due to its possession of a bureaucratic base from which to conduct its transformation of psychiatric services. The lack of such a bureaucratic base in England explains the meager success these equally dedicated reformers have had in creating decentralized, community-based alternatives to total institutional care. True, the English have "made-do" and have adopted the old asylum for many new purposes, but the intent of the 1959 Mental Health Act has never been as fully realized as compared with the U.S.'s CMHC Acts. Because the English also face problems of gaining community acceptance of local psychiatric treatment centers (local authorities are more conservative than the central government in England as well as the U.S.), it appears that local psychiatric services will have to be imposed in England as they were in the U.S. I can not see such a successful imposition taking place until an English equivalent of NIMH is established, with discretionary authority to not only fund research and personnel training, but also to advance the development of local treatment alternatives. The data reveal the dramatic shift in the U.S. locus of psychiatric care. Such a shift would be possible in England if the mental health reform movement, and its Parliamentary lobby, the All-Party Conference for Mental Health, realized that old-style lobbying for social reformers will not be effective in an era of bureaucratic domination of health and welfare services. The message from this comparative analysis is this: an effective reform movement must have an institute or bureau, with discretionary powers, that can do battle in the policy implementation war with other bureaus and their lobbies. In the modern welfare state such a bureaucratic-base for the pursuit of reform interests is essential if such interests are not to be thwarted by other, more strategically-placed and powerfully-armed interests. The dilemma of decentralization of psychiatric services is that such a devolution of care is best achieved by a bureaucratically-based central authority capable of overcoming the multiple sources of resistence to this approach to managing the distressed population of mentally disordered persons.

NOTES

1. For an assessment of an analogous policy implementation process, and the pit-falls contained therein, see C. L. Estes' (1979) analysis of the Older Americans Acts (cf. Armour, 1981, _et al._).

2. England's post-war welfare state has left many persons ill-housed, underfed, underemployed, and underserved by a variety of health and social services. Shelter and CPAG were formed in the mid-60's in response to the failures of the Socialist state to deliver on its promises. NAMH noted that CPAG was not just drawing attention to the thousands of families living below the official poverty levels with the aid of research studies conducted by noteable social scientists like Peter Townsend and W. G. Runciman. And, CPAG was gaining media recognition for its cause with terms like "poverty trap." Further, the CPAG was advancing its reform goals when its legal officer brought cases to the courts to dramatize the inequities inherent in anti-poverty programs.

CHAPTER X

CONCLUDING THEORETICAL OBSERVATIONS

This study of mental health policy making has been informed by a variety of concepts and has attempted to demonstrate the analytic utility of a typology of social reform movement. This typology suggested that the organizational form of a reform movement can be linked to the degree of specificity of a reform movement; that is, broad-aim reform movements are concerned with changing the value-structure of a society while norm-oriented movements focus on specific social changes. Second, the typology noted that broad-aim or specific reform movements may take on different organizational forms, depending upon whether they are led by a charismatic leader, or adopt a formal associational-mode of organization, or are based in a bureau that has social change as its objective. Further, the typology noted that social-change relevant evidence, knowledge, information was crucial for social reformers whatever their organizational form. This policy-making intelligence may range from the highly ideological to the scientific and is linked to the organizational form of a reform movement.

Revised Analytic Typology

Figure 3 presents a revised version of the analytic typology that has guided this analysis of the role of reformers in mental health policy making in the United States, England, and Sweden. The location of individuals and organizations in this typology reveals how aims of reform, the particular form of organization of a reform movement, and the type of intelligence utilized determines the placement of an individual or organization. For example, the broad reform aims of Benjamin Rush, coupled with the underdevelopment of 18th-century psychiatric theory, fixes him in a cell for broad-aim solo charismatic reformers using political-ideological intelligence. In contrast, the specific mental health aims of Philippe Pinel, combined with his bureaucratic position as an asylum director and the particular under-

305

FIGURE 3

BROAD-AIM REFORM AND SPECIFIC REFORM MOVEMENTS, ORGANIZATIONAL FORMS, AND INTELLIGENCE BASES

FORMS OF INTELLIGENCE EMPLOYED BY REFORMERS AND REFORM MOVEMENTS				
RATIONAL-SCIENTIFIC INTELLIGENCE	IMPRESSIONISTIC EVIDENCE FORMS OF INTELLIGENCE	POLITICAL-IDEOLOGICAL INTELLIGENCE		
RALPH NADER PRIOR TO THE ESTABLISHMENT OF HIS LAW CENTERS	HORACE MANN IN HIS EARLY CAREER	BENJAMIN RUSH	SOLO CHARISMATIC REFORMERS	BROAD-AIM REFORM MOVEMENTS
CHILD POVERTY ACTION GROUP (CPAG)	EARLY CHILD GUIDANCE MOVEMENTS	THE TOWNSEND PLAN OR POOR PEOPLES' MOVEMENT	FORMAL ASSOCIATION REFORM ORGANIZATIONS	
ENGLAND'S MINISTRY OF HEALTH UNDER A. BEVAN (1945-48)	NEW YORK STATE'S 19TH CENTURY CHARITY BOARDS	17TH CENTURY SWEDISH COMN'S ADMINISTRATIVE BOARDS	BUREAU-CRATICALLY BASED REFORMERS	
ALAIN ENTHOVEN AS ADVOCATE FOR U.S. HEALTH INSURANCE	MIKE GORMAN OR DOROTHEA L. DIX	WILLIAM TUKE	SOLO CHARISMATIC REFORMERS	SPECIFIC REFORM MOVEMENTS
AMERICAN PSYCHIATRIC ASSOCIATION	C. BEERS' NATIONAL COMMITTEE FOR MENTAL HYGIENE	NETWORK AGAINST PSYCHIATRIC ASSAULT (NAPA)	FORMAL ASSOCIATION REFORM ORGANIZATIONS	
U.S. NATIONAL INSTITUTE OF MENTAL HEALTH	SHAFTESBURY'S METROPOLITAN LUNACY COMMISSION	PHILIPPE PINEL AS ADMINISTRATOR OF BICETRE	BUREAU-CRATICALLY BASED REFORMERS	

development of psychiatric theory, yields a different location in this typology   others   than that of Rush.   In these
ways, the typology is a useful analytic tool, enabling the
researcher to classify mental health reformers   in a number
of theoretically-relevant dimensions and to employ this
classification scheme in constructing an explanation of the
process employed to enact and implement public policies.

Bureaucratically-based Reformers

The application of Figure 3 to the analysis of mental
health reform movements has revealed the superiority of
bureaucratically-based reform movements over movements not
linked with a reform-minded branch of government.

A marked contrast between the U.S., England, and Sweden
can be found in the way mental health associations participate in bureaucratized policy-making. As noted, the U.S.'s
NIMH provides an example of a dedicated cadre of bureaucratic reformers: Dr. Robert Felix and associates established
a new institute within NIH in 1946 which took on a totally
new function for the federal government.   Of this form of
bureau-creation process Downs (1967) says:

> "When a group of such zealots somehow conceive of
> a new function they believe their bureau should
> undertake, they form a nucleus, agitating for
> change.   Enthused by their idea, they persuade
> their superiors to give them some resources and
> manpower to develop it." (Downs: 6)

NIMH thus was not only a new bureau, but one which, due to
its mode of formation or creation, would attempt to maximize
its own interests.

Reforming the mental health detention laws (England,
1959; Sweden, 1966) and merging the psychiatric and somatic
hospital services (England, 1948; Sweden, 1968) are not comparable legislative victories. The creation of a separate
institute of health by and for a group of committed mental
health reformers would have enabled English and Swedish
reformers to more effectively battle for reform goals that

were and are similar to those of their U.S. counterparts. In my view, the lack of such a reformer-created bureau accounts for the relative failure of mental health reform forces to achieve parity with somatic health services in these European nations.

Organizational effectiveness of a bureaucratic-based reform. Weber (1978:956 ff.) viewed bureaucracy as the most efficient and effective form of domination. When reformers make use of rational-legal authority they would be more effective than a charismatic or associational reformer because they would be employing the best organizational weapon available to achieve an objective. This effectiveness would be enhanced by the degree to which a bureau was able to obtain and maintain organizational discretion to pursue its goals and objectives relatively free from the outside control or interference. In the case of NIMH, it grew rapidly, as measured by increases in its Congressional appropriations; it expanded the scope of its operations and despite attempts by other bureaus to grab NIMH's operations; it was able to preserve its organizational integrity vis-a-vis other branches of NIH.

The integrated mental health services in Sweden and England have been noticeably less successful in achieving their organizational goals. This is particularly true of the English mental health services. While the English have been notable as innovators in hospital-based treatment, industrial therapy, day-care hospital care, and the like, they have been told as of 1975 to postpone the day when the full dream of community-care would be realized. And the 1959 Mental Health Act that gave considerable organizational discretion in achieving community-care goals has not been amended. Under such a system, the English community-care advocates were at a relative disadvantage when compared to their U.S. counterparts. In sum, I have shown how crucial an organizational weapon--in this case, a bureau--can be in the cause of social reform.

Subgovernments and bureaucratic-based reformers. The bureaucratic-based reformers need allies to successfully realize their reform agenda. Figure 2 in Chapter Two notes that mental health reformers work within a dense organizational context to achieve their objectives. Elements of the government bureaucracy, legislations, professional associations and other groups play key roles in enabling a reform movement objective to be translated into law and then implemented. This network of policy-enabling actors has been called a subgobernment.

Ripley and Franklin's (1979) analysis of the policy-making and implementation processes suggest that the role of the subgovernment is crucial in sustaining a piece of legislation:

> "Subgovernments are small groups of political actors, both governmental and nongovernmental, that specialize in specific issue areas. Subgovernments in part are created by the complexity of the national policy agenda and they sustain that complexity. They are also the most prevalent and influential in the least visible policy areas." (Ripley and Franklin: 7)

In a non-crisis atmosphere such subgovernments insure that their policies and programs are sustained by continuing governmental appropriations. When new participants enter the policiy-making and implementing process, and when such participants do not share the subgovernment's perceptions, sentiments, and ideologies, the stage for conflict is set. Such a conflict occured during the Nixon-Ford Administrations in most domestic social policy arenas. The mid-70's battles over NIMH's CMHC budget appropriations reveals the effectiveness of the mobilized mental health reformers—reformers within and without the federal government—that directed, in subgovertnmental fashion, the implementation of Kennedy and Johnson mental health programs for community-care. The lesson of the Nixon-Ford defeats in the battle to de-fund CMHC's is that the bureaucratically-based reformers of NIMH, coupled with its allies in Congress, the mental health centers, professional psychiatric associations, voluntary associations, colleges and university-based trainers and researchers, can thwart the wills of Presidents.

Nixon and Ford probably never fully appreciated the fact that when a policy has assembled a powerful constituency, such a policy is much more likely to survive any one chief executive's ideological opposition to government spending program.

Reaganomics and social reform subgovernments. The electoral and legislative triumphs of Ronald Reagan, coupled with key defeats of members of subgovernments for various policies and programs, also supports the generalizations drawn from this detailed analysis of mental health policy making. When the relationships between elements of a reform coalition have been shattered, when many of the key members of a reform subgovernment have been removed from office, or retired, or died, the reform subgovernment is weakened to the point where it cannot defend its spending programs effectively.

In both England and the U.S. the post-war reform coalitions have been disrupted by personnel changes and losses. These developments have created the chances for President Reagan and Prime Minister Thatcher to attack and attempt to dismantle programs that were once considered sacrosanct and too well defended to be assaulted by politicians. Further, the attack and even erosion of the accomplishments of reform movements suggests that such bureaucratically-based reform movements are vulnerable to attacks by latter-day charismatic political leaders. In a word, the assault on the post-war health and welfare programs, including mental health services, suggest that charisma has not been extinguished by the rise of the bureaucratic-reformers and their subgovernmental allies.

Emergency of Latter-Day Charismatic Reformers

As noted in Chapter Two, reform movements are by their very nature opposed to the status quo. Whether such reform movements call for a return to past values and norms or for the imposition of new principles and procedures is not crucial. What is important is that all reformers are seeking to transform present conditions and activities. As such, reformers, and their movements, are faced with a dilemma:

310

on the one hand, reformers are anti-institutional, anti-establishment; on the other hand, reformers are seeking to institute and establish something new (or re-institute and re-establish something old). Thus, today's reformers may become tomorrows establishment that must itself be reformed. And, charismatic leadership is a chief mechanism for initiating reform activity aimed at overturning bureaucratic reformers that have become, in Alford's terms, structural-interest groups, that have something to lose and have vested interests in extant relationships and activities.

The new charismatic reformer. In the area of specific reformers, Mike Gorman illustrates the emergence of a new style reformer. Armed with the tools of the journalistic trade, convinced that the nation had again abandoned the mentally ill, certain that the National Association for Mental Health was limited in its vision and careerist in its approach, Gorman launched a one-man crusade that focused the attention of state and federal officials on the plight of the insant. In the area of broad-aim reforms, Ralph Nader is illustrative of this emergence of the latter-day charismatic reformer. Like reformers of a previous era, Nader affects a spartan life-style, eschewing the trappings of a successful professional. By assuming a modest life-style, Nader makes it difficult for others to coopt or corrupt him. He thus insulates himself from a political decision-making system which seeks to absorb and neutralize its critics by offering them rewards for compliance--rewards such as grants and jobs, positions of power, or badges of prestige. Thus, the latter-day social reformer emulates Weber's this-worldly -ascetic, one who struggles to overcome the corrupting influences of this world in the campaign to transform the world.

The routinization of latter-day reform charisma. Nader has not let his efforts to alter the historical relationship between the consumer and producer, citizen and government falter because he lacked the personal energy or interest to address the wide range of perceived inequities. Nader has regularized and rationalized the process of investigation and revealation by establishing The Center for Study of Responsive Law. The center's stated goal is to further the investigation into "the abuses of the public interest by

311

business and governmental groups." As a private, non-profit, tax exempt center, the "Nader group" is able to receive charitable donations and grants to further studies and has acted as a forum on a wide range of consumer interest projects, e.g., Nader's investigation of Congress, and his study of federal agencies regulating drug safety, automotive safety, pollution, pensions, nursing homes, and NIMH itself (see Chu and Trotter, 1974).

Nader's study groups and research center not only are illustrative of one type of routinized, charismatic social reform, but also demonstrate linkages of types of reform intelligence to the typology of reform organizations. Not only has Nader regularized investigation and reform, he and his associates have also employed a higher quality of intelligence in their analysis than was true of previous generations of American muckrakers, investigative reporters, and would-be reformers. Thus, a consideration of new forms of social reform movements raises the issue of the new forms of policy-relevant intelligence used by government crusaders. All have had to increase the quality of the knowledge used in the management of public affairs. Hence, the refinement of the intelligence used in policy analysis and a formalization of the process of developing and imparting this intelligence to new policy actors.

The New Intelligence Technologies, the Policy Process, and Bureaucracy

The rise of planned program budgeting systems (PPBS), the techniques of systems analysis, the development of a science of evaluation research, the adoption of quantitative analytic tools (e.g., econometrics), the emergency of "generic" schools of policy analysis--all these phenomena have altered the kinds and uses of intelligence in the policy formation and implementation process, both public and private. Ironically, these new techniques have created a new possibility for solo reformers or small groups of social reformers (cf. Wilensky, 1967: 18-19; 186-190; cf. Lynn, 1978).

312

The stated objective of all these new intelligence generating and analyzing technologies is to bring to the process of policy design, adoption and implementation, a predictability, accountability, cost-effectiveness, and control, in short, rationality. Weber (1978) had foreseen these developments; he viewed the central tendency of modern social forms as the demystification and disenchantment of the universe and the rise of impersonal, rational modes of domination, control, and production. The development of PPBS and other tools fulfills Weber's vision and represents efforts to gain greater mastery over the mode of domination which increasingly controls all spheres of modern life, the bureaucracy.

In a modification of the Weberian perspective, Downs' (1967) less tragic, more pragmatic view says simply: bureaucracy is here to stay because complex modern society must have non-market oriented organizations that can intervene in markets to assure that the relevant "costs and benefits enter into the decision-making process" (Downs, 1967:32 -33). An expansion in the scope of bureaucratic operations requires that the efforts increase the precision with which costs and benefits can be assessed. Since bureaucracies usually lack market mechanisms to make such assessments, methods like PPBS have risen to meet this evaluation need. For example, by attempting to link costs and benefits of producing services by bureaucratic modes, these techniques seek to aid producers and consumers of services in making intelligent production and consumption decisions.

The loss of value-neutral knowledge. Ironically, the very application of new forms of scientific intelligence to the policy-making process compromises and even erodes the objectivity, the value neutrality of such data collection and analysis methods. The bureaucracies are involved at all stages of the enactment and implementation of policy mandates. Their techniques lose their objective, value-neutral quality, and potentially become themselves part of the arsenal of tools available to reformers and anti-reformers alike. The so-called Pentagon Papers reveal how the knowledge of objective social, economic, and military conditions in Southeast Asia was distorted and misused by bureaucrats and consultants that sought to justify a bankrupt campaign

313

to support a corrupt dictatorship in Southeast Asia. The sad case of the Viet Nam war thus shows how modern policy analytic tools can be misused and intelligence rendered useless (cf. Wilensky, 1972).

<u>The emergence of the policy analyst.</u> These management techniques may not necessarily just enhance the control of bureaucrats, their masters, and those who do their bidding (e.g., consulting firms, "think tanks"), but can serve the new version of the solo-charismatic social reformer as well. That is, an age of bureaucratic control, new technologies, and forms of knowledge has witnessed the emergence of a new form of the social reform activist: the policy analyst. This new generalist is a person capable of employing a variety of generic skills and approaches in the service of the public sector.

And these skills of the policy analyst are now increasingly imparted in formal training programs in schools of public affairs, public management, and public policy. Just as the 19th-century reform activity took on a professional cast with the gradual formalization of the training of social workers (cf. Wilensky and Lebeaux, 1958), the founding of formal training programs in public policy analysis and management in the latter-half of the 20th-century coincides with both the qualitative and quantitative expansion of the areas of concern of the public sector and the refinement of the policy-relevant knowledge base (Lynn, 1978).

Policy actors are being not only trained in these new techniques of problem identification and solution—using the latest rational-scientific techniques—but also housed within colleges, universities, bureaus, agencies, and private "think tanks."

Thus, as the intelligence for policy-making has been altered in quality as well as the quantity of the data employed to support the arguments made for and against policy options, this so-called knowledge explosion, with its technical application in the policy arena, has also necessitated the creation of "counter-institutes and bureaus" of health, education, and the like (e.g., the American Enterprise Institute and Brookings Institution) that can develop and

314

marshall the information to support the critics of the establishment of governmental agencies.

The marketing of social reform. The modern era, with its instant, universal, accessible modes of mass communication has also transformed the voluntary formal reform associations. Marketing of social reform (or attempts to resist such reforms) is thus a by-product of the mass marketing of the goods and services of post-industrial, scientific age.

The modern reform association and professional societies as well as solo reformers and policy analysts must now be as conscious of the style and manner of their presentation as they are about the adequacy of the content of the policy intelligence they are seeking to make available for use in the policy-making process. As noted, the charismatic reformer has always been aware of the necessity of maintaining the appearance of impeccability and uncorruptability in public. The organizational heirs to solo reforms have also had to struggle with the problem of the public image, appearance, and perception of the routinized reform movements. Just as producers of goods and services seek to gain the maximum amount of information about markets, and employ that information in the production and distribution, so the solo reformers, organized reformers associations, structural-interest groups, bureaus, and the like all consiously design their campaigns to gain the attention of public officials with a view towards increasing the acceptability of not only their programs but also their image.

An example of this marketing of social reform can be seen in the English National Association for Mental Health's attempts to transform their media image by changing their name to MIND, and thereby enhance the prospects of success for their reform campaigns in an era when other reform movements have successfully crafted a media identity. Another example can be found in the Network Against Psychiatric Assault (NAPA), a California organization composed chiefly of former mental patients, their families, and friends, that seek to attract the public concern over patient abuse in an era of psycho-pharmacology. Both MIND and NAPA (Napa is also the location of a California state mental hospital) are organizations that are attempting to grab and hold media (particularly television) attention in an era when most knowledge of events is imparted in news reports that last several minutes at most on an evening news program. Names like MIND and NAPA--like product names--are designed to more quickly fix the public attention on issues of concern to social reformers and thereby enable reformers to impart their message and influence public officials more effectively.

Marketing of reform and policy-relevant intelligence. Valid and reliable policy-relevant intelligence in policy-making is no less crucial than truth in advertising consumer products in an era of mass marketing. As in commercial marketing in social reform, the cosmetic alterations of a reform association or a bureaucratic-based reform group are no substitute for good, hard intelligence in the service of reform. The success of new solo-social reformers (e.g., Ralph Nader) was initially based on the ability of such reformers to develop, analyze, and present the best evidence supporting their arguments for reform. In other words, attempts to market social reform proposals are no substitute for the development of rational-scientific evidence supporting a proposal for reform (e.g., imposing auto safety standards).

The case of the English National Association for Mental Health (MIND) provides evidence that a cosmetic name change can produce identity problems: the new name MIND for the NAMH creates an ambiguous, diffuse image that its designers did not intend and may even alienate potential supporters; unlike the name Shelter, MIND does not evoke an identifiable image and so does not really assist the English NAMH in its reform campaigns in the absence of new policy-relevant intelligence. MIND has sought such new knowledge in the review of mental health detention laws and voluntary treatment regulations. But such a review has not had a direct, policy-making, pay-off that had been anticipated (cf. Gostin, 1975). My study of MIND suggests that reform movements, seeking to alter one or another aspects of a society's normative order, cannot succeed merely by adopting the most fashionable media-age devices for marketing their proposals. Hard, reliable policy-relevant intelligence must be generated or gathered and made available to policy actors best positioned to make effective use of such knowledge.

Summary and Conclusions

In this chapter, I have suggested how to extend the theory of reform movements that integrates elements of Weber's organizational theory, Smelser's theory of collective behavior, Wilensky's concept of organizational intelligence, Alford's notion of structural-interest groups, and various definitions of lobbyists. With examples drawn from the study of mental health reform movements and from the recent history of public policy-making in other areas, one can see how the analytic typologies of Figures 1, 2, and 3 represent useful ways to conceptualize the process of creating social programs.

Only the further use of an integrated theory of reform movements will demonstrate the usefullness of this formulation and suggest modifications and elaborations. And the examination of these groups will be increasingly important because of the changing character of public policy making. Reform movements and the lobbyists connected with them, will play an larger role in shaping the outcome of legislative and executive decision making. Thus, a deeper understanding of the conditions under which reform movements form, their organizational patterns emerge, and the connections develop between reformers, lobbyists, and interest groups, becomes important. When traditional political party discipline is declining, when party manifestos are unenforceable, and the policy-making options are constrained, an understanding of the reformer and reform movement is crucial for the comprehension of the policy making process.

BIBLIOGRAPHY

This bibliography contains not only the references for citations in the text, but also additional material read in the course of preparing this work.

Aaron, Henry J. 1973. Why Is Welfare So Hard to Reform? Washington, D.C.: Brookings Institution.

Abel-Smith, Brian and Richard Titmuss. 1956. The Cost of the National Health Service. (Cambridge: Cambridge University Press National Institute of Economics and Social Research Occasional Paper #18).

Abel-Smith, Brian. 1960. A History of the Nursing Profession. London: Heinemann.

_____. 1964. The Hospitals: A Study in Social Administration in England and Wales. Cambridge: Harvard University Press.

_____. 1967. An International Study of Health Expenditure and Its Relevance for Health Planning. Geneva: WHO Public Health Paper #32.

Alaszewski, Andy, et al. 1981. "Another Dose of Managerialism? Commentary on the Consultative Paper 'Patients First.'" In Social Science and Medicine, 15A:3-15.

Alford, Robert R. 1975. Health Care Politics: Ideological and Interest Group Barriers to Reform. Chicago: University of Chicago Press.

Allison, Graham T. 1971. Essence of Decision: Explaining the Cuban Missile Crisis. Boston: Little, Brown and Company.

American Academy of Political and Social Science. The Annals. 1938. Social Problems and Policies in Sweden. Edited by Bertil Ohlin, Ph.D. Vol. 197 (May).

American College of Hospital Administrators. 1971. The Swedish Health Services System. Chicago: ACHA by University of Chicago Press.

American Psychiatric Association. 1968. Diagnostic and Statistical Manual-II. New York: American Psychiatric Association.

Angrist, Shirley S. 1968. "The Mental Hospital: Its History and Destiny." In The Mental Patient. Edited by Stephen Spitzer and Norman K. Denzin. New York: McGraw-Hill.

Ander, O. Fritiof. 1958. The Building of Modern Sweden: the Reign of Gustav V, 1907-1950. Rock Island, Ill.: Ansgnstana Book Concern.

Anderson, O. W. 1971. "Styles of Planning Health Services: The U.S., Sweden, and England." In International Journal of Health Service. Vol. 1, No. 2: 106-120.

_____. 1972. Health Care: Can There Be Equity? The United States, Sweden, and England. New York: Wiley.

Andren, Nils. 1968. Modern Swedish Government. (Second Edition). Stockholm: Almqvist and Wiksell.

Arieti, Silvano (Ed.). 1974. American Handbook of Psychiatry (Second Edition). New York: Basic Books.

Armour, Philip, C. L. Estes, and Maureen L. Noble. 1978. "Problems in the Design and Implementation of a National Policy on Again: A Study of Title III of the Older Americans Act." In Policy Studies Annual Review. Edited by Howard E. Freeman. Beverly Hills: Sage Publications.

_____. 1981. "Implementing the Older Americans Act." In Robert B. Hudson (Ed.) The Aging in Politics: Process and Policy. Springfield Ill.: C. C. Thomas.

Armstrong, John A. 1973. European Administrative Elite. Princeton: Princeton University Press.

Ashdown, Margaret and S. Clement Brown. 1953. Social Service and Mental Health: An Essay on Psychiatric Social Workers. London: Routledge & Kegan Paul.

Axelsson, Stellan and Ulf Nicolansson. 1977. "Community Health Nursing--Farthest Outpost of the Health and Medical Services." In Current Sweden (January). Stockholm: Swedish Institute.

Babchuk, Nicholas and John N. Edwards. 1965. "Voluntary Associations and the Integration Hypothesis." In Sociological Inquiry. (Spring).

Baker, A. A. 1976. Comprehensive Psychiatric Services. Oxford: B. H. Blackwell.

Bardach, Eugene. 1972. Skill Factor in Politics. Berkeley: University of California Press.

_____. 1974. "Upgrading the Quality of Residential Care for the Long Term Mentally Ill." An Address to Kings View Foundation Symposium on Community Mental Health and Developmental Disabilities.

_____. 1977. The Implementation Game. Cambridge: MIT Press.

Barnard, Keith and Kenneth Lee (Eds.). 1977. Conflicts in the National Health Service. London: Crown Helm.

Barten, Harvey and Leopold Bellak (Eds.). 1972. Progress in Community Mental Health. New York: Grune and Stratton.

Barton, Walter E. and Charlotte J. Sanborn. 1977. An Assessment of the Community Mental Health Movement. Lexington, Mass.: Lexington Books.

Barton, Walter E., et al. 1961. Impressions of European Psychiatry. Washington, D.C.: American Psychiatric Association.

Baruch, Geoff and Andrew Treacher. 1978. _Psychiatry Observed_. Boston: Routledge and Kegan Paul.

Bateson, Gregory., et al. 1956. "Toward a theory of schizophrenia." _Behavioral Science_. 1 (Oct.): 251-264.

Beers, Clifford. 1944. _A Mind that Found Itself_. New York: Doubleday.

Becker, Howard. 1963. _The Outsiders_. New York: Free Press.

Belknap, I. 1956. _Human Problems of a State Mental Hospital_. New York: McGraw-Hill.

Bellak, Leopold. (Ed.). 1961. _Contemporary European Psychiatry_. New York: Grove Press.

Bellak, Leopold, _et al_. 1973. _Ego Functions in Schizophrenics, Neurotics, and Normals_. New York: Wiley.

Bellak, Leopold. (Ed.). 1974. _A Concise Handbook of Community Psychiatry and Community Mental Health_. New York: Grune & Stratton, Harcourt Brace Jovanovich.

Beigel, Allan and Alan I. Levensen. 1972. _The Community Mental Health Center_. New York: Basic Books.

Bendix, Reinhard. 1960. _Max Weber: An Intellectual Portrait_. New York: Doubleday.

_____. 1963. _Work and Authority in Industry_. New York: Haper Torch Books.

_____. 1964. _Nation Building and Citizenship_. New York: Wiley.

Berger, Philip, Beatrix Hamburg, and David Hamburg. 1977. "Mental Health: Progress and Problems." In _Doing Better and Feeling Worse_. Edited by John Knowles. Daedalus 106 (Winter): 261-276.

Berube, Maurice R. and Marilyn Gittell (Eds.). 1969. Confrontation at Ocean Hill-Brownsville. New York: Praeger.

Bindoff, S. T. 1950. Tudor England. London: C. Nicholls.

Board, Joseph R. 1970. The Government and Politics of Sweden. New York: Houghton Mifflin.

Bond, Earl D. 1950. Thomas W. Salmon, Psychiatrist. New York: Norton.

Bransby, E. R. 1974. "The Extent of Mental Illness in England and Wales." In Health Trends 6: 56-59.

Brenner, Harvey. 1973. Mental Illness and the Economy. Cambridge: Harvard University Press.

Briggs, Asa. 1961. "The Welfare State in Historical Perspective." In Archives of European Sociology 11: 221-258.

Bromberg, Walter. 1963. "History of Treatment of Mental Disorders." In The Encyclopedia of Mental Health. Edited by Albert Deutsch and Helen Fishman. Vol. 3: 737-746. New York: Franklin-Watts.

Brooke, Eileen M. 1967. A Census of Patients in Psychiatric Hospitals Beds, 1966. London: HMSO.

Brothwood, John. 1973. "The Development of National Policy." In Policy for Action: A Symposium on the Planning of a Comprehensive District Psychiatric Service. Edited by Robert Cawley and Gorden McLachlan. London: Oxford University Press.

Brown, Bertram S., Lorrin M. Koran, and Frank Ochberg. 1977. "Community Mental Health Centers Impact and Analysis." In Lawrence Corey et al. (Eds.). Medicine in a Changing Society. 141-150. St. Louis: C. V. Mosby.

Brown, George W. and J. K. Wing. 1966. Schizophrenia and Social Care. London: Oxford University Press.

Brown, George W. 1973. "The Mental Hospital as an Institution." In Social Science and Medicine, 7: 407-424.

Burns, James MacGregor. 1963. The Deadlock of Democracy: Four Party Politics in America. Englewood Cliffs, N.J.: Prentice-Hall-Spectrum.

Burns, Kenneth E. 1978. "A Study of Methods Used in Planning Psychiatric Bed Needs". Atlanta, Georgia: Health Systems Research Center Paper.

Burrow, James G. 1977. Organized Medicine in the Pregressive Era: The Move Toward Monopoly. Baltimore: Johns Hopkins.

Caplan, Ruth B. 1969. Psychiatry and the Community in Nineteenth Century. New York: Basic Books.

Carstairs, G. M. 1959. "The Social Limits of Eccentricity: An English Study." In Culture and Mental Health. Edited by M. Opler. New York: MacMillan.

_____. 1966. "Psychiatric Problems of Overdeveloped Counties." In American Journal of Psychiatry 122: 12.

_____. 1968. "Problems in Evaluative Research." In Community Mental Health: An International Perspective. Edited by R. H. Williams and L. D. Ozarin. San Francisco: Jossey-Bass.

_____. 1973. "Psychiatric Problems of Developing Countries." In British Journal of Psychiatry, 123: 574 (September): 271-277.

Cartwright, F. F. 1977. A Social History of Medicine. London: Longmans.

Cawley, Robert and Gordon McLachlan (Eds.). 1973. Policy for Action: A Symposium on the Planning of a Comprehensive District Psychiatric Service. London: Oxford University Press for the Nuffield Provincial Hospital Trust.

Chapman, Brian. 1959. The Profession of Government. London: George Allen and Unwin.

Chu, Franklin D. and Sharland Trotter. 1974. The Madness Establishment Ralph Nader Study Group Report on NIMH. New York: Grossman Publishers.

Clark, Gary J. 1979. "In Defense of Deinstitutionalization." In Milbank Memorial Fund Quarterly Health and Society. 57: 4: 461-497. (Fall).

Clausen, John A. 1956. Sociology and the Field of Mental Health. New York: Russell Sage.

_____. 1961. "Mental Disorders." In Contemporary Social Problems, Second Edition. Edited by Robert K. Merton and Robert A. Nisbet. New York: Harcourt, Brace & World.

_____. 1966. "The Sociology of Mental Illness." In Sociology Today. Edited by Robert K. Merton. II: 485-508.

_____. 1970. "Social Psychiatry and Mental Health Programs in the United States". Presented at the 7th World Congress of Sociology, Committee on Psychiatric Sociology, Varna, Bulgaria, (September).

_____. 1972. "Sociology of Mental Disorder." In The Handbook of Medical Sociology. Edited by Howard Freeman et al. Englewood Cliffs: Prentice Hall.

Clausen J. A. and Carol Huffine. 1975. "Socio-cultural and Social Psychological Factors Affecting Social Responses to Mental Disorders." In Journal of Social Issues. 16.

Clausen, J. A. and M. L. Kohn. 1954. "The Ecological Approach in Social Psychiatry." In American Journal of Sociology. 60 (September): 140-151.

_____. 1959. "Relation of Schizophrenic to Social Structure of a Small City." In Epidemiology of Mental Disorders. Edited by Benjamin Pasamanick.

Washington: American Association for the Advancement of Science. Pub. No. 60.

_____. 1960. "Social Relation and Schizophrenia: A Research Report & Perspective." In The Etiology of Schizophrenia. Edited by Don D. Jackson. New York: Basic Books.

Clausen, John A. and Marian R. Yarrow (Eds.). 1955. "The Impact of Mental Illness on the Family." In Journal of Social Issues. Vol. XI: No. 4 (Entire issue).

Cole, Jonathan O. and Ralph W. Gerard (Eds.). 1959. Psychopharmacology: The Problems in Evaluation. Washington, D.C.: National Academy of Sciences. National Research Council Publication #583.

Cole, Margaret and Charles Smith (Eds.). 1958. Democratic Sweden: A Volume of Studies Prepared by Members of the New Fabian Research Bureau. London: George Routledge.

Coleman, James S., Elihu Katz, and Herbert Menzel. 1966. Medical Innovation: A Diffusion Study. Indianapolis: The Bobbs-Merrill Co.

Connery, Robert H. 1961. The Politics of Mental Health: Organizing Mental Health in Metropolitan Areas. New York: Columbia University Press.

Corey, Lawrence, et al. (Eds.). 1977. Medicine in a Changing Society. Second Edition. St. Louis: C. V. Mosby.

Council of State Governments. 1950. The Mental Health Programs of the Forty-Eight States: A Report to the Governors Conference. Chicago: Council of State Governments.

Carfoord, Clarence. 1976. "Changing Mental Health Services in Sweden." In Current Sweden. No. 114 (May). Stockholm: Swedish Institute.

Crocetti, Guido, et al. 1974. Contemporary Attitudes Toward Mental Illness. Pittsburg: University of Pittsburg Press.

Culyer, A. J. and P. Jacobs. 1972. "The War and Public Expenditure on Mental Health Care in England and Wales." In Social Science and Medicine 6: 35-36.

Dahrendorf, Ralf. 1959. Class and Class Conflict in Industrial Society. Stanford: Stanford University Press.

Dain, Norman. 1964. Concepts of Insanity in the United States, 1759-1865. New Brunswick, N.J.: Rutgers University Press

David, Henry P. (Ed.). 1966. International Trends in Mental Health. New York: McGraw-Hill.

Davis, Kingsley. 1938. "Mental Hygiene and the Class Structure." In Psychiatry 1 (February): 55-56.

Denner, Bruce and Richard Price (Eds.). 1973. Community Mental Health: Social Action and Reaction. New York: Holt Rinehart and Winston.

Deutsch, Albert. 1944a. "Military Psychiatry: The Civil War, 1861-1865." In One Hundred Years of American Psychiatry. Edited by J. K. Hall, et al. New York: Columbia University Press.

_____. 1944b. "The History of Mental Hygiene." In One Hundred Years of American Psychiatry. Edited by J. K. Hall, et al. New York: Columbia University Press.

_____. 1944c. "Military Psychiatry in World War II." In One Hundred Years of American Psychiatry. Edited by J. K. Hall, et al. New York: Columbia University Press.

_____. 1948. The Shame of the States. New York: Harcourt, Brace.

_____. 1949. <u>The Mentally Ill in America.</u> New York: Columbia University Press.

Deutsch, Albert and Helen Fishman (Eds.). 1963. <u>Encyclopedia of Mental Health.</u> New York: Franklin-Watts.

Dicks, H. V. 1970. <u>Fifty Years of the Tavistock Clinic.</u> London: Routledge and Kegan Paul.

Dickens, A. G. 1966. <u>Reformation and Society in Sixteenth Century Europe.</u> London: Thames and Hudson.

Dohrenwend, Bruce P. and Barbara Dohrenwend. 1969. <u>Social States & Psycholigical Disorder: A Causal Inquiry.</u> New York: Wiley.

Douglas-Wilson, I. and Gordon McLachlin. 1973. <u>Health Service Prospects: An International Survey.</u> Boston: Little Brown.

Downs, Anthony. 1967. <u>Inside Bureaucracy.</u> Boston: Little Brown.

Drew, Elizabeth. 1967. "The Health Syndicate: Washington's Noble Conspirators." In <u>The Atlantic,</u> (Dec.): 75-82

Duhl, Leonard (Ed.). 1963. <u>The Urban Condition: People and Policy in the Metropolis.</u> New York: Simon and Schuster.

Duhl, Leonard and Robert L. Leopold. 1968. <u>Mental Health and Urban Social Policy: A Case Book of Community Actions.</u> San Francisco: Jossey-Bass.

Durkheim, Emile. 1951. <u>Suicide.</u> Translated by John A. Spaulding and George Simpson. New York: Free Press [1897].

Dysinger, Robert H. (Ed.). 1953. "Mental Health in the United States." In <u>The Annals of the American Academy of Political and Social Science.</u> Vol. 286 (March). Entire issue.

327

Eckstein, Harry. 1958. The English Health Service: Its Origin, Structure, and Achievements. Cambridge: Harvard University Press.

_____. 1960. Pressure Group Politics: The Case of the British Medical Association. Stanford, California: Stanford University Press.

Ehrmann, Henry W. (Ed.). 1964. Interest Groups in Four Countries. Pittsburg: University of Pittsburg Press.

Eisenstadt, S. N. 1968. Weber on Charisma and Institution Building. Chicago: University of Chicago Press.

Ellenberger, Henri. 1974. "Psychiatry From Ancient to Modern Times." In Silvano Arieti (ed.) American Handbook of Psychiatry. Vol. 1: 3-27.

English National Association for Mental Health. 1961. Emerging Patterns for the Mental Health Services: Annual Conference Report. London: National Association for Mental Health.

_____. 1974a. Co-ordination or Chaos? The Run-down of Psychiatric Hospitals. MIND Report No. 13. (May). London: NAMH (MIND).

_____ (MIND). 1974b. Annual Report for Year 1973-74. London: NAMH (MIND).

_____. 1975a Annual Report 1974-75. London: NAMH (MIND).

_____. 1975b. Sanity and Society. London: NAMH (MIND).

Enthoven, Alain. 1978. "Consumer-Choice Health Plan." In New England Journal of Medicine 298: 650-658 and 709-720. (March 23 & 30)

Erikson, Erik H. 1950. Childhood and Society. New York: Norton.

Erikson, Kai. 1966. <u>Wayward Puritans</u>. New York: John Wiley.

Estes, C. L. 1979. <u>The Aging Enterprise</u>. San Francisco: Jossey-Bass.

Estes, C. L. and Howard E. Freeman. 1976. "Strategies of Design and Research for Intervention." In <u>Handbook of Aging and Social Sciences</u>. Edited by R. H. Binstock and E. Shanas. New York: Van Nostrand Reinhold.

Fabian Society. <u>The Fifth Social Service</u>. Glasgow: Civic Press, Ltd.

Falk, I. S. 1977. "Proposals for National Health Insurance in the USA: Origins and Evolution and Some Perception for the Future." In <u>Health and Society</u> (Spring): 161-191.

Farndale, James. 1964. <u>Trends in the National Health Service</u>. New York: Macmillan for Pergaman Press.

Feldman, Saul. 1973. <u>Administration of Mental Health Services</u>. Springfield, Ill.: C. C. Thomas.

Felicetti, Daniel A. 1975. <u>Mental Health and Retardation Politics: The Mind Lobbies in Congress</u>. New York: Praeger.

Felix, Robert and Morton Kramer. 1953. "Extent of the Problem of Mental Disorders in Mental Health in the United States." In <u>The Annals of the American Academy of Political and Social Science</u>. Vol. 286 (March).

Felix, Robert. 1967. <u>Mental Illness: Progress and Prospects</u>. New York: Columbia University Press

Ferrer, H. P. (Ed.). 1972. <u>The Health Services-Administration, Research, and Management</u>. London: Butterworths.

Finkel, Norman J. 1976. <u>Mental Illness and Health: Its Legacy, Tensions, and Changes</u>. New York: Macmillan.

Fischer-Hamberger, Esther. 1975. "Germany and Austria." In
World History of Psychiatry. Edited by John W. Howells.
New York: Bruner and Mazel.

Fleisher, Frederic. 1967. The New Sweden: The Challenge
of a Disciplined Democracy. New York: David McKay.

Foley, Henry A. 1975. Community Mental Health Legislation:
The Formative Process. Lexington, Mass.: Lexington
Books

Foucault, Michael. 1965. Madness and Civilization. New
York: Pantheon.

Frank, Jerome D. 1963. "Psychotherapy." In The
Encyclopedia of Mental Health. Edited by Albert
Deutsch. New York: Franklin-Watts.

Freedman, Alfred M., Harold I. Kaplan and Benjamin J.
Shadock (Eds.). 1975. Comprehensive Textbook of
Psychiatry--II. Baltimore: Williams and Walkins.

Freeman, Howard E. 1972. Handbook of Medical Sociology.
Second Edition. Englewood Cliffs: Prentice-Hall.

Freeman, Hugh and James Farndale (Eds.). 1963. Trends in
the Mental Health Services. Oxford: Pergaman Press.

_____. 1967. New Aspects of the Mental Health
Services. Oxford: Pergaman Press.

Freud, Sigmund. 1964. New Introductory Lectures on
Psychoanalysis. New York: Norton translated by James
Strachey. [1933]

_____. 1968. A General Introduction to
Psychoanalysis. New York: Washington Square Press
[1924].

Fried, Max. 1964. "Effects of Social Change on Mental
Health." In Personality and Social Structure. Edited by
N. J. Smelser and W. Smelser. New York: Wiley.

Freidson, Eliot. 1970. The Profession of Medicine. New York: Harper and Row.

Furniss, Norman and Timothy Tilton. 1977. The Case of the Welfare State: From Social Security to Social Equality. Bloomington: Indiana University Press.

Furman, Sylvan S. 1965. Community Mental Health in Northern Europe. Washington, D.C.: U.S. Public Health Service Document. No. 1407

Gemmill, Paul F. 1960. Britain's Search for Health: The First Decade of the National Health Service. Philadelphia: University of Pennsylvania Press.

Gerth, Hans and C. Wright Mills. 1946. From Max Weber. New York: Galaxy-Oxford University Press.

Giddens, Anthody. 1973. Class Structure of Advanced Societies. London: Hutchinson.

_____. 1977. Capitalism and Modern Social Theory. Cambridge: Cambridge University Press

Gilbert, Bently B. 1970. British Social Policy 1914-1939. London: B. T. Batsford.

Glaser, Barney G. and Anselm L. Strauss. 1967. The Discovery of Grounded Theory: Strategies for Qualitative Research. Chicago: Aldine

Glennerster, H. 1976. Social Service Budgets and Social Policy: British and American Experience. London: Allen and Unwin.

Goffman, Erving. 1961. Asylums. Garden City, N.J.: Doubleday-Anchor.

Goldhamer, H. and W. H. Marshall. 1953. Psychosis and Civilization: Two Studies in the Frequency of Mental Disease. New York: The Free Press.

Goodman, Paul. 1960. Growing Up Absurd: Problems of Youth in the Organized Society. New York: Random House.

Gore, Charles P., Kathleen Jones, Wallis Taylor, and Brian Ward. 1964. "Needs and Beds: A Regional Census of Psychiatric Hospital Patients." In The Lancet (August 29): 452-460.

Gore, W. R. 1970. "Societal Reaction as an Explanation of Mental Illness: An Evaluation." In American Sociological Review 35: 5: 873-883.

Gorman, Mike. 1956. Every Other Bed. Cleveland: World Publishing.

Gostin, Larry O. 1975. A Human Condition: The Mental Health Act from 1959 to 1975. Vol. 1. London: National Association for Mental Health (MIND).

Grad, Jacqueline C. 1968. "A Two-Year Follow-up." In Community Mental Health: An Internal Perspective. Edited by R. H. Williams and L. D. Ozarin. San Francisco: Jossey-Bass.

Greenland, Cyril. 1970. Mental Illness and Civil Liberty: A Study of Mental Health Review Tribunals in England and Wales. London: G. Bell & Sons., Occationals Paper on Social Administration No. 38.

Grob, Gerald N. 1966. The State and the Mentally Ill: A History of Worcester State Hospital in Massachusetts, 1830-1920. Chapel Hill: University of North Carolina Press

_____. 1973. Mental Health Institutions in America: Social Policy to 1875. New York: The Free Press

Gruenberg, Ernest M. 1966. Evaluating the Effectiveness of Community Health Services. Milbank Memorial Fund Quarterly 1 (January).

Gursslin, Orville R. and Raymond G. Hunt and Jack L. Roach. 1959-60. "Social Class and the Mental Health Movement." In Social Problems 7:3 (Winter): 210-218.

Guttman, Damil and Barry Willner. 1976. The Shadow Government. New York: Pantheon Books Random House.

Hall, Calvin S. 1954. A Primer of Freudian Psychology. Cleveland: World Publishing.

Hall, M. Penelope. 1952. The Social Services of Modern England. London: Routledge and Kegan Paul.

Hall, Phoebe. 1976. Reforming the Welfare. London: Heineman.

Halsey, A. H. (Ed.). 1972. Trends in British Society Since 1900. London: Macmillan.

Hamilton, Samuel W. 1944. "The History of American Mental Hospitals." In One Hundred Years of American Psychiatry. Edited by J. H. Hall et al. New York: Columbia University Press.

Hammond, Kenneth R. and C. R. B. Joyce. 1975. Psychoactive Drugs and Social Judgment Theory and Research. New York: Wiley Interscience.

Hancock, M. Donald. 1972. Sweden: The Politics of Post-Industrial Change. Hinsdale, Illinois: Dryden Press.

Harris, Jose. 1977. William Beveridge: A Biography. Oxford: Clarendon Press.

Hartz, Louis. 1955. The Liberal Tradition in America. New York: Harcourt, Brace & World.

_____. 1964. The Founding of New Societies. New York: Harcourt, Brace & World.

Hay, J. R. 1975. The Origins of Liberal Welfare Reforms 1906-1914. London: Macmillan.

Heclo, Hugh. 1974. Modern Social Politics in Britain and Sweden. New Haven: Yale University Press.

Heidenheimer, Arnold J., C.T. Adams, and Hugh Heclo. 1975. Comparative Social Policy. New York: St. Martin's Press

Hill, Christopher. 1969. Reformation to Industrial Revolution. Harmondsworth: Pelican Books

Hobsbawn, Eric. J. 1968. Industry and Empire: From 1750 to the Present Day. London: Weidenfeld and Niclson.

Hodgkinson, Ruth E. 1967. The Origins of the National Health Service. Berkeley: University of California Press.

Hoenig J. and M. H. Hamilton. 1969. The De-Segregation of the Mentally Ill. London: Routledge and Kegan Paul.

Hollingshead, A. and R. C. Redlich. 1958. Social Class and Mental Illness. New York: Wiley.

Höjer, Alex. 1938. "Public Health and Medical Care." In Social Problems and Policies in Sweden. Edited by Bertil Ohlin. The Annals of the American Academy of Political and Social Science. Vol. 197 (May): 104-119.

Holmberg, Gunnar. 1972. The Integration of Continued Rehabilitation. Stockholm: National Board of Health and Welfare.

Honigsbaum, Frank. The Struggle for the Minister of Health 1914-1919. London: Bell.

Howard, Anthony. 1963. "We Are the Masters Now." In The Age of Austerity. Edited by Michael Sissons and Philip French. London: Hodder and Stoughton.

Howells, John G. 1975. World History of Psychiatry. New York: Brunner/Mazel.

Howells, John G. and M. Livia Osborn. 1975. "Great Britain." In World History of Psychiatry. New York: Brunner/Mazel.

Humes, Samuel and Eileen M. Martin. 1961. The Structure of Local Governments Throughout the World. The Hague: Martinus Nijhoff.

Huntington, Samuel P. 1968. Political Order in Changing Societies. New Haven: Yale University Press.

Illich, Ivan. 1976. Medical Nemisis: The Expropriation of Health. New York: Pantheon

Jackson, Don D. (Ed.). 1960. The Etiology of Schizophrenia. New York: Basic Books.

Jaco, E. G. 1960. The Social Epidemiology of Mental Disorders. New York: Russell Sage.

Jacoby, Henry. 1973. The Bureaucratization of the World. Berkeley: University of California Press.

Jahoda, Marie. 1958. Current Concepts of Positive Mental Health. New York: Basic Books.

Janowitz, Morris. 1976. Social Control of the Welfare State. Chicago: University of Chicago Press.

Jeffreys, Margot. 1965. An Anatomy of Social Welfare Services. London: Michael Joseph.

Jewell, Malcolm and Samuel C. Patterson. 1977. The Legislative Process in the United States. Third Edition. New York: Random House

Jewkes, John. 1961. The Genesis of British National Health Service. Oxford: Blackwell.

Joint Commission on Mental Health and Illness. 1961. Action for Mental Health. New York: Basic Books.

Jonas, Steven (Ed.). 1977. Health Care Delivery in the United States. New York: Springer Publishing.

335

Jones, Kathleen. 1960. Mental Health and Social Policy 1845-1959. London: Routledge and Kegan Paul.

_____. 1962a. "Address to the Royal Medico-Psychological Association." London: (February).

Jones, Kathleen and Roy Sidebotham. 1962b. Mental Hospitals at Work. London: Routledge and Kegan Paul.

Jones, Kathleen. 1963a. "Administrative Problems in the Mental Health Service." In Public Health LXXVIII: 1.

_____. 1963b. "Revolution and Reform in the Mental Health Services." In Trends in the National Health Service. Edited by W. A. J. Farndale. London: Pergaman Press.

_____. 1964. "Too Few Psychiatric Beds." In New Society. (10 September).

_____. 1971. "Moral Management and the Therapeutic Community" An Address to the Society for the Social History of Medicine. (July 3).

_____. 1972. A History of the Mental Health Services. London: Routledge and Kegan Paul.

_____. 1979. "Deinstitutionalization in Context." In Milbank Memorial Fund Quarterly Health and Society. 57:4. (Fall):552-569.

Joseph, Sir Keith. 1973. "Introduction." In Policy for Action. Edited by R. Cowley and Gordon McLachlan. London: Oxford University Press.

Kaplan, Bert (Ed.). 1964. The Inner World of Mental Illness. New York: Harper and Row.

Katz, Michael. 1978. "Origins of the Institutional State." In Marxist Perspectives 1: 4 (Winter): 6-22.

Kennedy, John F. 1963. Message Relative to Mental Illness and Mental Retardation: Feb. 5, 1963; 88th Congress, Document No. 58. Washington, D.C.: U.S. House of Representatives.

Kesey, Ken. 1962. One Flew Over the Cuckoo's Nest. New York: Viking Press.

Kessell, W. I. W. 1966. "The Whirligig of Time: A Cautionary Tale." In Community Mental Health: An International Perspective. Edited by R. Williams and L. D. Ozarin. San Francisco: Jossey-Bass.

King, Clarence Wendell. 1956. Social Movements in the United States. New York: Random House.

Klarman, Herbert E. 1977. "The Financing of Health Care." In Daedalus. Edited by John Knowles. 106:1 (Winter): 215-234.

Klein, Rudolph. 1973a. "Policy Problems and Policy Perceptions in the MHS." In Policy and Politics. Vol. 2: 3.

_____. 1973b. "National Health Service: After Reorganization." In The Political Quarterly 44 (July-Sept.): 316-328.

_____. 1973c. Complaints Against Doctors. London: C. Knight.

Knowles, John H. (Ed.). 1977. "Doing Better and Feeling Worse." In Daedalus 106:1 (Winter). Entire issue.

_____. 1977. "The Responsibility of the Individual." In Daedalus. Edited by John H. Knowles. 106:1 (Winter): 57-80.

Koran, Lorrin M. 1977. "Mental Health Services." In Health Care Delivery in the United States. Edited by Steven Jonas, et al. New York: Springer Publishing Co.

337

Kohn, M. L. and J. A. Clausen. 1955. "Social Isolation and Schizophrenia." In American Sociological Review 20 (June): 265-273.

Kramer, Morton. 1968. "The History of the Efforts to Agree on an International Classification of Mental Disorders." In Diagnostic and Statistical Manual of Mental Disorders. Washington, D.C.: American Psychiatric Association.

_____. 1969. Applications of Mental Health Statistics. Geneva: World Health Organization.

_____. 1973. "Some Perspectives on the Role of Bio-statistics and Epidemiology in the Prevention and Control of Mental Disorders." A paper presented at Reina Lapouse Mental Health Epidemiology Memorial Award Session (WN8). San Francisco, California.

_____. 1977. Psychiatric Services and the Changing Institutional Scene, 1950-1985. Washington, D.C.: DHEW, NIMH.

Kramer, Ralph M. 1969. "Ideology, Status, and Power in Board-Executive Relationships." In Readings in Community Organization Practice. Edited by Ralph M. Kramer & Harry Specht. Englewood Cliffs, N.J.: Prentice-Hall.

Krause, Eliot. 1968. "Functions of a Bureaucratic Ideology: Citizen Participation." In Social Problems. 16:2. (Fall):129-143.

_____. 1977. Power and Illness: Political Sociology of Health and Medical Care. New York: Elsevier-North Holland

Kuhn, Thomas S. 1962. The Structure of the Scientific Revolution. Chicago: University of Chicago Press.

Langfeldt, Gabriel. 1961. "Scandinavia." In Contemporary European Psychiatry. Edited by Leopold Bellak. New York: Grove Press.

Larson, M.S. 1977. *The Rise of Professionalism: A Sociological Analysis*. Berkeley: University of California Press.

Leavitt, Ruth. 1976. *The Reorganized National Health Service*. London: Croom Helm Ltd.

Leche, H.G. 1970. *Some Viewpoints on Swedish Psychiatry Today*. Stockholm: The Swedish National Board of Health and Welfare, The Psychiatric Division (March 1).

Leigh, David. 1961. *The Historical Development of British Psychiatry*. (Vols. 1 and 2). Oxford: Pergaman Press.

Leighton, Alexander H., John A. Clausen, and Robert N. Wilson. 1957. *Explorations in Social Psychiatry*. New York: Basic Books.

Levitan, Sar A. and Robert Taggart. 1976. *The Promise of Greatness*. Cambridge, Mass.: Harvard University Press.

Lewis, Aubrey. 1961. "Great Britain." In *Contemporary European Psychiatry*. Edited by Leopold Bellak. New York: Grove Press.

Lewis, Nolan D.C. 1974. "American Psychiatry From Its Beginnings to World War II." In Silvano Arieti (Ed.) *American Handbook of Psychiatry*, Vol 1. New York: Basic Books.

Lindgren, S. Ake. 1970. *Health Services in Sweden: Planning and Implementation*. Stockholm: National Board of Health and Welfare.

Lindsey, Allmont, 1962. *Socialized Medicine in England and Wales*. Chapel Hill: University of North Carolina Press.

Lipset, S. M. 1963. *First New Nation: United States in Historical and Comparative Perspective*. New York: Basic Books.

Lynn, Laurence (Ed.) 1978. Knowledge and Policy: The Uncertain Connection. Washington, D.C.: National Academy of Sciences.

Macalpine, I. and R. Hunder. 1969. George III and the Mad-Business. Harmondsworth: Allen Lane.

Manning, Christine. 1974. The Reorganized National Health Service. London: Health and Social Service Journal.

Marmor, Theodore. 1973. The Politics of Medicare. Chicago: Aldine.

Marshall, T.H. 1964. Class, Citizenship and Social Development. Garden City, N.J.: Doubleday-Anchor.

_____. 1970. Social Policy in the Twentieth Century. London: Hutchinson.

Martin, E. W. (Ed.). 1972. Comparative Developments in Social Welfare. London: Allen and Unwin.

Martindale, Don and Edith Martindale. 1971. The Social Dimensions of Mental Illness, Alcoholism, and Drug Dependence. Westport, Conn.: Greenwood.

Marx, John H. et al. 1974. "The Sociology of Community Mental Health: Historical and Methodological Perspectives." In Sociological Perspectives on Community Mental Health. Edited by P. M. Roman and H. Trice. Philadelphia: F. A. Davis.

Marx, Karl. 1972. "The Eighteenth Brumaire of Louis Bonaparte." In Marx and Engles Reader. Edited by Robert C. Tucker. New York. W. W. Norton [1851].

Mathews, F. B. 1954. Mental Health Services (Second Edition). London: Shaw and Shaw.

Matza, David. 1966. "The Disreputable Poor." In Class, Status, and Power. Edited by R. Bendix and S. M. Lipset. New York: Free Press.

Maunder, W. F. (Ed.). 1974. _Review of United Kingdom Statistical Sources_. Vols. I and II. London: Heinemann.

May, A. R. 1976. _Mental Health Services in Europe: A Review of Data Collected in Response to a WHO Questionnaire_. Geneva: World Health Organization.

Maynard, Alan. 1975. _Health Care in the European Community_. London: Croom Helm.

McCarthy, Carol. 1977. "Planning for Health Care: In _Health Care in the United States_. Edited by S. Jonas. New York: Springer.

McConnell, Grant. 1966. _Private Power and American Government_. New York: Knopf.

Mechanic, David. 1969. _Mental Health and Social Policy_. Englewood Cliffs, N.J.: Prentice Hall.

_____. 1973. _Politics, Medicine and Social Science_. New Yori: Wiley.

_____. 1978. _Medical Sociology_ (Second Edition). New York: Free Press.

Menninger, William C. 1946. "Lessons from Military Psychiatry for Civilian Psychiatry." In _Mental Hygiene_ Vol. 30.

Merton, Robert K. 1967. _Social Theory and Social Structure_. New York: Free Press.

Michaelsen, Jacob B. 1976. "Implementation." In _Policy Analysis_ Vol. 2, No. 1: 165-8.

Milbrath, Lester W. 1963. _The Washington Lobbyists_. Chicago: Rand-McNally.

Miles, Rufus E. 1974. _The Department of Health, Education and Welfare_. New York: Praeger.

Mora, George. 1974. "Recent Psychiatric Developments Since 1939." In The American Handbook of Psychiatry (Second Edition). Silvano Arieti (ed.) Vol. 1. New York: Basic Books.

_____. 1975. "Historical and Theoretical Trends in Psychiatry." In Comprehensive Textbook of Psychiatry--II. Edited by Alfred M. Freedman, et al. Baltimore: Williams and Wilkins.

Moore, Barrington, Jr. 1966. Social Origins of Dictatorship and Democracy. Boston: Beacon Press.

Morris, Mary. 1969. Voluntary Work in the Welfare State. London: Routledge and Kegan Paul.

Moynihan, Daniel Patrick. 1969. Maximum Feasible Misunderstanding. New York: Free Press.

_____. 1973. The Politics of a Guaranteed Annual Income. New York: Vintage Books.

Mutso, David. 1975. "Whatever Happened to Community Mental Health?" In The Public Interest 39 (Spring: 53-79.

Myrdal, Gunnar. 1960. Beyond the Welfare State. New Haven: Yale University Press.

Nelson, George R. (Ed.). 1953. Freedom and Welfare: Social Patterns in the Northern Countries of Europe. Published by the Ministries of Social Affairs of Denmark, Finland, Iceland, Norway and Sweden.

Nisbet, Robert. 1953. The Quest for Community. New York: Oxford University Press.

Nordick Statistisk Skriftserie. 1973. (Statistical Reports of the Nordic Countries, No. 24). Social Security in the Nordic Countries: Expenditures on and Scope of Certain Social Security Measure 1970. (1970.71). Stockholm: Socialstyrelsen.

Noyes, Arthur P. and Lawrence C. Kolb. 1958. <u>Modern Clinical Psychiatry</u>. Fifth Edition. Philadelphia: W. B. Saunders.

Oakley, Stewart. 1966. <u>The Story of Sweden</u>. London: Faber and Faber.

Office of Health Economics. 1975. <u>Medicines Which Affect the Mind</u>. London: OHE.

Ohlin, Bertil (Ed.). 1938. <u>The Social Problems and Policies in Sweden</u>. Entire issue of <u>The Annals of the American Academy of Political and Social Science</u>. Vol. 197 (May).

Olson, Mancur, Jr. 1965. <u>The Logic of Collective Action</u>. Cambridge: Harvard University Press.

Overholser, Winfred. 1944. "The Founding and the Founders of the Association." In <u>One Hundred Years of American Psychiatry</u>. Editors J. K. Hall <u>et al</u>. New York: Columbia University Press.

Palmer, R. R. and J. Colton. 1965. <u>History of the Modern World</u>. 3rd Edition. New York: Knopf.

Parry-Jones, William L. 1972. <u>The Trade in Lunacy</u>. London: Routledge and Kegan Paul.

Pasamanick, Benjamin, F. R. Scarpitti, and S. Dinitz. 1967. <u>Schizophrenics in the Community</u>. New York: Appleton-Century-Crofts.

Pinker, Robert. 1966. <u>English Hospital Statistics, 1861-1938</u>. London: Heinemann.

_____. 1971. <u>Social Theory and Social Policy</u>. London: Heinemann.

Piven, Francis Fox and Richard Cloward. 1971. <u>Regulating the Poor: The Functions of Public Welfare</u>. New York: Random House (Pantheon).

Polanyi, Karl. 1957. <u>The Great Transformation: the Political and Economic Origins of Our Time</u>. Boston: Beacon [1944].

Powell, J. Enoch. 1961. "Opening Remarks." In the NAMH Conference on <u>Emerging Patterns for the Mental Health Services and the Public</u>. London: National Association for Mental Health.

_____. 1968. <u>A New Look at Medicine and Politics</u>. London: Pitman Medical.

_____. 1969. <u>Freedom and Reality</u>. New Rochelle: Arlington House.

Pressman, Jeffrey L. and Aaron Wildavsky. 1979. <u>Implementation: How Great Expectations in Washington Are Dashed in Oakland</u>. Berkeley: University of California Press. [1973].

Redcliffe-Maud, Lord and Bruce Wood. 1972. <u>English Local Government Reformed</u>. London: Oxford University Press.

Redlich, Fredrick and Daniel Z. Freedman. 1966. <u>The Theory and Practice of Psychiatry</u>. New York: Basic Books.

Redlinger, Lawrence John. 1970. "Making Them Normal." In <u>American Behavioral Scientist</u> (Dec.).

Redman, Eric. 1973. <u>The Dance of Legislation</u>. New York: Simon & Schuster.

Rehin, G. F. and F. M. Martin. 1968. <u>Patterns and Performance in Community Care</u>. Oxford: Oxford University Press.

Retterstol, Nils. 1975. "Scandinavia and Finland." In <u>World History of Psychiatry</u>. Edited by John W. Howells. New York: Fruner and Mazel.

Ridenour, Nina. 1961. <u>Mental Health in the United States: A Fifty Year History</u>. Cambridge. Harvard University Press.

_____. 1963. "The Mental Health Movement." In
Encyclopedia of Mental Health. Edited by Albert Deutsch
and Helen Fishman. Vol. 3: 1011-1102. New York:
Franklin-Watts.

Rifkin, Alfred H. "A General Assessment of Paychiatry." In
American Handbook of Psychiatry. Edited by Sivano
Arieti Vol. 1: 117-130. New York: Basic Books.

Rimlinger, Gaston V. 1971. Welfare Policy and
Industrialization in Europe, America, and Russia. New
York: Wiley.

Ripley, Randall and Grace Franlkin. 1980. Congress, the
Bureaucracy, and Public Policy. Homewood, Ill.: Dorsey
Press.

Roberts, Nesta. Mental Health and Mental Illness. London:
Routledge and Kegan Paul.

Robinson, Kenneth. 1968. Partnership in Medical Care.
Glasgow: Jackson, Son & Co.

Robson, William Alexander & Bernard Crick. 1970. The
Future of the Social Services. Harmondsworth: Penguin.

Roman, Paul M. and Harrison M. Trice (Eds.). 1974.
Sociological Perspectives on Community Mental Health.
Philadelphia: F. A. Davis.

Roof, Madeline. 1957. Voluntary Societies and Social
Policy. London: Routledge and Kegan Paul.

Rosen, George. 1968. Madness in Society.
Chicago: Chicago University Press.

Rosenthal, Albert H. 1967. The Social Programs of Sweden:
a Search for Security in a Free Society. Minneapolis:
University of Minnesota Press.

Rosenweig, Norman. 1975. Community Mental Health Programs
in England. Detriot: Wayne State University Press.

Rothman, David J. 1971. <u>The Discovery of the Asylum:</u>
<u>Social Order and Disorder in the Republic.</u> Boston:
Little Brown.

_____. 1980. <u>Conscience and Convenience.</u>
Boston: Little Brown.

Rowse, A. L. 1950. <u>The England of Elizabeth.</u>
New York: Macmillan.

Rustow, Dankwart. 1969. <u>The Politics of Compromise.</u> New
York: Greenwood Press.

Sainsbury, Peter. 1968. "Research Methods in Evaluation."
In <u>Community Mental Health: An International</u>
<u>Perspective.</u> Edited by Richard H. Williams and Lucy D.
Ozarin. San Francisco: Jossey-Bass.

Samuelsson, Kurt. 1968. <u>From Great Power to Welfare State.</u>
London: George Allen and Unwin.

Scheff, T. J. 1966. <u>Being Mentally Ill: A Sociological</u>
<u>Theory.</u> Chicago: Aldine.

Schriftgiesser, Karl. 1951. <u>The Lobbyists: The Art and</u>
<u>Business of Influencing Lawmakers.</u> Boston: Little
Brown.

Schulz, James. 1980. <u>The Economics of Aging.</u> Belmont,
Ca.: Wadsworth.

Schumpeter, Joseph A. 1962. <u>Capitalism, Socialism and</u>
<u>Democracy.</u> New York: Harper Torchbooks.

Schwartz, Donald A. 1972. "Community Mental Health in
1972--An Assessment." In <u>Progress in Community Mental</u>
<u>Health</u> Vol. II. Edited by Harvey H. Barten and Leopold
Bellak. New York: Grine & Stratton.

Schweiker, Richard J. 1979. Hearings on Mental Health
System Act, 1979. Washington, D.C. U.S. Senate
Subcommittee on Health and Scientific Research.

Scott, Franklin D. 1977. _Sweden, the Nation's History._
Minneapolis: University of Minnesota Press.

Selznick, Philip. 1943. "An Approach to a Theory of
Bureaucracy." In _American Sociological Review._ 8: 49.

Shanas, Ethel _et al._ 1968. _Old People in Three Industrial
Societies._ New York: Atherton Press.

Sidel, Victor W. and Ruth Sidel. 1977. _A Health State: An
International Perspective on the Crises in United States
Medical Care._ New York: Pantheon.

_____. 1979. "Medical Care in Sweden:
Planned Pluralism." In _Social Change in Sweden_ 10
(February).

Sigerist, Henry E. 1944. "Psychiatry in Europe at the
Middle of the Nineteenth Century." In _One Hundred Years
of American Psychiatry._ Edited by J. K. Hall, _et al._
New York: Columbia University Press.

Sissons, Michael and Philip French (Eds.). 1963. _Age of
Austerity 1945-1951._ London: Hodder and Stoughton.

Sjogren, T. 1948. "Genetic-Statistical and Psychiatric
Investigations of a West Swedish Population." In _Acata
Psychiatrica et Neurologica._ Supplement 52.

Skultans, Veida. 1975. _Madness and Morals: Ideas on
Insanity in the Nineteenth Century._ London: Routlege
and Kegan Paul.

Smelser, Neil J. 1959. _Social Change in the Industrial
Revolution._ Chicago: University of Chicago Press.

_____. 1962. _The Theory of Collective Behavior._
London: Routlege and Kegan Paul.

Smelser, Neil J. and R. Stephen Warner. 1975. _Sociological
Theory: Historical and Formal._ Morristown, N.J.:
General Learning Press.

Soddy, Kenneth and Robert Ahrenfeldt (Eds.). 1965. <u>Mental Health in a Changing World</u>. Vol. I: Report of an International and Interprofessional Study Group Convened by the World Federation for Mental Health. Philadelphia: Lippincott.

_____. 1967. <u>Mental Health and Contemporary Thought</u>. Vol. 2. London: Tavistock. Philadelphia: Lippincott.

_____. 1967. <u>Mental Health in the Service of the Community</u>. Vol. 3. London: Tavistock. Philadelphia: Lippincott.

Speer, Albert. 1970. <u>Inside the Third Reich: Memoirs of Albert Speer</u>. New York: Macmillan.

Spitzer, Stephen and Norman K. Denzin. 1968. <u>The Mental Patient: A Reader in the Sociology of Deviance</u>. New York: McGraw-Hill.

Srole, Leo <u>et al</u>. 1962. <u>Mental Health in the Metropolis: The Midtown Manhattan Study</u> (2 vols.) New York: McGraw-Hill.

Stanton, A. H. and M. S. Schwartz. 1954. <u>The Mental Hospital</u>. New York: Basic Books.

Stanton, Esther. 1970. <u>Clients Come Last: Volunteers and Welfare Organizations</u>. Beverly Hills: Sage Publications.

Steiner, Gilbert. 1971. <u>The State of Welfare</u>. Washington, D.C.: The Brookings Institution.

Stinchcombe, Arthur L. 1978. <u>Theoretical Methods in Social History</u>. New York: Academic Press.

Strecker, Edward A. 1944. "Military Psychiatry: World War I, 1917-1918." In <u>One Hundred Years of American Psychiatry</u>. Editors J. K. Hall <u>et al</u>. New York: Columbia University Press.

Swazey, Judith P. 1974. <u>Chlorpromazine in Psychiatry</u>.
Cambridge: MIT Press.

Sweden National Board of Health and Welfare. 1973. <u>The
Basic Plan for Psychiatric Care</u>. Stockholm: NBHW,
Psychiatric Division SN3 (June).

_____. 1975. <u>This is the National Board of
Health and Welfare</u>. Stockholm. National Board of
Health and Welfare.

_____. Sociolstyrelsen. 1973.
<u>Forhandsredorisning av vissa tabeller</u>. (i AHS 1973).
Stockholm: Socialstyrelsen.

_____. 1974. <u>Abstracts from Public Health in
Sweden</u>. 1972. Stockholm: Socialstyrelsen.

_____. Swedish Institute. 1975. <u>The
Organization of Medical Care in Sweden</u>. Stockholm: The
Swedish Institute (July).

Szasz, Thomas. 1961. <u>The Myth of Mental Illness</u>. New
York: Harper and Row.

Taylor, A. J. P. 1965. <u>English History, 1914-1945</u>.
Oxford: Oxford University Press.

Thomas, Lewis. 1974. <u>The Lives of a Cell: Notes of a
Biology Watcher</u>. New York: Viking Press.

_____. 1977. "On the Science and Technology of
Medicine." In <u>Daedalus</u>. Edited by John H. Knowles.
106:1 (Winter): 35-46.

Thompson, E. P. 1968. <u>The Making of the English Working
Class</u>. Harmondsworth: Penguin Books.

Titmuss, Richard M. 1950. <u>Problems of Social Policy</u>.
London: HMSO and Longmans, Green.

_____. 1958. <u>Essays on the Welfare State</u>
(Second Edition). London: Unwin.

_____. 1961. "Community Care--Fact or Fiction." In *The Emerging Patterns for the Mental Health Services*. London: National Association for Mental Health.

_____. 1970. *The Gift Relationship: From Human Blood to Social Policy*. London: Allen & Unwin.

_____. 1974. *Social Policy: An Introduction*. London: Allen & Unwin.

Tocqueville, Alexis de. 1955. *Old Regime and the French Revolution*. Translated by Stuard Gildert. Garden City, New York: Anchor Books. [1865].

_____. 1961. *Democracy in America*. Two Volumes. Translated by John Reeve. New York: Schocken Books. [1840].

Toóth, G. C. and Eileen Brooke. 1961. "Trends in the Mental Health Population and Their Effects on Future Planning." In *The Lancet* (1 April): 710-713.

Trattner, W. L. 1979. *From Poor Law to Welfare State*. New York: Free Press.

United Kingdom. 1932 and various years. Board of Control. *Annual Reports*. London: HMSO.

_____. Department of the Environment. Welsh Office. 1974. *Local Government in England and Wales: A Guide to the New System*. London: HMSO.

_____. Department of Health and Social Security. 1968. *National Health Service: Twentieth Anniversary Conference*. London: HMSO.

_____. 1970. *National Health Service: The Future Structure of the National Health Service*. London: HMSO.

_____. 1971. *Hospital Services for the Mentally Ill*. (December). London: HMSO.

_____. 1972. The Facilities and Services of Psychiatric Hospitals in England and Wales, 1970. Stat. & Research Reports Series, No. 2. London: HMSO.

_____. 1972. Psychiatric Hospitals and Units in England and Wales: In-Patient Statistics from Mental Health Enquiry Year, 1970. Stat. and Research Report Series No. 4. London: HMSO.

_____. 1973a. The Facilities and Services of Psychiatric Hospital in England and Wales, 1971. Stat. & Research Report Series no. 4. London: HMSO.

_____. 1973b. Psychiatric Hospitals and Units in England and Wales: In-Patient Statistics from the Mental Health Enquiry Year, 1971. Stat. & Research Report Series, No. 4. London: HMSO.

_____. 1974a. Proceedings of the Conference on Psychiatric Case Registers at the University of Aberdeen, March 1973. Stat. & Research Report Series No. 7. Edited by D. J. Hall, N. C. Robertson, and R. J. Eason. London: HMSO.

_____. 1974b. Providing a Comprehensive District Psychiatric Service for the Adult Mentally Ill. Proceedings of a Conference held jointly by the Department of Health and Social Security and the Royal College of Psychiatrists on 22 June 73. Report on Health and Social Subjects, No. 8. London: HMSO.

_____. 1974. Health and Personal Social Service Statistics for England, 1974. London: HMSO.

_____. 1975. Better Services for the Mentally Ill. Cmnd. 6233. London: HMSO.

_____. 1977. Health and Personal Social Services Statistics for England, 1977. London: HMSO.

_____. Ministry of Health. Board of Control. 1932. Annual Report. London: HMSO.

_____. Ministry of Health. 1944. A National Health Service. London: HMSO.

_____. 1946. National Health Services Act, 1946: Provisions Relating to Mental Health Services. London: HMSO.

_____. 1948. National Health Services Act, 1946: Provisions Relating to Mental Health Services. London: HMSO.

_____. Ministry of Health. National Health Service. 1964. A Hospital Plan for England and Wales. (Revision to 1973-74). London: HMSO.

_____. Royal Commission on Law Relating to Mental Illnesses & Mental Deficiency, 1954-57. (Report of the Percy Commission) Cmnd. 169. London: HMSO.

United States. Department of Commerce. Bureau of the Census. 1976. Historical Statistics of the United States: Colonial Times to 1970. 2 Volumes. Washington, D.C.: U.S. Government Printing Office.

_____. Health Education and Welfare Public Health Service, NIMH. 1968. The Community Mental Health Centers Act (1963). Public Health Service Pub. No. 1298. Rockville, MD.: USHEW:NIMH.

_____. National Center for Health Statistics. 1971. Health Manpower: A County and Metropolitan Area Data Book. Rockville, Md: USHEW:NCHS.

_____. Alcohol, Drug Abuse Mental Health Administration. NIMH. 1977. Evaluating Community Mental Health Services. Edited by Isabel Davidoff et al. Rockville, MD.: NIMH.

_____. President's Commission on Mental Health. 1978. Report to the President from the President's Commission on Mental Health. 4 Volumes. Washington, D.C.: The White House.

_____. Senate. 1979. Subcommittee on Health
and Scientific Research. Reappraisal of Mental Health
Policy, 1979. Washington, D.C. Senate Committee on
Labor and Human Resources.

_____. Senate. 1979. Subcommittee on Health
and Scientific Research. Mental Health Systems Act,
1979. Washington, D.C. Senate Committee on Labor and
Human Resources.

Ullman, Leonard P. 1967. Institutions and Outcome.
Oxford: Pergammon Press.

Vail, David J. 1965. The British Mental Hospital System.
(Springfield, Ill.: Charles C. Thomas).

_____. 1968. Mental Health Systems in
Scandinavia. (Springfield, Ill.: Charles C. Thomas).

Vallier, Ivan (Ed.). 1971. Comparative Methods in
Sociology. Berkeley: University of California Press.

Watkin, Brian. 1975. Documents in Health and Social
Services, 1934 to the Present. London: Methuen & Co.

_____. 1978. The National Health Service: The
First Phase, 1948-1974 and After. London: Allen and
Unwin.

Walzer, Michael. 1965. The Revolution of the Saints.
Cambridge: Harvard University Press.

Whitehorn, John C. 1944. "A Century of Psychiatric
Research in America." In One Hundred Years of American
Psychiatry. Edited by J. K. Hall et al. New York:
Columbia University Press.

Weber, Max. 1946. "Bureaucracy." In From Max Weber.
Edited by Hans Gerth and C. Wright Mills. New York:
Oxford University Press. [1922].

_____. 1947. The Theory of Social and Economic
Organization. Translated by T. Parsons and A. M.
Henderson. Glencoe, Ill.: Free Press. [1922].

_____. 1978. Economy and Society. Edited by Guenther Roth and Claus Wittich. Berkeley, Ca: University of California Press. [1922].

Wildavsky, Aaron. 1964. The Politics of the Budgetary Process. Boston: Little Brown.

_____. 1977. "Doing Better and Feeling Worse." In Daedalus. Edited by John H. Knowles. 106: 1 (Winter): 105-124.

Wilensky, Harold L. and Charles N. Lebeauz. 1958. Industrial Society and Social Welfare. New York: Russell Sage.

Wilensky, Harold L. 1967. Organizational Intelligence. New York: Basic Books

_____. 1972. "Intelligence, Crises, and Foreign Policy: Reflections on the Limits of Rationality." In Surveillance and Espionage in a Free Society. Edited by Richard H. Blum. New York: Praeger

_____. 1975. The Welfare State and Equality. Berkeley: University of California Press.

_____. 1976. The 'New Corporatism', Centralization, and the Welfare State. Beverly Hills: Sage Publications.

Willcocks, Arthur J. 1967. The Creation of the National Health Service. London: Routlege and Kegan Paul

Williams, Richard H. & Lucy D. Ozarin (Eds.). 1968. Community Mental Health: An International Perspective. San Francisco: Jossey-Bass.

Wing, John K. 1978. Reasoning About Madness. Oxford: Oxford University Press.

Wing, John K. and Authea M. Hailey (eds.) 1972. *Evaluating a Community Psychiatric Service: The Camberwell Register, 1964-71.* London: Oxford University Press

Wooton, Barbara. 1963. *Social Science and Social Pathology.* London: Allen & Unwin.

World Health Organization. 1953. *Report of Third Expert Committee on Mental Health.* Geneva: WHO Technical Report Series No. 73.

Yardley, D. C. M. 1974. *Introduction to British Constitutional Law.* (Fourth Edition). London: Butterworths.